Y0-CBF-685

Donald W. Douglas

OTHER BOOKS BY WILBUR H. MORRISON

Hellbirds: The Story of the B-29s in Combat

The Incredible 305th: The "Can Do" Bombers of World War II

Wings over the Seven Seas: U.S. Naval Aviation's Fight for Survival

Point of No Return: The Story of the Twentieth Air Force

Fortress without a Roof: The Allied Bombing of the Third Reich

Above and Beyond: 1941–1945

The Elephant and the Tiger: The Full Story of the Vietnam War

Baja Adventure Guide

Donald W. Douglas

A HEART WITH WINGS

Wilbur H. Morrison

IOWA STATE UNIVERSITY PRESS / AMES

WILBUR H. MORRISON is a full-time writer at his home in Fallbrook, California. He was a radio news commentator for fifteen years before and after World War II; an air force lieutenant colonel, who flew five hundred combat hours, during the war; and a public relations manager with the Douglas Aircraft Company and the Lockheed-California Company during parts of 1954 through 1969.

First edition, 1991

Library of Congress Cataloging–in–Publication Data

Morrison, Wilbur H.
    Donald W. Douglas, a heart with wings / Wilbur H. Morrison. — 1st ed.
        p.   cm.
    Includes index.
    ISBN 0–8138–1834–6
    1. Douglas, Donald W. (Donald Wills), 1892–1981. 2. Aircraft industry—United States—Biography. I. Title.
TL540.D65M67 1991
338.7'6291'0092—dc20
[B]   90–48685

For Ed Heinemann

Contents

Preface

I n each generation the lives of a few men and women make such a difference that mankind is benefited to an incalculable extent. In the twentieth century, Donald W. Douglas was one of these men. More than any other individual he helped to create the modern miracle of global air transportation. With two thousand dollars of his wife's savings, Douglas created an enormous heritage as a brilliant design engineer and a producer of airplanes who literally made it possible for the world's airlines to free themselves from their reliance on government subsidies. During one period in the 1930s more than 50 percent of all air travelers flew in Douglas commercial transports.

His company's contribution to the defenses of the United States helped to make the nation invincible in the air during World War II, and in all wars since then. Douglas combat aircraft, justly recognized for their reliability and safety, have always been mainstays of America's armed forces since the company was founded in the early 1920s. The Douglas Army Air Corps World Cruisers completed the first around-the-world flight in 1924, marking the beginning of a series of record flights by the company's airplanes through the years. The SBD Dauntless, developed by E. H. Heinemann and his engineers at the Douglas El Segundo Division, won the battle at Midway during World War II by sinking all four carriers of the Japanese fleet. The C-47, a derivative of the highly successful DC-3 transport, served around the world, and was given credit by General Dwight D. Eisenhower as one of four American developments that contributed most to Allied victory.

America's preeminence in space exploration owes much to Douglas's insistence upon structural integrity of the company's products, which became the standard for the industry. The company built one of the vital stages that helped to put the Apollo astronauts on the moon. Later, Douglas built Skylab, the nation's first earth-orbiting space station to demonstrate that people could work and live in space.

Outside his own family few people really got to know Donald Douglas. He was a private person in his dealings with company employees—many of his top executives never got to know him intimately. He not only was an outstanding engineer, but had a natural gift of authority. He managed his company by delegating authority as it grew into a huge organization. His basic rule was to place top-notch administrators in primary positions and give them the authority they needed to carry out their assignments without constantly looking over their shoulders.

By nature a quiet, introspective man whose love for the sea dominated his life, he had a marvelous sense of humor, and loved a good joke, whether on himself or on a friend. He married twice, and both marriages were turbulent, but he was a deeply emotional man who kept feelings to himself and a few intimates. His loyalty to those whom he trusted is legendary.

I worked for the Douglas company in public relations for almost ten years. I served as public relations manager of the Long Beach Division during the period when the DC-8 jetliner was conceived and placed in production. Much of my work involved relations with the sales department as hundreds of the world's leaders came to Douglas Long Beach to be briefed about the company's first commercial jet transport. During those years, I was privileged to be a part of a small but vital group, including Mr. Douglas, who briefed the heads of the world's airlines. I shall never forget the respect and admiration they all expressed for Donald Douglas. He did not believe in a "hard-sell" technique, and after experts completed their briefings, he would simply say, "I've always stood behind our products, and the DC-8 is no exception. If anything goes wrong, we'll fix it. You have my word."

They never doubted his integrity because they had learned that in buying a Douglas transport they were not buying just another airplane; they were buying the integrity of the company's founder. In his low-keyed, soft-sell approach, he was the most effective salesman I have ever known. Today's industrialists would benefit by following his example.

The material for this book was not derived from published records, most of which are inaccurate or so limited in scope that they are useless for the preparation of a book. During my ten years at the Douglas Company, I wrote hundreds of stories about the company's people and its history. Before I left in 1964, knowing I would eventually write a book about Donald Douglas, I gathered all pertinent data from the company's files for my personal collection. This proved to be a wise move because the McDonnell Corporation, after it absorbed the Douglas Company, destroyed most of this historical material as it was considered unimportant and too costly to store in its dozens of files. This was shortsighted and tragic, but fortunately for me, I retained copies of the most important papers. This material, along with many interviews with former Douglas executives and my personal recollections, made it possible for me to write the book.

I sent the manuscript to Mr. Douglas shortly before he died. After reading it he wrote me a short note: "Dear Will, Reads very well. Wish you luck. Don Douglas"

Acknowledgments

THE AUTHOR OWES a special debt of gratitude to Edward H. Heinemann who helped immeasurably in recreating the Douglas years. The late Arch C. Wallen, Barbara Douglas Arnold, Arthur F. Raymond, Jackson R. McGowen, T. D. MacGregor, the late Crosby Maynard, Charles R. Chappell, Ren Briggs, and Jean Murphy each were helpful in various ways and the author expresses his appreciation.

Donald W. Douglas

A Born Leader

Donald W. Douglas, descended from a distinguished lineage of stalwart, proud Scotsmen, was inspired throughout his life by the persistence and imagination of his forebear, James Douglas. First to bear the name Douglas, or *dhu glas* (Gaelic for "black water"), James was one of the heroes of Scotland's fight for independence from England and the family member who inspired the coat-of-arms. James Douglas was born in 1286. As friend to the great Scottish leader Robert Bruce, after his death in 1329, Sir James set out for the Holy Land with Bruce's heart in a silver casket to satisfy a deathbed wish. He intended to symbolically complete a vow that Bruce had made as a young man to go on a crusade, but instead James met his own death by Moors in Spain.

In remembrance of this tragic event, the Douglas coat-of-arms carries a human heart to symbolize the courage and fortitude of James Douglas. Since that time, the Douglas family has been an illustrious one in Scotland and around the world. And Donald W. Douglas, as a pioneer designer and industrialist, has created a distinguished heritage in his own right.

In 1799 John Duncan Douglas came to America and established an American line of the family. His grandson William Douglas, like most members of the Douglas clan, began life in the business world in a small way by working as an errand boy in a coffee and tea house, before becoming a runner for the National Park Bank, and later rising to assistant cashier. Upon achieving this position he married a lovely woman by the name of Dorothy Hagen-Locher who was of German and Scandinavian descent. They bought a home in Brooklyn and their first son, Harold, was born in 1890. Their second son, Donald Wills Douglas, was born April 6, 1892.

Donald's father was a distinguished-looking man with the large mustache popular in those days, who always maintained a calm outlook on life. Donald grew up with many of his relaxed, fun-loving father's characteristics, but he often said his enthusiasm and determination were inherited from his mother. She had a practical, no-nonsense view of life.

During childhood, Donald developed interests that remained with him all his life: a love of the sea, an appreciation for good poetry, and a strong interest in the history of Scotland.

His early heroes were all but forgotten after a visit to the Smithsonian Institution with his father, where he was particularly intrigued by Charles M. Manley's experimental aircraft engine. While working for Professor Samuel P. Langley, Manley designed a lightweight, five-cylinder radial engine for aircraft that later was recognized as the first modern aircraft engine.

From then on Douglas devoured books on flying, particularly stories about Langley's successful experiments with a flying model and his early attempts to fly a heavier-than-air machine. So intense was Douglas's enthusiasm for anything pertaining to flying that he began to build model airplanes.

After powered flight became a reality on December 17, 1903, Douglas followed the advancements made by Orville and Wilbur Wright. He was present on July 30, 1909, when Orville made his final tests to qualify the Wright Flyer for acceptance by the United States Army. He was fascinated as the machine circled the field at speeds averaging forty-two miles an hour. Witnessing the miracle of powered flight for the first time, Douglas was almost overwhelmed by emotion.

Before he graduated from Trinity Chapel preparatory school in the spring of 1909 he decided that his two great loves—airplanes and the sea—could best be advanced by attending the Naval Academy at Annapolis. His brother, Harold, had entered the academy two years before, and he was anxious to follow in his footsteps. He was successful in the exams and entered the academy that fall, where he became known as "Doug" or "Little Doug."

Although there was no aviation course at Annapolis, he continued his experiments flying model airplanes. His efforts were not appreciated by the faculty, and he was often told that he was wasting his time at the academy.

His brother graduated in 1911. The following year Donald resigned from the academy. Although he could not describe his exact reasons to his parents, he had a strong inner conviction that the right course for him was in aeronautical engineering. His parents agreed, so he decided to attend Massachusetts Institute of Technology.

When he reported to the college in the fall of 1912, he learned that there was no course in aeronautical engineering. In those days M.I.T. was *the* engineering school, and a good one, although it had no course in aeronautical engineering nine years after the first Wright flight. He was told it would take him four years to graduate, despite his three years at Annapolis.

"I'll do it in two years," he told college officials.

Douglas enrolled in mechanical engineering, in which he had to choose among such elective subjects as boiler, locomotive, and cotton mill design.

He was popular at M.I.T. and was pledged to the Number Six Club, the campus name for the Tau Chapter of Delta Psi fraternity. The club's finances were in bad shape, and he was elected treasurer. In a short time, his innate sense of thrift and orderliness had the fraternity on a paying basis. Even in those years he had a reputation for frugality—one that would last him throughout his business life.

Although he had told his professors he would graduate in two years, they were amazed when he actually did so, graduating in 1914 with a bachelor of science degree.

At this time, due to apathy in government, aviation was still in its infancy in the United States, while in France rapid strides were being made. Louis Blériot had already built over 800 airplanes of 40 different types.

While Donald was trying to decide what his first step should be in the business world, he received word from Comdr. Jerome C.

Hunsaker that he had been assigned to the M.I.T. Department of Naval Architecture, where he was to help build the college's first wind tunnel and start a course in aerodynamics and aeronautical engineering. Hunsaker said he was looking for an assistant, and Douglas happily accepted his offer to work for him at a salary of $500 a year.

Douglas found Hunsaker an inspiring teacher, and they became good friends. Engineers in the 1910s had meager information to support their efforts. The limited basic knowledge of aircraft design in the United States was gained primarily from wind tunnel research in England, France, and Germany.

The Wrights had built a small tunnel in the early 1900s, and there was another tunnel at the Washington Navy Yard, but the M.I.T. tunnel was more advanced in style and operation. The wind tunnel's balance had to be purchased from the British National Laboratory. The first tests Hunsaker and Douglas made in Cambridge confirmed the results of foreign experiments.

Years later Hunsaker said:

> In this pioneer research, Douglas showed originality, technical competence, and a persistence in the face of difficulties that indicated to his colleagues he would go far as a scientist. We knew that he was a leader. But we expected him to lead along the paths of research. Evidently Douglas had those qualities of leadership which guarantee attainment along any path.
>
> In creative design, and as an industrialist, he has changed the trend of aviation development throughout the world, but it is only natural to wonder what the world may have lost by his leaving the laboratory for the factory.

In the spring of 1915 Hunsaker obtained a consulting job for Douglas in New Haven with the Connecticut Aircraft Company, which won the bid to build the D-1, the United States Navy's first nonrigid dirigible. In those days lighter-than-air craft vied actively with the airplane.

At Connecticut Aircraft, he met Capt. Tom Baldwin, a designer of airships and a graduate of the old circus hot-air balloon days. He piloted both lighter-than-air craft and airplanes, and Douglas quickly learned that Baldwin knew more about airships than any other man at the company. His one failing was that he could not make a sketch or an engineering drawing. He and Douglas got along famously because Baldwin would show him what he wanted and Douglas would translate Baldwin's thoughts into an engineering drawing. Once, Baldwin had to cut a design out of wrapping paper so Douglas could understand how he wanted a safety valve made. This was all very elementary and unscientific, but that was the way things were done in those days. Douglas profited by the experience by learning the practical aspects of engineering.

Douglas did not find his work at Connecticut Aircraft challenging, so once the dirigible was completed, he left to devote his efforts to heavier-than-air vehicles.

About this time, he turned down an offer to work for Thomas Alva Edison. He and Edison's son had been fraternity brothers and roommates in college. Although Douglas appreciated the offer from the famed scientist, he turned down the job because he wanted to make a career for himself as an aeronautical engineer.

Glenn L. Martin, a man who was to play an important role in Douglas's early years, had moved from Santa Ana, California, to Los Angeles and constructed an aircraft factory prior to the start of World War I. By 1915, he was successfully building army training planes. That year Hunsaker received a letter from Martin asking him to recommend an aeronautical engineer. He asked Douglas if he wanted the job, and Douglas eagerly assured him that he did.

Douglas boarded a train for Los Angeles in August for his first full-time job in aviation. He was to meet Martin at the Hayward Hotel. When he walked into the Hayward he appeared even more youthful than his twenty-three years—a slim figure with a stubborn chin and prominent nose, and brown eyes that twinkled when he was amused. Martin knew him only by name and reputation, and had no idea what he looked like. Douglas had seen so many pictures of the bespectacled Martin, however, that he recognized him immediately. "Mr. Glenn L. Martin?" Douglas said as he approached.

Martin eyed the young man without interest. "I am. Sorry I can't talk to you now. I'm waiting for someone. If you're interested in a job, come to the plant later."

Douglas was nonplused by his reception and walked away,

sitting across the lobby, and watching Martin. Finally, seeing that Martin kept darting anxious glances at the front entrance, he decided to approach him again. "I don't want to disturb you, Mr. Martin, but I think you're waiting for me."

Martin looked at the young man incredulously. "You?" He laughed. "I'm waiting for a chief engineer for my airplane factory—not a high school boy." He grinned affably. "Now, if your name was Donald W. Douglas . . ."

"I am Donald W. Douglas."

Martin looked at him with disbelief. "You're just a boy. A boy engineer!" Martin finally was convinced, and they completed arrangements for Douglas to report for work.

The Martin plant was a three-story brick building that had once been used by the manufacturers of such early automobiles as the Durocar and the Tourist. When Martin showed Douglas around the plant his first day on the job, Martin's shop foreman, George Strompl, eyed him speculatively. In response to a query from one of his mechanics, the rotund Strompl said, "Whoever he is, he isn't old enough to be buyin' no airplanes."

Strompl and the other workmen shook their heads in disbelief when Martin said, "Boys, meet our new chief engineer, Don Douglas."

Strompl's doubts about him were reemphasized when Douglas began to send detailed drawings to the shop. Explosive by nature, Strompl made it clear that he considered drawings superfluous, saying they had never needed them in the past. Later, Strompl became one of Douglas's strongest boosters because detailed drawings made his job easier, and they became close friends.

During the year Douglas spent at Martin, he grew to admire not only Strompl but Ross Elkins, pilot Eric Springer, and Harry Wetzel. The latter was not an employee, but a government inspector of military aircraft. Douglas vowed then that if he ever opened his own plant, he would ask all four to join him.

One day Martin took Douglas out to see a biplane that had been designed before his arrival. It was set up on sawhorses and Douglas's eyes popped when Martin climbed into the cockpit of the little airplane and bounced it around rather energetically while he checked the wires and fittings. Everyone looked on with great interest, but

Douglas was baffled. "What's going on?"

Martin looked at him with astonishment, shocked that his new chief engineer could be so stupid. "I'm testing it to see if it's strong enough," he said haughtily.

Douglas shook his head in wonder. His engineering background was such that he knew Martin's test had nothing to do with the stresses the airplane would have to bear in flight.

Douglas proceeded to change Martin's way of doing things after he settled into the job. He made stress analyses, and told the factory's fifty workers they would get detailed drawings for each part. They called him the "boy engineer" behind his back, and frankly thought he was a bit off his rocker.

In view of their skepticism Douglas was particularly pleased when the Model S, Douglas's first airplane for Martin, exceeded its performance specifications. A seaplane manufactured for Holland, with six on order for the Army Signal Corps, the S was designed to fly at seventy MPH, and it attained a cruising speed of seventy-two MPH. It also set three world altitude records and for three years held the world's flight duration record.

Douglas often said that designing an airplane was 99 percent mathematics, and his fellow workers grudgingly admitted that maybe he was right.

In those days pusher-type planes were giving way to tractor designs, although many pushers continued to be built. Virtually all planes were small and of relatively low power. A big order for a firm was six or eight airplanes a year, and they were priced between ten and fifteen thousand dollars each.

Douglas was privileged to meet many men who later became famous in the industry, including Lawrence "Larry" Bell who later founded his own company. At Martin, he was factory manager. He and Douglas quickly agreed each would be master in his own domain—he in manufacturing, and Douglas in engineering—and they would not try to poach on one another.

Douglas's enthusiasm for his work was infectious, and he made many friends, including Floyd Smith, Martin's colorful and excellent chief test pilot. Smith and his wife worked the county fairs, where he did some fancy stunt flying, while she did parachute jumping.

Edmund R. Doak became a friend and later a top Douglas executive for many years until he founded his own Doak Aircraft Company.

While Douglas worked at Martin he met Charlotte Marguerite Ogg, a visitor from Marion, Indiana, on a blind date arranged by his roommate Art Barry. The following June he and Charlotte were married at Riverside, California. The black-haired, blue-eyed bride had been known as a string bean as a teenager because she was tall and thin. Although she was not a Roman Catholic, she received most of her normal schooling at a Catholic convent. Charlotte had hoped to become a doctor, but she had to support herself because her mother died when she was three years old and her father passed away when she was nine. When she met Douglas she was a registered nurse. Throughout her life she was known as very generous with her time and money.

Martin's first airport was at Griffith Park, but when this proved inadequate, flights were shifted to a field that later became Los Angeles International Airport. Seaplanes such as the Model S were tested in a large freshwater lake that stretched from 55th and Main streets nearly to the Los Angeles harbor.

When Donald's father came west to visit his son, noting the intense enthusiasm with which he spoke of his work, he shook his head doubtfully. "Why don't you build motorcycles like other air pioneers? This business is too risky." His son was well aware of the risks, but that did not deter him from staying in an industry he loved.

On the West Coast Douglas got to know many early pioneers but he never met Glenn Curtiss, and it was not until the late 1920s that he met Orville Wright. One reason was that California was four grimy days by train from the East. Although Douglas did travel for Martin, most trips were confined to San Diego. He did not particularly like the isolation from most of the industry because he felt he was too far from centers of activity that could broaden his aeronautical knowledge.

So, in November 1916 Douglas left Martin, and he and Charlotte went to Washington, D.C., where he accepted a position as chief civilian aeronautical engineer for the Army Signal Corps. An Army officer who had been at M.I.T. with him, Colonel Clark, had written to ask if he would become head of a new engineering department that the corps was creating.

Douglas and Charlotte registered at the Raleigh Hotel while he waited for word on where to take his Civil Service examination. While he chafed at government bureaucracy, the Signal Corps tried to find someone who could make out a test. It finally was agreed that no one in government knew as much about aeronautical engineering as Douglas so they decided to forego the examination.

He was sent first on a tour of all eastern aircraft plants to collect information on what everybody was doing, thus broadening his knowledge to his immense satisfaction. During this period the government brought over quite a few well-known British and French aircraft, types then in service on the Western Front. Rather quickly, he was able to gather extensive information about what was going on in the world of aviation. When some of these planes were gathered in a building belonging to the Smithsonian Institution, he was instrumental in seeing that all American aircraft company officials had a chance to benefit from the latest knowledge and techniques of aircraft design and construction.

Douglas worked diligently to improve the status of the Aviation Section. It was not in high favor among army brass, despite the efforts of the army's first aeronautical engineer, Grover Loening, who was one of the most brilliant engineers of his time. Douglas strove to improve the Aviation Section's image, although he was frustrated more than once by the failure of army generals to understand the importance of airpower.

When the United States entered World War I in 1917 the navy had only 38 pilots, 163 enlisted men, 6 flying boats, 45 seaplanes, 3 land-based airplanes, 7 balloons, and 1 nonrigid airship. The army was in even worse shape with only 54 training planes.

Government insensitivity had put the United States far behind other nations despite the fact that it had flown the first heavier-than-air machine. American industry was not prepared for the mass production of airplanes, and when Congress passed an appropriation of $649 million to build them, Douglas and others wondered how 20,000 combat planes and 9,000 trainers could ever be built. Standardization was the word most often used to get the job done. In other words, airplanes should be built like automobiles.

Douglas's main job during the year he spent in Washington was to work on redesigning British airplanes. During his government service he argued forcefully for the design of stronger airplanes but each time he had a new airplane to propose, orders came down from above to scrap it. Douglas was often bitter, but he stubbornly kept up with new designs although all of them were rejected.

Throughout this period he was made particularly unhappy by the fact that automobile executives were brought in to run the aircraft production program. He readily conceded that they were good men at mass production techniques, but he was also aware that these men knew little or nothing about the production of airplanes.

After Glenn Martin opened a new plant in Cleveland in the spring of 1918 he asked Douglas to join his firm again, and he gladly accepted. Douglas's first assignment with Martin was to help design a large twin-engine bomber. When the design was offered to the Aviation Production Board Douglas was told that no new American bomber design would be considered. The board was reorganized shortly thereafter, however, and Martin was asked to build the new bomber with Liberty engines.

Martin insisted his company be given a free hand and, despite the fact he refused to promise specific performance characteristics, such was his reputation and that of Douglas that the offer was accepted. For the first time in years Douglas was happy with what he was doing, feeling free of all government interference, and left alone to design an airplane to his own high standards.

All of this experience was a great lesson for Douglas, and of value to him and the nation in later years when he spoke forcefully about the inadequacies of military procurement. The frustration he and many others felt about aircraft procurement policies during the war caused them to think seriously about the problem in later years and attempt to do something about it.

Although $1.5 billion had been spent on aviation, only 200 American-built aircraft ever reached the front. There was no doubt, however, that if the war had lasted another year America's aircraft industry would have proven itself because a rate of 21,000 aircraft a year had been reached in 1918.

2

On His Own

August 17, 1918, was not only an auspicious day for the Martin Company, but also for Douglas because he had designed an airplane that he was sure would be superior to anything produced in Europe. The flight was scheduled for early afternoon and a large crowd had gathered to watch the new bomber take the air. There were delays, however, and it was not until 7 P.M. that pilot Eric Springer was able to take off.

Douglas watched the plane intently as it moved to the end of the runway, where Springer revved the two engines. He held his breath as the big plane slowly gathered speed and lifted gracefully into the air.

After Springer and the plane returned, he told Douglas and Martin, "This is the best job I've ever flown. I went to 9,000 feet and could have gone higher."

"How fast did she fly?" Douglas asked eagerly.

"I reached 120 miles an hour. And I turned off one engine and climbed to 3,000 feet."

They were impressed by the words of the tall distinguished-looking Springer. Because of his methodical way and honesty of expression, they began to think they had a winner.

The war ended before the new bomber could have an impact on operations in Europe, but the airplane proved so good that orders remained on the books because it surpassed the performance of every competitor.

In describing the airplane later, Douglas said, "The general characteristics which made the machine stand out are its flying qualities and high efficiency, which serve to assure us that the utility and practicability of large machines for all uses, both civil and military, definitely have been realized."

Springer lauded the airplane because of its many comfort features, and because even with a full load and with either one or both engines operating, it answered all controls readily. He told Douglas that it was possible to climb the bomber, turn against a dead engine, and land on a small field.

Despite its size, Springer frequently looped the aircraft and, he said, even when the controls were reversed, it pursued a steady and stable course for an indefinite period. He also described how he could leave the controls and walk around in the cabin and the plane would continue to fly well.

The Douglas-designed bomber took off easily with a heavy load either with or against the wind. Its landing speed was slow, too, adding an additional measure of safety to the crew that heretofore was unknown. The bomber had an official high speed of 118.5 MPH, with a full bomb load, and it could climb to 10,000 feet in fifteen minutes to reach a service ceiling of 17,000 feet.

The design of the airplane was so versatile that Douglas told Martin it could be used as a light bomber, a day bomber, or a long-distance reconnaissance airplane. As a night bomber, it was equipped with three flexible machine guns, one on the front turret, another in the rear, and a third inside the fuselage so it would be protected at all angles from enemy fighters. It also could carry 1,500 lbs of bombs, and its radio telephone had a range of 600 miles so it could communicate with ground stations.

Douglas was so enthused with prospects for the airplane that he recommended the Martin Twin be adapted to carry passengers, mail, and express, and for use in aerial mapping. As a commercial transport, it could carry twelve passengers in addition to its two-man crew for a distance of 600 miles. Powered by two twelve-cylinder Liberty engines, the Martin Twin had a wing span of seventy-one feet, five inches, and was forty-six feet long, with an overall height of fourteen feet, seven inches.

The airplane helped Martin to survive after the end of the war, which saw dissolution of 90 percent of the aircraft industry. Despite the fact that the bomber could be converted to a commercial transport, both Martin and Douglas realized the time was not ripe to develop it, because the army was selling surplus planes at any price.

Douglas and his engineering staff went to work on a new three-place sports plane called the Comet, but he was more anxious than ever to form his own company. In the east, he found it impossible to get financing to start such a company.

The Douglases found living conditions in Cleveland extremely difficult, and they moved continually from one apartment to another in family hotels. Douglas refused to buy furniture because he did not intend to stay with Martin, so their problems were aggravated by the need to move from one furnished place to another as families who had previously occupied their apartment returned to reclaim it.

The family now consisted of two children—Donald, Jr., born in 1917, and William, born in 1918.

During the winter of 1919–1920 the weather was so bad in Cleveland that Charlotte decided to take the children to California for a time. In January, she and the children set off while Donald stayed behind to help Martin try to sell his big planes.

He also helped to design a new plane, based on the bomber, which was to be used for a transatlantic flight. Unfortunately, it was destroyed in its hangar on Long Island when a hurricane swept the area. Martin did manage to sell the Post Office Department a commercial version, but other sales failed to materialize.

In March, Douglas went to California to see his family. Although Martin had been good to him, paying him $10,000 a year in salary, even though he was only twenty-eight years old, he still wanted to establish his own company. He believed his experience and background had been extensive enough so that such a company would be a success. It was a difficult decision to make. He was well aware that $10,000-a-year jobs were few in number and that his future at Martin was assured.

One of the motivating factors in his decision was a conviction that the airplane had a bright future as a civilian transport. He had a dream that airplanes could bring people all over the world closer together, and through greater understanding, eliminate disastrous wars such as the one the world had just experienced. He was well aware how radical such an idea was in 1920.

Before he left for Los Angeles, he had completed the design of a torpedo plane that was destined for navy use. But, reunited with his family, he discussed the possibility of resigning from Martin and moving to California to set up his own business. He talked to Charlotte honestly about the risks, and the fact he had less than $1,000 in savings.

"You'll have to make the decision yourself," she said.

In late March, his mind made up, he wired his resignation. Martin tried to change his mind, telling him the market was flooded with war-surplus airplanes selling for $200 or less, but Douglas would not be dissuaded. His decision to make the move was based on several considerations. First, he wanted a better climate for his children, and he knew that a plant in California would permit him to build airplanes cheaper because more work could be done outdoors. And flying conditions were almost ideal because flights could be made almost the year round.

In later years, when he talked about his start as an independent businessman, he said it began as a fledgling industrial enterprise. "Sure it was a business," he said. "After all we had to eat. But it was more than that. It was an adventure. I never felt that I, at my drafting table, was 'in business.'"

In reminiscent moods, he often talked about the feeling of adventure that inspired all who shared in it. "It was a tremendously creative force. We early adventurers gave life to something that has had a profound impact on the life of all mankind and whose ultimate achievements we can but vaguely guess—even years later." All who knew him agreed that aviation succeeded better than most fields of endeavor in keeping alive that sense of adventure that produces creative power.

In modern aircraft plants, engineering departments use vast electronic computers to accomplish in a matter of seconds what these early engineers sweat out for hours or even days.

In establishing his own firm, Douglas joined with other aviation pioneers in helping to pave the way for the hundreds of thousands who followed them. He had the stubborn determination to succeed and always refused to be intimidated by seemingly insurmountable obstacles.

Once Douglas made the decision to establish ownership of his own company, he made the rounds of the financial institutions to borrow money. At first, they all turned a deaf ear. With the collapse of so many aeronautical firms following the war, bankers considered such an investment too risky. In desperation, he turned to an old friend who was a sports editor for the *Los Angeles Times*. Bill Henry, who later became one of the nation's finest correspondents and radio commentators, had been with Martin in Cleveland for a time in public relations. Henry listened sympathetically to his friend's plea.

"I'll try, Don. Perhaps I can find someone to help you out."

Shortly afterwards, Henry talked to David R. Davis, a wealthy sportsman, who wanted an airplane in order to fly across country nonstop. It had never been done before, and he was anxious to compete for the prize money that had been offered. Davis, who had known Douglas for several years, was interested in what Henry had to say and Bill went back to talk to his friend. "I've got your man, Don. He'll finance you, but only for one airplane."

"Just one, Bill?" Douglas's face showed how crestfallen he was that only one airplane was involved.

"That's all. If I were you, I'd forget about building a lot of commercial planes. Get this one to fly across country, and you'll win support for other designs. It's a start."

It was a start, and Douglas expressed his gratitude. He had, however, long set himself a goal that once he started building airplanes they would be designed in series, each incorporating the seed for the next one.

After Douglas met Davis again arrangements were completed to incorporate the Davis-Douglas Airplane Company in South Dakota. Douglas's wife Charlotte put up her husband's share of $2,000 from her personal savings to start the company. She had such faith in him that she never doubted that he would succeed.

Bill Henry filled in as a vice-president, although he never actively engaged in the company's operations. When Douglas told him he had set aside shares in the company for him, Henry protested. "Everything I did was on the basis of friendship. I don't want to become involved in anything but the newspaper business."

Douglas insisted because, he said, "I've always appreciated your help. The shares are yours, and I want you to keep them."

Henry reluctantly agreed.

Once incorporation papers were signed, Douglas wired friends in Cleveland. With typical honesty and candor he wrote George Strompl on June 21, 1920,

I'm not sure of anything until I get it because I'm not in the habit of claiming business before I have a contract.

I expect, however, to work up a strong business in a conservative manner and have something worthwhile in another year or so.

I want you like the dickens but I cannot promise big money nor any future beyond the next six months.

Best in the world to you, old top.

DOUG

This short letter expressed Douglas's basic beliefs, and revealed much about the character of the man.

On July 20, 1920, five friends from Martin arrived in Los Angeles to join the company. They were Ross Elkins, who later returned to Martin, but rejoined Douglas again in 1928; Jim Goodyear; George Borst, a mill expert who died in 1928; Henry Guerin; and George Strompl.

It was a young industry that Douglas was getting into as an independent businessman, and he surrounded himself with young people who matched his own foresightedness. It was a precarious time for anyone to start a new aviation company because the industry was in such a chaotic state that even the mighty Curtiss Aeroplane and Motor Company had gone into bankruptcy.

With his typical thrift, Douglas rented an office on Pico Boulevard behind a barber shop. When his Martin friends arrived outside, they looked at one another with disbelief.

Strompl turned to the others. "Who's playing a practical joke on us? This can't be the right address."

Guerin looked at the number on the building. "That's the one Don gave us."

Strompl peered into the barber shop where several men were getting haircuts. "Wonder which chair Don has?" he said with a grin. "If he bought the shop, he must have the first chair. Here we've quit our jobs with Martin and come all the way from Cleveland, and what do we find. A barber shop!"

Then they noticed a small sign off to one side that said Davis-Douglas Airplane Company, with an arrow pointing to the rear.

They located Douglas and greeted him with great hilarity. While they were exchanging greetings, the building shook wildly as an earthquake rocked the structure. Douglas's friends looked at one another, wondering what in the world they had gotten themselves into.

The next day they went to look for a factory building. When they saw the Koll Planing Mill near the Southern Pacific station in downtown Los Angeles, they agreed the second floor easily could be converted into a factory, although it was dark and had a fairly low ceiling.

When Bill Waterhouse was added to the payroll, the engineering department grew to three, with Goodyear and Douglas the other members. Douglas appointed Strompl purchasing agent because he was so persuasive: the type of aggressive individual who refused to take no for an answer, and whose talents would be most needed because material would have to be purchased largely on credit.

Strompl bought material from the Ducommun Hardware Company when he worked for Martin, so he went there first. After he met Charles Ducommun, he said, "Remember me? I'm George Strompl. Used to work for Glenn Martin. I'm now purchasing agent for the Davis-Douglas Airplane Company."

Ducommun eyed him suspiciously. He said cautiously, "Well, yes, I remember you. Did you say Davis-Douglas Company? Never heard of it."

Strompl opened his mouth to speak, but Ducommun interrupted. "Well, sir, our books are full of red ink on aircraft credits."

Strompl squirmed uneasily.

"Why didn't you get into a business with a future?" Ducommun said.

"I have!" Strompl said indignantly, and then proceeded to explain the organization of the new company and its plans.

Ducommun eyed him thoughtfully. "I've heard of Douglas and the work he did at Martin. Don't know much about him, though, but I've heard a lot about Davis."

He looked at the perspiring Strompl. "Here's what I'll do. You can have anything you want." A broad smile appeared on Strompl's face. "Up to $100 on credit! Remember, I want regular payments the end of the first week of each month."

Ducommun's decision paid dividends in later years that he never dreamed of at the time. As long as Douglas had his company, Ducommun shared in his success.

Work on the new plane proceeded quickly at Koll Mill. Tools were rented from the piano factory downstairs so all the company had to purchase was a $25 hand drill.

It was a frugal time for everyone. To help feed his family, Douglas started a garden in his backyard and hoed potatoes and vegetables. Once his workers pooled their limited funds to pay for a new tire for Douglas's car so he could come to work. The six men of the fledgling company worked long hours, missing paychecks occasionally, while Charlotte organized their wives to sew the fabric on the airplane.

Douglas made sure that his workers eventually received every cent due them, and they were remembered by him for the rest of their lives. They had jobs as long as they wanted to work.

One day when Bill Henry came to the mill to see how work was progressing, he talked to Douglas about the company's prospects. "I'll write the local angle for the *Times* when you make the flight successfully."

Douglas nodded soberly, looking at the partially completed airplane, confident this creation would justify his faith.

When Henry Guerin joined them, he said, "Say, Don, ever read Trowbridge's poem about flying?"

Douglas nodded. "Used to be in all schoolbooks."

Guerin read several stanzas while they listened with smiles on their faces.

"Remember the moral?" Douglas said with a twinkle in his eyes.

Guerin flipped the pages until he got to the end. "And this is the moral, stick to your sphere."

Douglas broke in. "Or if you insist, as you have the right, on spreading your wings for a loftier flight, the moral is—take care how you light." Douglas chuckled, and the stern lines on his face relaxed.

He loved a good joke, and his sense of humor would stand him in good stead through many a trying period in the future.

"First," Bill Henry said, "you'll have to see she gets in a position to light."

"She will," Douglas said with conviction, and the firm resolve on his face was so profound that neither Henry nor Guerin had the least doubt of the airplane's ultimate success.

3

"A Real Cloud Duster"

The airplane was built in sections because the small factory was on the second floor and assemblies had to be lowered separately down an elevator shaft. When it was nearly completed, the plane was taken by truck to the Goodyear blimp hangar at Ascot Park, between South Park and Florence Street in Los Angeles, where final touches were made in a rented shed and the skin was placed on the framework and the gas tanks installed.

It had taken a year to build and Eric Springer and Douglas watched while it was rolled out, with its wings spreading fifty-six feet, and its powerful 400-horsepower Liberty engine gleaming in the nose. Springer said, "You've got a real cloud duster, Doug." The name was shortened and, thereafter, she became known as the *Cloudster.*

Springer, Douglas's old friend from his Martin days, was the latest recruit to join the company. Douglas had urged him to come because he respected Springer as one of the finest fliers of the time, and one who had successfully flown his Martin bomber.

Springer's first attempt to get the plane into the air was aborted when he ran out of runway, had to ground loop, and ended up in a cauliflower field. The plane suffered no damage, but the farmer sued for $55.00 in crop damage.

When the *Cloudster* made its first flight, a sixteen-year-old named E. H. "Ed" Heinemann watched enthralled as the short stacks of the Liberty engine spewed four-foot flames. He was surprised how long the plane took to get off the ground, but learned later that this distance was quite normal for such a heavy airplane.

He also learned that the flames that shot out of their exhaust stacks were caused by the engine running on too rich a mixture. He carried with him ever after a vivid memory of the care with which Douglas and his associates tuned that engine. He was particularly impressed by Douglas's youth, and how nice he was in answering his countless questions.

After the successful flight of the *Cloudster,* Davis's niece, Jane Pearsall, broke a bottle of champagne on the nose officially christening the airplane.

In the weeks that followed, Springer made several flights, breaking the Pacific Coast altitude record on March 29 by reaching 19,160 feet. Even though he was clothed in a fur-lined suit, he almost froze in the -16°F temperature aloft. After he landed, he was greeted by members of the Aero Club of California. Everyone was jubilant. He had bettered Frank Clark's record of 15,819 feet in a Fokker scout plane.

Flights continued during April and May while the *Cloudster* was prepared for its transcontinental flight. With added fuel, a longer runway was needed so Douglas decided to use the army's March Field at Riverside. Springer, Davis, and the ground crew went there with the *Cloudster* on a truck, while Douglas remained in Los Angeles.

For days, early mornings were fogbound and, when Davis and Springer awoke before dawn on June 27, 1921, it appeared as if they would again have to cancel the flight. Although the transcontinental flight was a momentous occasion, it had aroused no press interest so there was no one in attendance other than company men. Davis and Springer stood by the airplane, peering disgustedly at the thick fog as it swirled around them. With the rising sun, it started to lift. Springer pulled on his leather jacket. Turning to Davis, he said, "Today's the day."

"Think we can take off about six?" Davis said doubtfully.

Springer nodded. He turned to the mechanics. "Get her warmed up."

The powerful engine thundered into action, echoing around March Field. They both knew they had a long and hard flight ahead—2,500 miles to Curtiss Field, Long Island—and that it would take thirty hours. After tests during the preceding weeks, they were confident of their calculations that the *Cloudster* could maintain an 85 MPH speed for thirty-three hours over a distance of 2,800 miles. The reserve seemed adequate, and they were confident of the plane.

Davis glanced at his watch. "Wish Don were here instead of back at the plant working on that new torpedo plane."

"That's like him," Springer said. "He'd rather stick to his drawing board."

Davis glanced again at his watch. "Time to go."

They both looked across the field when they heard an Army DeHavilland warming up. Springer turned inquiringly to an officer who walked up to them.

"Thought we'd provide an honorary escort until you're on your way," the officer said with a grin. "That's our way of saying good luck."

"Thank you," Springer said. "We're ready to leave."

Davis and Springer climbed into the cockpit and the *Cloudster*'s engine broke into a loud roar as they taxied away, waving their hands to those behind them. Springer guided the airplane to the end of the runway, ran up the engines, and then pushed the throttle full forward. They gathered speed slowly due to the heavy load of fuel, and the airplane at first did not want to take to the air. Springer watched a farmhouse off the runway straight ahead as it got closer and closer while the *Cloudster* clung to the ground.

"I must get her up," he thought anxiously, as the house loomed larger by the second.

Each time he pulled back gently on the stick, the *Cloudster* rose a few inches only to settle back again to the runway. At last, the *Cloudster* stopped bouncing and was airborne; it barely cleared the farmhouse.

Davis let out an explosive sigh. "New York, next," he said with relief.

"That's right," Springer said happily. "We're on our way."

The *Cloudster* handled beautifully now that it was in the air and Springer looked at Davis with a smile. His enthusiasm for the airplane had been high ever since the first flight because it was the first airplane in history to carry the equivalent of its own weight in payload. In addition, the streamlining that had gone into its design was unique in the industry. Douglas, with his accustomed concern for crew safety, had installed gas-dump valves, the first airplane to have them, so that a heavy load of fuel could be jettisoned in case of emergency. And there were landing flares and rockets for signaling.

Davis and Springer watched the countryside unfold beneath them as they crossed Arizona and New Mexico and headed across Texas. There, without warning, the engine quit and Springer frantically tried to restart it, but he quickly realized they had to get down in a hurry. Springer swung the airplane in circles as the propeller wind-milled.

"Believe the timing gear's stripped," he told Davis. "We'll have to land at Fort Bliss."

Although they both wore parachutes, they gave no thought to bailing out and leaving the airplane to crash. Expertly, Springer brought the *Cloudster* down to a dead-stick landing at the army base near El Paso. They had flown 785 miles in eight hours and forty-five minutes, attaining a peak altitude of 8,000 feet.

Davis and Springer were disconsolate as they rode in the truck that towed the *Cloudster* to the workshops. The rain poured down and vicious streaks of lightning swept across the sky. Then a high wind came up, blowing the airplane sideways, and damaging a wing tip and the tail.

Springer surveyed the damage. He said sadly to Davis, "That'll take some real repair work. You'd better call Doug."

Back in the Los Angeles plant, Douglas picked up his phone and the operator told him Fort Bliss was calling. Associates gathered around soberly while he talked with Davis.

At the end of the call, in which Davis described the extent of the damage, he turned to the anxious group behind him. "The *Cloudster*'s down." To Strompl and Guerin, he said, "You two get out to Fort Bliss and see what needs to be done." Without another word he turned back to his drawing board.

It took three weeks to repair the *Cloudster* so that it could be flown to California for further work. While it was being repaired, Army Lieutenants Oakley G. Kelly and John A. Macready flew nonstop from New York to San Diego in a Fokker T-2.

With the success of the Army flight, Davis's competitive spirit evaporated, and he lost interest in the *Cloudster*. He sold it to Thornton Kinney, whose family owned a cigarette company and who also was one of the founders of Venice, California, and to Benjamin Brodsky, head of the Consumers Water Company.

At a small hanger at Clover Field in Santa Monica, the *Cloudster* was redesigned as a seven-passenger commercial transport. By now, the plane had received much publicity but Kinney and Brodsky's attempts to make money by carrying passengers came to naught because most people were still afraid to fly.

In 1925 the *Cloudster* was sold to T. Claude Ryan who wanted it for transporting prospective real estate buyers from San Diego to San Clemente. Again the plane was rebuilt. This time it was fitted with plush carpets and comfortable seats. There was a center aisle inside the cabin with six seats on each side.

Ryan kept it only a year before he sold it to a firm in Baja California, which used it to transport illegal liquor to California during prohibition. It met an ignominious end when its pilot became confused in a storm and landed on a beach. The crew escaped, but high tide engulfed the *Cloudster* and destroyed it.

After the *Cloudster*'s aborted transcontinental flight, Douglas submitted a design to the United States Navy for a torpedo plane that was based, in part, on the *Cloudster*'s design. It was considered so outstanding that three airplanes were ordered and given the designation DT-1.

Unlike the thousands of pages of data later required to interest the government in a new airplane, the navy contract was only eighteen pages long.

Davis was so disillusioned when the *Cloudster* failed to win the prize that he withdrew from the company, selling his shares for $2,500 on a promissory note. The company was renamed the Douglas Company and reincorporated in California.

Davis's departure was a blow to Douglas because he liked Davis and needed his financial support, but he shrugged his shoulders and went back to work, wondering how he was going to get financing now that he had a government contract.

During these trying times, austerity was the rule at the Douglas home on 10th Street in Santa Monica. It was a small, two-bedroom frame house and it was only partly furnished. It remained that way until after Douglas delivered his torpedo planes.

The contract with the navy called for the government to make a partial payment on the cost of designing and building the airplanes, but Douglas needed an additional $15,000 to proceed. After going from one bank to another, he grew more and more discouraged. They told him frankly he was a fool to start such a business, and that he ought to get out of it. The fact the Douglas Company had a contract for $120,000 meant nothing to them.

One of the problems he had in getting financial support was his youthful appearance. Some time before he had grown a mustache in the hope he would look more mature. Even this did not work so he turned, in desperation, to Bill Henry, his sports editor friend with the *Los Angeles Times,* who had been given a 25 percent interest in the company for his help in getting the Davis contract.

Henry listened patiently. "Let me talk to Harry Chandler."

Chandler, publisher of the *Times,* met young Douglas and listened to his plea for a loan of $15,000. "I'm a publisher, Douglas, and I know nothing about aviation. Perhaps your airplane will be a success. I just don't know. However, I'm interested in the growth of Los Angeles. We need people like you and new plants so I'm going to help." He dictated a letter, saying that when nine other local businesses agreed to back Douglas, he would guarantee a loan of $15,000.

Douglas was jubilant and thanked him profusely.

His next step was to visit the office of C. F. Brant, vice-president of the Title Insurance and Trust Company. Brant's secretary at first refused to even ask Brant whether he would see Douglas. "He's too busy!" she said tartly.

Douglas persisted until she agreed to take Chandler's letter in to Brant. Douglas's eyes fastened hopefully on the closed door of Brant's private office. A few minutes later, the secretary came out and gave him Chandler's letter without comment. He was crestfallen until he glanced at the letter. On the bottom, Brant had signed his name, adding, "Me, too."

After that others quickly fell in line and he received backing from other prominent businessmen. One banker, who agreed to a loan, told him kindly, "Shave it off, kid. You're not fooling anybody!"

He did, and never grew another mustache.

After he received the money, Douglas almost wished he had asked for more to cover all contingencies, but it just went against his frugal nature. With money problems out of the way for the time being, the torpedo planes went into production at the Goodyear hangar in east Los Angeles.

Douglas's uncompromising standards were spelled out early in his career in the rather quaint advertising language of 1921. "The users of airplanes, whether they be purchasers of rides, private owners, transportation companies, or government departments, demand and get the utmost in performance consistent with sturdy and conservative construction.

"Without these basic characteristics, airplanes cannot be satisfactory from the point of performance nor as a sound financial investment.

"Those who know most of the importance of superfine quality and workmanship find the cost of quality a small item when measured in terms of satisfactory performance. Quality is the basic feature of all successful aircraft."

Quality workmanship was a theme that was a distinctive part of Douglas's basic philosophy and no one who ever worked for him was allowed to forget it.

The atmosphere at the Douglas plant was so informal that, if one had a problem, he just went up to Douglas and told him about it. His new general manager, Harry Wetzel, was a former government inspector he had known during his years with Martin. Wetzel was against such informality, and he told his boss the workers should be advised to go through channels.

Douglas replied, "Horseshit!"

The makeshift nature of the Goodyear plant was not adequate for aircraft production so Douglas began to look elsewhere. Originally, he wanted to establish his plant at Long Beach, but he could not find a suitable place near the city. One day in 1922 Douglas drove his Elgin roadster along Wilshire Boulevard, then a two-lane road lined with eucalyptus trees that ended in the beach resort of Santa Monica. He stopped at 24th Street and Wilshire where stock promoters had built a movie studio that failed to become a profitable enterprise. He noted that the buildings seemed to have lots of floor space that would be suitable for assembling airplanes, and that the field in back was flat and suitable to take off and land airplanes. After a follow-on contract for eighteen additional DT airplanes was approved by the United States Navy, Douglas bought the property and the number of employees rose to forty-two. Six torpedo planes were delivered to the navy during 1922 from the old movie studio.

At home Charlotte gave birth to Barbara Jean Douglas on November 25, 1922.

The following year his first true production line was set up to complete the DT-2 order for thirty-eight planes, and even more employees were needed from the sleepy town of Santa Monica.

The Engineering Department, composed of Douglas, John "Jack" Northrop, and Arthur Mankey started to design a cargo plane.

Harry Strangman, who later joined the company, became a good friend in 1924. He ran his own accounting office, and this former Alaskan adventurer often went sailing with Douglas.

George Strompl, the blustery shop foreman, was an awesome sight to new employees until they got to know him and realized his bark was worse than his bite. For the slightest infraction Strompl would roar, "You're fired!" Then he would insist that the person return to work.

Bill Henry, who had helped to secure the original *Cloudster* order from Davis, now decided to bow out completely from the company. Although he was proud of what Douglas had accomplished, he had no interest in being involved in an industrial enterprise. He sold his quarter interest to Douglas's father for $25,000. The father had to borrow on his life insurance to raise the money. Thirty years later, the stock Henry sold for $25,000 was worth $70 million.

First Around the World

So successful was the DT series that other organizations were contracted to build them. In early 1924, the Naval Aircraft Factory built six, and the Dayton Aircraft Company became the largest builder outside of Douglas. During the summer of 1923, a young army officer appeared at the plant. He told a worker, "I'd like to see Mr. Douglas. I'm Lt. Erik Nelson." When he learned Douglas was back east, he talked to company engineers, explaining the army wanted to buy four airplanes to fly around the world.

This was exciting news, but only Douglas could make the decision, so they wired him and he returned immediately to Santa Monica. Nelson and Douglas discussed the matter at length, and then Douglas said, "We can do it."

Arthur Burr Stone and Holger "Al" Wictum, inspectors from the procurement division of the Materiel Division of the United States Army, joined Nelson at the company to oversee the design. When they were satisfied, they took Douglas's drawings to Maj. Gen. Mason M. Patrick, chief of the air service, who was so pleased that he approved them on August 1, 1923. He authorized five planes, one to be used as a trainer.

Nelson returned to the company to supervise production. The lieutenant and Douglas frequently clashed while plans were finalized, but each had great respect for the other. Work was started on the five planes in the fall, and tests were completed by the middle of March the following year.

The world flight was planned to demonstrate the feasibility of aerial communications and transportation around the world. Gen. Patrick, who personally planned the flight, was anxious to bring the value of air transportation forcefully to the public, knowing that only a dramatic flight would capture everyone's imagination. Patrick was a visionary. He was aware that the general public was not conscious of the contributions airplanes could make to world transportation, so he was anxious to demonstrate their inherent possibilities.

The World Cruisers were designed for either land or water operations, and their wings were made to fold for easy storage. The reliable Liberty engine was selected, and the airplane was designed to cruise at 100 MPH.

The world flight was a masterful undertaking because supplies had to be shipped to twenty-two countries where the aircraft would land. Only one country, the Soviet Union, refused to permit them to cross or make a stop.

Major F. L. Martin was the pilot of the first airplane and S. Sgt. A. L. Harvey was assigned as mechanic. The second ship was commanded by Lt. Lowell Smith with T. Sgt. A. H. Turner. Lieutenant Leigh Wade was pilot of number three with S. Sgt. A. H. Ogden. Lieutenant Erik H. Nelson was given command of number four, and also was designated engineering officer for the flight with Lt. John Harding, Jr., as maintenance officer. The fifth plane at first was used as a trainer.

There were numerous farewell parties, but the man most responsible for making the around-the-world flight possible was not at any of them. Douglas and his entire family were sick with whooping cough.

Santa Monica held a World Flight Day celebration at Clover Field on March 16, 1924, the day before the start of the round-the-world flight. The four aircraft departed the following morning at 9:30, but Martin's plane had to make an emergency landing in the San Joaquin Valley.

The official starting point was Seattle. There, Sergeant Turner on ship two had to be replaced by Lt. Leslie P. Arnold when he became ill. The start of the world flight was scheduled to begin April 4 from Lake Washington, but a heavy fog delayed departure. The next day, the propeller of Major Martin's plane broke, and the flight was delayed again.

Douglas, getting these reports from the crews, began to wonder if the flight was jinxed from the start. It was certainly having more than its share of problems.

Once they did take off from Seattle, Martin was forced to land at Portage Bay on the flight to Alaska, and a new engine had to be installed. In an effort to catch up, he took a short cut and found himself in a deep fog. In trying to climb out of the soup, his plane hit a mountain peak. Although the plane was badly damaged, neither Martin nor his mechanic was injured. As far as the Air Service and Douglas officials knew, the airplane had just disappeared.

Martin and Sgt. Harvey stayed near the wrecked airplane for two days and nights until the weather cleared and they could walk out. They found a cabin and later made their way to Fort Moller, where they wired their superiors and Douglas with details of what had happened.

Meanwhile, the other three airplanes flew across the Pacific to Japan, and then on to China where they were royally welcomed. Across the continent of Asia and then on to Paris all went well, and they arrived jubilantly at the French capital on July 14.

Hard luck returned, however, when ship three was forced to land in the Atlantic on its way home. A U.S. Navy ship rescued Wade and Ogden and, taking the airplane in tow, proceeded to within a mile of shore before heavy seas capsized the World Cruiser and it sank. At Nova Scotia, Wade and Ogden were given the fifth cruiser, flown from Santa Monica by Victor Bertrandias, so they could rejoin the others on their way to the West Coast. Few people knew of the substitution at the time.

As the three airplanes flew triumphantly over Clover Field at 2:25 P.M. on September 3, Lt. Erik Nelson noted with amazement the 200,000 or more people who had gathered to watch them land. Nelson's plane was first to touch down, his propeller wash flinging rose petals behind his plane as it swept through an acre of the field, which had been strewn with flowers. As his plane drew up to a grandstand, Nelson noticed that a fenced parking area also was covered with rose petals.

As the pilots crawled out of their airplanes, guards fought to contain the huge crowd. It was an impossible task, and the crews soon were mobbed. Souvenir hunters tore buttons from their uniforms, and Nelson feared for their planes as people slashed at them in a frenzy to obtain anything as a memento. One woman cut a chunk of cloth out of Nelson's collar with a knife, while another slashed at his pants. It took the crews forty-five minutes to reach the reviewing stand.

Nelson's first words were, "Where's Donald Douglas? He's built the most successful plane yet perfected. I want to tell him personally that he certainly knows how to build airplanes."

Douglas had left the reviewing stand to accept a silver and gold plaque from Santa Monica officials. In endeavoring to return, he was stopped by security guards and, because they did not recognize him, refused entrance to the reviewing-stand area. After some frustrating moments while he established his identity, he was allowed to enter.

People congratulated him as he slowly worked his way to meet the crew members. His eyes flooded with tears and his voice cracked as he stepped to the reviewing stand to thunderous applause.

After this tremendous celebration, the flight to Seattle to officially end the flight was anticlimactic.

For its time, the round-the-world flight was one of incredible fortitude and courage on the part of the men who flew it, but they were unanimous in saying it could only have been made in a Douglas airplane. Their longest flight had been from Reykjavik, Iceland, to Fredriksdal, Greenland, a distance of 875 miles. In all, the World Cruisers flew 27,550 miles, approximately 3,000 more than the official distance around the earth as measured on a great circle route.

This flight, more than any previous one, brought aviation to the fore, and the company was the first to benefit from renewed interest in aviation. The Norwegian government not only bought a plane similar to the World Cruisers, but obtained manufacturing rights to build them in their own country. These airplanes served Norway for over ten years.

Following this flight, the Douglas Company adopted the slogan "First Around the World."

Typically, Douglas took the historic World Cruiser flight in stride, never ceasing his constant endeavors to design new and better airplanes, looking only to the challenge of the future.

As orders poured in, the company expanded, reaching a level of 112 workers by January 1925, with an annual payroll of $248,867. Through all this intense activity, Douglas had been working on the design for an observation plane, and also the design for a new cargo aircraft.

Obsolete airplanes such as the DH-4s still were the mainstay of the army even in the mid-1920s. As a result, U.S. airpower was ranked in fifth place in the world. Such a condition was intolerable, so the United States Army announced a competition for a new observation plane. Douglas told his staff to design a plane to be called the XO-2, and to continue work on a cargo plane for possible use as a mail plane. In February 1925, the O-2, despite the stiffest competition in the business, won the army trials and the company was given a contract to build forty-six observation planes for $750,000.

Douglas knew the success of the World Cruisers had helped to win the competition against major eastern companies, despite the fact they had produced the bulk of World War I aircraft. The eastern press and members of Congress demanded an investigation. The army was accused of misspending the major part of its aviation budget for airplanes produced by a small outfit in California that would build them in a barn in Santa Monica formerly occupied by the Herrman movie studios. An impartial investigation was held, and it soon became evident that the award had been granted strictly on merit.

In the summer of 1925 a young man appeared at the employment offices to seek a job as an engineer. Arthur E. Raymond, who was later to become the company's vice-president of engineering, had graduated from Harvard with honors in 1920, and later studied aeronautical engineering at M.I.T., where he received his master of science degree. Although he wanted to make a future for himself in the aircraft business, during the early years of the 1920s engineering jobs were hard to find, so he had been working for his father, who owned the Raymond Hotel in Pasadena.

When Raymond appeared at the company's offices, he sought an interview with Douglas, but as he was not available, Raymond talked to Ed Doak. Doak listened sympathetically, noting the young engineer's credentials with approval. "There's nothing open now in engineering," he said, "but we've got a bid in for a new observation plane. If we get the job, we can use you."

With all the confidence of youth, Raymond quit his job with his father and rented a house in Santa Monica for him and his wife on the strength of what really was not a strong hope for a job. For several weeks he haunted the employment office each day until finally he was asked if he would take a job in the shop. Eager to do anything to get in the business, he agreed and spent six weeks working for the turbulent George Strompl filing fittings and drilling holes.

Shortly afterward Douglas wrote his old friend Jerome Hunsaker to seek his help in finding an aerodynamacist for engineering analysis work. Hunsaker wired back, saying, "You have an excellent man out there. His name is Arthur Raymond, and he's working in your shop." Douglas checked with George Strompl and, sure enough, graduate engineer Raymond was doing menial work filing the rough edges off fittings. Raymond was transferred immediately to the Engineering Department where his talents proved far more valuable. His pay was raised to $30 a week, and he joined such others as Edward F. Burton, Jack Northrop, and Jerry Vultee. Each of these talented individuals later distinguished himself in the industry.

Shortly after Raymond joined the company, Douglas brought in James H. "Dutch" Kindelberger as chief engineer. The gregarious Kindelberger had replaced Douglas as chief engineer at Martin. A big man physically, Kindelberger's boundless energy and colorful, earthy sense of humor made him a wise choice for the job, permitting Douglas to phase out his own work on detailed drafting so he could concentrate full time on running his company.

In the fall of 1925, the Engineering Department moved into a new and larger building behind the old one, which fronted on Wilshire Boulevard. While Douglas and Wetzel remained in the front offices, the Engineering Department moved to new quarters in the rear. Informality remained the rule; most employees wore golf knickers to work.

Behind Engineering, Douglas had renovated a large concrete reservoir by removing its wooden roof and installing a court for volleyball or tennis. Some employees played during lunch.

Raymond learned to respect and admire Douglas and Wetzel. As general manager of the company Harry Wetzel was a penny pincher who remained somewhat aloof from the rest of the staff, but underneath his craggy features was a very human individual.

After Raymond had been with the company several months, he walked into Douglas's office. "Do I have a future at Douglas?"

Douglas eyed him for a moment. "The future here is unlimited."

Raymond, inspired by such talk, said, "Mr. Douglas, I think I should have a raise."

His boss looked at him thoughtfully before replying. "I agree. How about $10 more a week?"

This was more than Raymond had expected, so he decided to wait around a few more minutes to see what else might develop. He left when Douglas made it obvious that he had pushed his luck as far as it would go.

With the press in attendance, the XO-2 flight evaluation tests were held at McCook Field in Dayton, Ohio. Douglas's chief test pilot Eric Springer demonstrated that it was thirty miles an hour faster than the DeHavilland entry, with a lower landing speed and a higher altitude ceiling.

With the Los Angeles area expanding at an unprecedented rate, Santa Monica also began to grow, helped by companies such as Douglas, whose payroll exceeded 500 men and women.

The O-2 proved to be the first in a series that lasted for ten years in production because the United States Army Aviation Service adopted it as their standard observation plane to replace the aging DeHavillands of World War I.

Douglas turned next to an earlier idea for a plane that could carry mail economically. With a number of prominent businessmen, he discussed the possibility of starting airmail service between Los Angeles and Salt Lake City. When an airline to be called Western Air Express was proposed, Douglas was asked if his company could design and build six cargo planes to carry the mail. He assured them his company could do so and on July 13, 1925, Western Air Express was incorporated by a number of businessmen in Los Angeles and Salt Lake City, including Harry Chandler of the Los Angeles *Times* and its sports editor Bill Henry.

The M-2 airplane that resulted was a variation of Douglas's

original design for a cargo carrier. Along with mail sacks, the M-2 was designed to carry two passengers, but they would have to sit on the sacks of mail. Western Air Express, later renamed Western Air Lines, purchased six M-2s for their routes.

Betty Dern, the daughter of Utah's governor, christened the M-2 with a bottle of Great Salt Lake water on April 17, 1926, before it took off with a load of mail for Los Angeles. Charles N. "Jimmy" James was at the controls. After leaving Salt Lake City, he saw he was getting so far ahead of schedule that he would arrive too soon in Los Angeles where the welcoming committee was planning a celebration. He stopped in Las Vegas, Nevada, to kill time, and then took off for Vail Field in Los Angeles, where he landed at 5:12 P.M.

Jumping jauntily out of the cockpit, he waved at officials and the crowd. "Well, folks, here's your mailman."

The same day, another Western M-2 piloted by Maury Graham left Los Angeles from a runway improvised in the middle of a hay field for the return trip to Salt Lake City.

The M-2 was the first Douglas aircraft to fly for a scheduled airline. It had a speed of 110 MPH, and it could fly 600 miles without refueling. Significantly, Western Air Express made a small profit by the end of 1926.

Ed Heinemann, the teenager who had witnessed the first flight of the *Cloudster,* dropped out of Manual Arts High School in the fall of 1925 after three and a half years, much to the dismay of his drafting teacher August Flam who had taken a liking to the kid. Ed had finished everything but his English course, and, with typical teenage cockiness, told his drafting teacher, "Who needs English?" He could not be persuaded to finish high school.

Heinemann had been so impressed by Donald Douglas that he went to his company first to see about a job. He was told that they were hoping to get a government tracing job for O-2 aircraft, but until they did no one could be hired.

Heinemann, whose aircraft designs years later would be marked by unusual foresight and genius, started his working career by designing elaborate and expensive picture frames for the Bachman Picture Frame Company. This job lasted two months until his former teacher at Manual Arts recommended him for a drafting job with the Yankee Motor Body Company. For the next year he designed ice wagons, moving vans, and school buses. Ed proved an apt pupil and his boss James Yankee pushed him along in the business as fast as his progress dictated.

In late 1926 Heinemann received a call from Arthur Mankey, the Douglas Company's chief draftsman, who offered him a job as a tracer and draftsman. "You'll have to come in for an interview," Mankey told him. "If you get by that, the pay is $18 a week. What do you say?"

Ed assured him of his interest, promising to see him the next day. When Heinemann appeared at the Douglas plant on Wilshire in Santa Monica, he learned that Mankey was not in. A red-haired secretary—Ed learned later all of Douglas's early secretaries were red-haired—took him in to see Dutch Kindelberger, the chief engineer. Ed noted that Kindelberger wore knickers, with long socks that were a loud green and brown in color. Heinemann answered questions as the shaggy-haired Kindelberger queried him in a casual but deliberate manner.

After Dutch explained that Douglas had been granted a tracing contract by the Army Air Service's Wright Field, he said, "Do you think you can do the job?"

"Yes. I've done tracing." He handed Dutch a drawing he had completed of a Dodge engine at Manual Arts High School. A Dodge dealer had given the youngster a cross-section of the engine, and he had scaled it full size, with every part of the engine drawn out.

Kindelberger was impressed. "Okay," he said. "You've got the job if you don't mind tracing." At the time, drawings were made on vellum and then traced on cloth with ink.

Ed assured him again that he did not mind. Later, he learned that college-educated engineers resented tracing work, believing such activity was beneath them. Jerry Vultee, who later founded his own aircraft company, was hired a few weeks later to do similar work despite the fact that he had just graduated from the University of Michigan with an aeronautical degree. Sitting at a desk next to Heinemann, Vultee constantly groused about tracing work.

One of Heinemann's most enduring memories of those early days was the peculiar odor of banana oil in the dope that was used to coat the linen surfaces of airplanes.

Soon after Ed was hired, Mankey left Douglas and Courtland

Hertel was appointed chief draftsman. After finishing his tracing work, Heinemann worked directly under Jack Northrop on the T2D, a unique convertible land-sea torpedo plane.

Ed got to see Douglas quite often because the Engineering building, behind the front office, did not have a men's room— everyone had to use the one in the front office. He quickly learned that in working for Douglas everything had to have a purpose, leaving little room for emotion in the design of airplanes. He found Douglas's thoroughness challenging because he was a very clear-thinking person who would not tolerate anyone who stuck to pet ideas once they were proven wrong.

To the rear of the plant, airplanes were built in a 65- by 120-foot building that formerly was used to make motion pictures. There, the pervasive smell of banana oil dominated everything.

The Wilshire plant was filled to capacity, with twenty people in the Engineering Department alone. Although Douglas did some drafting, by and large he left the Engineering Department in the hands of Chief Engineer Kindelberger. The boss stayed up front with Vice-President-Treasurer Harry Wetzel and Purchasing Agent Ed Doak.

In his conversations with Douglas, Heinemann realized their mutual love for boats was one thing they had in common. At the time Douglas had a twenty-one-foot boat that he sailed frequently to Catalina and back with a few cronies. As a lover of sailboats, Heinemann recognized Douglas as a superb sailor. Douglas's first sailboat was followed later by a larger boat he named *Barbara Jean,* after his daughter.

Heinemann's first job at Douglas lasted eleven months. When the government contract was finished, the company was in a tight spot financially, so at the age of eighteen, Heinemann and half of the twenty-man Engineering team were laid off. Douglas felt so highly about Ed and a few others that he called the plant manager at Standard Oil's El Segundo division to recommend them. Douglas's reputation for hiring top-notch people was well known, so Standard Oil was only too happy to hire all of those laid off by Douglas.

While he worked at Standard, Heinemann decided to take flying lessons. At the time, there were three airports on Western Avenue in Los Angeles. The first was run by Burdett "Pop" Fuller who owned three WWI Jennies and a new International biplane called the F-16

Violet. The second was operated by Jack Frye and Paul Richter, who ran the Eaglerock Agency, selling a frail airplane that was built by a Wichita, Kansas, company. Ed watched the Eaglerock airplanes land with misgivings. They seemed almost to fly backwards when head winds were strong, even under full power.

He decided to take instructions from Pop Fuller. Ed's first landing in a DH-4 was so perfect that Pop could not believe he had never flown before. Heinemann, with his usual thoroughness, had studied the controls thoroughly during taxi runs, and soon became an expert pilot although in later years he had little time to enjoy the pastime.

Douglas submitted designs for four experimental airplanes to the U.S. Army in 1927, winning three of them amid tough competition.

While production of the O-2 observation planes continued for the army, C-1C aircraft were used as the army's standard cargo, medical evacuation airplane and troop transport.

Until 1927, most mail planes in the country had been DeHavillands, but the Post Office Department decided they must be replaced because they were so outmoded. In the competition that followed, Douglas received an order for fifty-one mail planes—one of the company's largest orders during that period.

His Elgin automobile, a venerable machine that had long since seen its best days, had been repaired again and again by Jack Northrop. When he asked Jack if he could fix it up again, Northrop responded loyally, "Sure, Doug. I'll fix it."

"Good. You can have it."

The astounded Northrop gaped at his boss, wondering what had happened that he had finally decided to part with the ancient Elgin. Douglas's frugality had kept him patching up the old car, even to the extent of using rope to hold one door shut because it would no longer function properly. Now, with business on the upswing, with a large and diversified backlog of airplanes in production, Douglas decided to splurge a bit and he bought a new air-cooled Franklin.

Although the Douglas Company was in good financial health, eastern aircraft companies were not because the United States

Congress was turning down one appropriation after another for new aircraft for the army and navy.

Brigadier General William S. "Billy" Mitchell tried to arouse an apathetic public to the dire straits the country was in with an ineffective and diminishing air fleet. The Army Air Service, he pointed out in 1926, was down to 60 pursuit aircraft and 169 observation planes. There were no bombers or attack planes available. Mitchell's strong arguments so upset the bureaucracy, particularly his insistence on a separate air force for the United States, that he was courtmartialed for insubordination. Despite his conviction, he carried his campaign to the public through books, speeches, and magazine articles.

Many believed aviation's future lay in lighter-than-air craft such as dirigibles, which had been developed by the Germans during World War I. Now, German engineers were imparting the knowledge gained by the Zeppelin Works at Friedrichshafen during the recent war to interested persons in the United States, Italy, and Great Britain. Later, the losses of Italy's *Roma,* and the fiery death of the *Hindenburg* at Lakehurst, New Jersey, plus losses of the United States Navy's dirigibles, convinced most experts that aviation's future lay in heavier-than-air craft. Douglas was in wholehearted agreement.

5

The Challenge of the 247

The reputation of the Douglas Company now was established throughout the world, and was perhaps best expressed in the words of an Army Air Service inspector who wrote his superiors, "The type of work turned out is of high standard, and everyone concerned seems anxious to turn out a good product."

In the next few years, production of the O-2 and C-1C continued for the army, and fifty O-2Ms were produced for the United States Post Office, ten of which were later redesignated M-3s and the others M-4s. In addition, the government of Mexico bought ten O-2s.

A navy production order arrived in 1927 for a twin-engine, multipurpose aircraft for land or carrier operations. This one was designed by the navy and it was called the T2D1.

Production continued at a high level after the army ordered sixty-two O-2Hs to replace the O-2C. The latter proved so successful in service that the Army adopted it as its standard observation plane. The H was an improved version that cruised at 110 miles an hour with a top speed of 126. Its landing speed was exceptional, down to an extremely safe 58 MPH.

Although the Wilshire plant was adequate to maintain production, its adjoining field posed severe limitations on flight operations. Therefore, planes had to be trucked to Clover Field in Santa Monica, two miles away, so they could be flight-tested. This situation could not last so Douglas signed orders to abandon the Wilshire field in early 1927.

Shortly thereafter, workers at the plant were astonished to hear an airplane overhead. They rushed out of the factory to wave the plane off, but it came in regardless of their frantic hand waving. Out of the plane stepped a tall, slim young man who apologized profusely. Indicating the man behind him, he said, "Just flew up from San Diego with a man from Ryan. He wants to see Donald Douglas."

One of the Douglas engineers escorted them to the plant office. "Work for Ryan?" he said to the younger man.

"No. Been flying the airmail. I'm Charles Lindbergh."

The visitors had their meeting with Douglas and then took off. Lindbergh was the last pilot to use the small pasture field.

By 1928, the number of passengers and the amounts of mail and cargo had increased three-fold over the previous year as airlines expanded their operations and larger airplanes became available.

That year, Ed Heinemann was again out of a job so he went back to Douglas and talked to Kindelberger. Heinemann was rehired at the Wilshire plant, this time to work on the XA-14 attack bomber. Later, he was transferred to help prepare drawings for the Ambassador, a high-wing monoplane built for commercial use. Douglas thought the time was ripe for entering the commercial field with this two-seater airplane, but the Ambassador found no buyers.

At this time the Moreland Company, which made all forgings for the couplings used to drill oil wells, sold stock with a value of $500,000 to start the Moreland Aircraft Company. Its prospects were so appealing that several Douglas engineers left to join the new company, and Heinemann told Dutch he also wanted to leave. Kindelberger asked him to finish the drawings for the Ambassador before he left, saying he would raise his weekly salary to $55, and Ed agreed to do so. When he finished his work at Douglas, Heinemann joined the Moreland Company at its new factory in El Segundo. While there he designed a high-wing training plane, and became the company's chief engineer.

The 1929 depression only aggravated the problem of starting up a new airplane company, and the Moreland trainer, despite its excellence, failed to sell, and the company folded. Throughout the aircraft industry there were many obscure people who were developing revolutionary designs and making them work. There were 300 aircraft factories in 1929, but most were little more than barns in fields where one had to scare away the cows to see the airplanes.

Heinemann left the Moreland Aircraft Company and went to work for the Northrop-Burbank Company, a new subsidiary of United Aircraft. After a year, United decided to move some of its plant personnel to Wichita. Neither Jack Northrop nor Heinemann was interested in moving to Kansas, so they refused offers to accept jobs with United in the Midwest. Later, they returned to Douglas.

As the decade of the turbulent 1920s drew to a close, Douglas decided to review his earlier designs, all biplanes that for the most part were made of fabric and wood. These planes were made with spruce spars and contoured wing ribs covered with linen, which was sewn to the ribs by women such as Christina I. St. Clair and dozens of other skilled seamstresses. Fuselages also were fabric-covered, but they had Shelby tubular frames.

Douglas realized the industry had stayed too long with outmoded ideas, and that metal should be used for greater strength and durability on wings and fuselages to replace fabric. The entire industry was moving in the direction of greater use of light-gauge aluminum alloys not only for structural tubing for the fuselage, but also for internally stressed wings. The Aluminum Company of America (ALCOA) had developed techniques to manufacture the odd shapes needed for airframe construction. Meanwhile, Ford, Junkers, Fokker, and Handley-Page had been experimenting with all-metal monoplanes that used corrugated metal skin surfaces.

The external surfaces of the Ford Motor Company's trimotors were made of such surfaces, with internal metal brackets in the wing attached to beams, or spars, thereby making the wing self-supporting once it was attached to the fuselage. Douglas was now convinced that monoplanes could be built that were stronger than biplanes, and that a drastic change in the design of aircraft was long overdue.

Every weekend in the late 1920s, the Douglas family took the *Barbara Jean,* a small forty-foot schooner, to Catalina Island. There were days when heavy winds kicked up such massive waves in the Pacific that the schooner heeled over and shipped green water. At times, Barbara, Don, Will, and Charlotte were overcome with fright as they were deluged under a cascade of water, but Douglas, Sr., scoffed at their fears and loved every minute of these trips.

At an early age, Douglas taught Don and Will to navigate, and how to use a sextant to determine their position by the stars. At night, anchored off Catalina, the children sat bundled up as their father identified the principal stars. They never forgot these moments of intimacy.

Oftentimes a popular figure called Carl would stop by with fresh lobsters or abalone for sale. Douglas always invited him on board for a drink of scotch, and they had long chats about fishing.

On each trip to Catalina, Douglas took his bagpipes along. Often he wrote American words to popular Scottish ballads, but there were other songs he liked. One of his favorites was "Endymion," which tells the story of a beautiful youth who, in Greek mythology, was loved by the goddess of the moon Selene.

Douglas entered the Inter-Island Races each year, and frequently won. The course extended around San Clemente, Santa Rosa, Catalina, and the other channel islands. During these races Charlotte always went along, turning out fabulous dinners despite the boat's small galley and the constant agony she suffered from seasickness, which she never completely overcame. Her husband was never sick, and he always ribbed those who suffered from the malady. When Don and Will were older, they joined their father in the Inter-Island Races, which lasted two or three days.

Douglas and his father, William E. Douglas, were sole owners of the company in 1928, and from 1921 to 1928 they earned a profit of $1.2 million. William Douglas, a former banker with New York's National Park Bank, which merged with Chase Manhattan in 1928, had earlier agreed with his son that profits during this period should be used to expand the company, although they gave themselves a $40,000 dividend in 1927.

The company had grown so much that another reorganization became necessary. On November 30, 1928, the Douglas Aircraft Company was incorporated in Delaware to purchase assets of the old Douglas Company. Although 1,000,000 shares were authorized, only 300,000 were issued. Douglas personally received 200,000 shares, and the remainder were sold to the public.

Douglas had been reluctant to go public, but was persuaded by

Latham R. Reed of E. A. Pierce and Company, and J. Cheever Cowdin of the Bancamerica-Blair Corporation. These two companies purchased the remaining stock for $1,000,000 and resold it. Douglas spent almost half of the million dollars to construct a new 7 3/4-acre plant at Santa Monica, adjoining Clover Field. He put the rest of the money into the company's cash account, where it remained unspent until 1934. Douglas's thrifty nature had earlier prescribed that development costs of a new airplane had to be written off each year although, at times, such conservative action resulted in lower dividends for stockholders.

For several years Douglas had considered building a flying boat. In 1929 he designed one, and in an era when flying boats had been successfully produced by other firms, the PD-1 proved itself despite the competition. It was a twin-engine flying boat built for the United States Navy. The hull was made of duraluminum as were the wing frames. Orders for twenty-five came in and work proceeded despite the October crash on Wall Street, and the tight credit that followed.

For some time Douglas had been concerned about the company's reliance on military orders—a concern that was to last throughout his industrial career. With foresight, he designed an airplane for the commercial market—the Dolphin—a sturdy amphibian that was to last for decades in service.

Douglas was rapidly becoming the world's number one man in aviation engineering. He had that rare instinct to recognize talent when he saw it. One did not have to have an aeronautical degree to impress Donald Douglas, and many of his finest engineers never went to college. Some, like Heinemann, never even graduated from high school. Along with Douglas's inherent ability to spot talent, he had an unerring knack for recognizing a phony.

In the decision-making process, he was absolutely fearless and always ready to try something new. Douglas was one of the first to build a thick wing, which he knew was possible on the basis of aerodynamics. The Wright brothers started with one-sided wings on biplanes, but Douglas was one of the first to realize the greater efficiency of monoplanes over biplanes because they eliminated many interwing struts and wires, which lowered the aerodynamic efficiency of the aircraft. He had recognized early that there was a critical wing thickness, or excessive drag would build up. In designing wings, he built right up to that drag limit.

With his early biplanes, Douglas learned the hard way that if the upper wing was in line with the lower wing, bad spin characteristics resulted. Therefore, he ordered the use of staggered wings, with the upper wing placed farther forward than the lower.

With consummate skill, Douglas bet on monoplanes at the right time. He had analyzed biplanes such as the Curtiss Condor, and learned that was not the way to go for a commercial airplane. There was too great a speed penalty.

His first successful monoplane was the Dolphin. It had a high wing and was powered by two Wright Whirlwind 300-horsepower engines. Priced at $45,000, the Dolphin sold well, although it was produced at the start of the Great Depression. Wilmington-Catalina Airline was one of the first to purchase.

Douglas shook his head in wonder at one Dolphin sale after a chauffeur-driven automobile came to the Santa Monica plant in 1933. Out of the car stepped an impeccably dressed young man who asked to see Mr. Douglas. He identified himself as Armand Esders. When he was shown into Douglas's office, he produced a scrapbook that had every advertisement ever published by the company about the Dolphin. He came right to the point. "Mr. Douglas, I'd like to buy a Dolphin."

Douglas eyed the young man appraisingly. "Indeed you can, but you must realize they are rather costly."

"I know. I have a check for $57,000. Will that cover it?"

Douglas looked at the check, then at the young man, and sat back in his chair. "More than enough."

The young man said politely, "There are several special features I want in my airplane."

Douglas raised his eyebrows, still wondering if the check was good. Among the things Esders wanted was a bar, and Douglas assured him that he could have whatever special features he wanted. When the young man left, Douglas checked up on him and found that his check was not only good, but that he was a prominent

French millionaire. Undoubtedly, Esders was one of the first to get an executive airplane precisely tailored to his wishes.

The next few years were grim for the nation at large, but Douglas's conservative instincts now paid off. While companies were folding right and left, Douglas Aircraft continued to grow and prosper. There was no depression at Douglas as the 1930s opened, because the company had delivered 430 airplanes in the previous decade, and it still had orders for 10 airplanes for China, 18 for the United States Navy, and 53 for the United States Army Air Service.

Airline operations had always depended on government subsidies for subsistence. Airplanes were not economical enough to operate strictly by carrying passengers. Most airplanes were underpowered and, like the Ford trimotor, were used to excess so they could not stand the strain of years of daily operations. In addition, passenger airplanes carried an average of eleven passengers—not enough to break even. Accidents were common and safety devices were unheard of, so only an intrepid few regularly used airplanes to travel. Douglas's first love had always been to build commercial transports, but conditions hadn't been right so he waited.

When Knute Rockne was killed in the crash of a commercial airliner on March 31, 1931, there was a tremendous hue and cry in the world's press about obsolescence and lack of safety of commercial transports. The public outrage was so great that the crash of the Fokker trimotor, which suffered a structural failure because of its wood construction, almost dealt a mortal blow to the infant airline industry. The Civil Aeronautics Authority insisted on so many modifications to the Fokker that further operations of the trimotor were impossible.

To survive, airlines knew they had to procure better and safer airplanes, so they appealed to the industry. It was clear that a totally different kind of airliner had to be designed—an all-metal airplane that would be bigger than anything heretofore used.

While this crisis developed in the aviation world, there was good news at home for the Douglases with the birth of twin boys. James and Malcolm increased Douglas's family to four sons and a daughter. When Barbara Jean was nine years old she went to Burbank

Airport to christen a C-1. Her mother was so shy that she turned such duties over to her daughter. Barbara thoroughly enjoyed such events, with their picture-taking ceremonies while her mother stood to one side beaming proudly.

Charlotte adored her husband Doug, often referring to him as her handsome husband, much to his embarrassment. She was five feet, ten inches in height, the same as her husband, with long, black, thick hair, blue eyes, and a small upturned nose. All but one son inherited the prominent German nose of Douglas's mother Dorothy. Malcolm, one of the twins born in 1931, was the only one of the Douglas children who resembled his mother.

In a "Dear Pa" letter, Douglas wrote his father October 8, 1931, to announce the birth of the twins a week after the event, saying they seemed to be getting along fine.

> Charlotte is still at the hospital and will be for another week, but is feeling well and gaining back her strength.
>
> We have given the little fellows some strong Scotch names, and I hope they will grow up to fit them. The oldest one, who has been just the picture of ruddy health from the first, is very dark with (new in our family) a heavy head of black hair and so he is called James Sholto. The younger lad had a lot of difficulty to start with. He was the same size as James and well built but something went haywire with his elimination system at first. He has got going now, however, and he is absolutely o.k. He seems to be fair and possibly red-haired, so we named him Malcolm Angus after the red end of the clan.
>
> They both weighed 5 3/4 pounds at birth, and I believe, according to all the experts, are as handsome a pair as you could find and yet do not look alike.
>
> Charlotte had the finest doctor for such matters in town (MacNeil) and got along fine. He uses a modified twilight sleep and it worked out wonderfully.
>
> The children are all very thrilled and interested, particularly Barbara Jean. They are all anxious to see their mother and brothers home as they are not allowed to visit them at the hospital at all on account of their ages and communicable diseases carried by youngsters.
>
> We have arranged things at the house so that we can have a nurse there at all times to take the bulk of the work from Charlotte. I have been pretty busy keeping the older ones going at their lessons, etc. We are, and have been, looking for a house or property

to build on and hope soon to have that settled. There are some bargains these days, but things you like don't seem any cheaper.

With the letter, Douglas enclosed a dividend check for $23,750. He explained that part of the dividend was earned on his own stock and he asked his father to deposit his share to his personal account at Chase. In a numerical table he indicated that his father's share of the stock dividend, figured on the basis of 50 cents for 25,000 shares, amounted to $12,500 which, he said, should be deducted from the total and the remainder, $11,250, deposited.

He told his father that the dividend was being paid to them somewhat in advance because they might want to buy some "stuff" in the market.

> It may be a time to buy a few stocks, although that still takes considerable courage. Mayo thinks a few are all right such as Gen'l Motors, Int. Harvester, Amer. Tel. and Tel., Con Gas N.Y. and Sears Roebuck. If you buy any bonds I believe they should be mainly in utilities and those only of operating companies (no holding co's) and of the highest character. Personally I am sticking to high grade States and Liberty 3 1/2 E. on account of expected tax burdens, particularly a Calif. Income Tax.

In conclusion he asked his father to do some straight talking to someone as high as possible in Chase about the possibility that a radical and frightened Congress might attempt to pass some bill such as the silver evaluation or other measure that would distinctly lower the value of the nation's currency.

> Such an inflation would give the stock market a great rise, but kill the bond market. I'm afraid the New York bankers might side in with some such move on account of their position in the stock market. Try and find out if the bankers seem friendly to such talk. If it is so, we will have to move out of most of our bonds even at heavy losses and Lord knows we all have them on paper now. This is very important. Don't forget what happened to the creditors in Germany when this was done.

His concern was valid because that is exactly what the Congress did. Douglas closed his letter saying he hoped his father and mother could come to see them soon, and get acquainted with the new members of the clan.

After World War I, airlines in Europe were subsidized by their governments. In the United States, commercial aviation suffered because surplus military airplanes, which were completely inadequate for civilian use, were dumped on the market at a fraction of their original cost. Equally bad, military airfields were closed and there were few good landing fields in or near major United States cities.

Secretary of Commerce Herbert Hoover tried to rectify this situation in 1922 by proposing legislation to the Congress that would help commercial aviation. He was not successful until February 1925 when the Congress passed the Kelly Bill, which authorized the postmaster general to contract for airmail service. Bidders had to be private operators, with experience in the field and available aircraft. As an added inducement, each operator was advised that he could keep up to four-fifths of the revenues earned by hauling mail.

When bids were sought in October to serve eight "feeder" routes, Colonial Air Transport received the one between Boston and New York. Colonial was run by an enterprising twenty-six-year-old by the name of Juan Terry Trippe. He immediately bought two Fokker trimotors that could carry six passengers and the mail. National Air Transport (NAT) received the Chicago-Dallas-Fort Worth route. Later, NAT took over the eastern route from New York to Chicago. The Chicago to San Francisco route was won by Puget Sound airmail pioneers William Boeing and Edward Hubbard, who formed Boeing Air Transport and placed twenty-five Boeing 40s into service. The Boeing transports carried two passengers in an enclosed cabin, as well as mail.

The cornerstone for modern commercial aviation in the United States was laid in May 1926 when Congress passed the Air Commerce Act. It created a Bureau of Aeronautics in the Department of Commerce authorized to license all American planes and pilots, set up and enforce air traffic rules and regulations, investigate accidents, and test all new engines and aircraft for safety.

After the 1931 crash of the Fokker trimotor that killed Knute Rockne, it was ironic that the Ford Trimotor, which owed so much of its design by William B. Stout to the pioneering work done by Tony Fokker, became queen of the skies.

Planes owned by Henry Ford, who had financed William Stout's early experiments with all-metal airplanes, were the first private carriers to fly domestic mail. Stout had been convinced since 1920 that biplanes used too much power to overcome drag. His first single-engine airplane, therefore, was an unorthodox monoplane. Ford had started freight service between Detroit, Cleveland, and Chicago in 1925. After Stout designed an all-metal trimotor transport, Ford bought him out and announced publicly that his airline would carry passengers as well as freight.

Stout was a gifted designer, but his Ford trimotor owed much to earlier designers. Hugo Junkers built his first all-metal airplane during World War I, using corrugated materials similar to the kind used by Stout. In 1919, German designer Adolf Rohrback, knowing that corrugated skin, while increasing structural strength, also caused high drag that reduced an aircraft's performance, started producing airplanes with smooth metal surfaces. The concept of "stressed skin" gained adherents because the wing's covering added strength to the entire structure.

Rohrback continued development of such wing structures and, in conjunction with Anthony Fokker, who extended his operations to the United States during the 1920s, the monoplane soon developed more backers and became more competitive in the minds of those who had always favored biplanes. But the biplane concept died slowly.

The Ford trimotor, designed by Stout, had many innovations. It was made with a corrugated metal skin, and had an enclosed cockpit and a thick, cantilevered wing attached to the top of the passenger cabin. It seated twelve people, but its noisy engines made comfort almost impossible except for a deaf person. To the delight of passengers, each person had his own window.

The *Tin Goose,* as it was affectionately dubbed, made possible the first successful passenger service, run by Stout Air Services. The company inaugurated the nation's first full-freight service, started the practice of serving meals on board, and even provided airport limousine service.

The Ford trimotor was a true pioneer, but its lifespan along airline routes was short. Although the Stout-designed trimotor was used for decades in a variety of roles after it was first introduced and doomed all other wood and fabric commercial airplanes, its service with scheduled airlines lasted only from the late 1920s to the early 1930s when it was superseded by more modern commercial transports.

The 1920s had been years of great innovation by individual designers. In addition to the work Stout was doing to revolutionize the science of aircraft design, Vincent J. Burnelli, an American designer, built a biplane in 1924 in which the fuselage, which enclosed the engine, contributed to the overall lift of the aircraft. British designer Handley-Page devised a slotted wing and Orville Wright invented split flaps, both of which improved control, adding to an airplane's performance and safety.

William E. Boeing established his Boeing Airplane Company in 1915, and he was Douglas's chief competitor during the 1920s. Eleven years older than Douglas, he had taken flying lessons from the Glenn L. Martin School of Aviation in Los Angeles while Douglas was at M.I.T. Afterwards, he bought a Martin flying boat for his personal use. Unlike Douglas, Boeing was wealthy. His family had earned millions through their lumbering and mining interests. Boeing considered flying a hobby, and he knew nothing about the design of airplanes. Along with the establishment of his airplane company, he also set up Boeing Air Transport, the foundation for United Air Lines. Former banker W. A. "Pat" Patterson started in the business with Boeing Air Transport.

For the first ten years of its industrial life, the Boeing Company built flying boats and seaplanes equipped with pontoons. Despite his own company's expertise in this field, Boeing bought a Douglas Dolphin for his personal use. Boeing departed from seaplanes in 1930 when engineer Claire Egtvedt designed a plane called the Monomail that was first flown in May. The original low-wing monoplane was designed for two engines later and was sold to the Army Air Corps as the B-9. The plane appeared to have commercial possibilities, so the Boeing company moved in that direction, and design work began on the 247.

Standard Airlines was one of the few airlines of this period to make money flying passengers and mail. Using a Fokker F-7, it carried movie stars to vacation spots in the Southwest. Harris M. Hanshue offered $1 million for Standard and, after it was accepted in 1928, he merged it with his Western Air Express. Jack Frye, one of Standard's founders, came with the deal.

Charles A. Lindbergh agreed to lend his name to Transcontinental Air Transport. This line provided rail and air service across the central United States. Passengers took a train across the Allegheny or Rocky mountains, where they could sleep peacefully in Pullmans, and then transferred to airplanes to fly over the lower, and safer, elevations. Such combination plane/rail transportation saved little time and quickly lost its appeal.

Three major transcontinental carriers survived the bitter struggle for survival as the decade drew to a close. Many smaller companies went bankrupt. In March 1929, Walter F. Brown, President Herbert Hoover's postmaster general, started an investigation. The Post Office Department had always believed commercial aviation should be encouraged in the interest of national defense. Brown was convinced that government subsidies to airlines to carry the mail were counterproductive. He told members of Congress that expansion of passenger air travel was impossible as long as airlines found it more profitable to carry subsidized mail. He asked Congress to amend the original Kelly Act and eliminate the pound-per-mile rate for airmail and pay operators on the basis of available cargo space. He argued such payments would encourage airlines to buy larger commercial transports and force them to carry more passengers to fill the extra space.

Brown was successful, and Congress passed the McNary-Watres Bill which offered rewards to airlines who purchased multiengined transports equipped with the most modern navigational aids. There were high hopes that this bill would increase competition among commercial carriers so that the airline industry eventually would become self-sufficient.

The reverse proved true, and the industry reduced its numbers even further as smaller carriers were squeezed out of the market. Western Air and Transcontinental Air Transport were merged to form Transcontinental and Western Air (TWA) Lines in 1930. Western Air Express's Jack Frye was promoted to vice-president of flight operations, and TWA inaugurated an all-air service across the country.

Earlier that year, in March, United Air Lines, which flew between the west coast and Chicago, bought out National Air Transport and extended its service to New York. And a number of small airlines, serving the southern section of the country, developed into American Airways, which became the most profitable airline during this period.

TWA and United now emerged as the nation's largest carriers. United's routes carried passengers and freight from New York across the northern part of the country, whereas TWA was given the central route between New York and Los Angeles. They both had lucrative airmail contracts, but were dedicated rivals when it came to getting passengers. Officials of both companies knew that the airline that got a new and better airplane first would have a competitive advantage. Postmaster Brown was so disturbed by emergence of these two giant airlines that he awarded American Airways the southern mail and passenger route.

Ed Heinemann rejoined the Douglas Aircraft Company as an engineering checker in late 1931. After Jack Northrop received Donald Douglas's approval to form a subsidiary with Douglas as sponsor with a 51 percent controlling interest, Heinemann asked permission to work for his old friend. Douglas granted Heinemann's request early in 1932, and he found himself working at his old desk in the former Moreland factory at El Segundo where Northrop established his plant.

Before he made the transfer Heinemann helped Douglas and the others move the Engineering Department from Wilshire Boulevard to its new location in Santa Monica. Each employee carried his own gear to the new plant, with a minimum of expense to the company.

Heinemann at last truly felt at home. He admired both Northrop, who was president of the Douglas subsidiary and chief engineer, and Douglas's chief engineer Dutch Kindelberger. He considered them brilliant, despite their lack of a college education.

Work began on two noted Northrop aircraft: the single-engine Gamma and Delta monoplanes. They were somewhat similar, each made of aluminum alloy, but the Delta had a larger fuselage to accommodate passengers. Douglas followed the design and production of the Northrop airplanes closely because they were all metal, and completely different from anything his company had built. The Gamma was designed primarily for freight and mail.

The first Gamma was made for Frank Hawks, and was called the *Texaco Fire Chief.* It was built in just eleven months. The second airplane, the *Polar Star,* was manufactured for millionaire Lincoln Ellsworth for use on an Antarctic expedition. This airplane was tested by Bernt Balchen. A Gamma, with Howard Hughes at the controls, flew coast-to-coast in 1936 to set a new record of nine hours and twenty-six minutes.

Heinemann loved his early years in the airplane business; he felt part of a close-knit family. He was saddened later when, as the industry expanded, personal relationships became less intimate.

When Boeing announced plans to build the 247 commercial transport, the race was on for a big new market. United Air Lines promptly signed to purchase the first sixty. TWA also tried to order but learned they would have to wait until United received its order. At the time, Boeing was affiliated with United because Boeing Air Transport, a subsidiary of the Boeing Company, had been merged with National Air Transport and Varney Airlines to form United Air Lines.

Jack Frye, vice-president of operations for TWA, got his engineering staff together to draw up plans for submission to the aircraft industry. He asked them to come up with ideas for a wholly new kind of airliner, one it was hoped would be better than the 200 MPH, ten-passenger Boeing 247, which was first to use engine cowls, and which could fly on one engine if necessary. The following summer Frye sent copies of a brief letter to Douglas, Martin,

Consolidated, Curtiss-Wright, Sikorsky, and General Aviation.

The letter to Douglas read, "Transcontinental and Western Air Lines is interested in purchasing 10 or more trimotored transport planes. I am attaching our general performance specifications, covering this equipment and would appreciate your advising whether your company is interested in this manufacturing job.

"If so, approximately how long would it take to turn out the first plane for service tests?"

Dated August 2, 1932, this letter became what Douglas later said was the "birth certificate of the modern airliner." The specs were stiff because they called for a transport that could carry at least twelve passengers, with more leg room than ever offered in previous passenger airplanes, a cruising speed of 145 miles an hour, a minimum service ceiling of 21,000 feet, and a range of 1,080 miles. Douglas also noted that the landing speed could not exceed 65 MPH, and the plane must have the very latest radio and instrumentation equipment for night flying.

Although no mention was made in Frye's letter about price, Douglas personally believed his company should go ahead and bid on the airplane. He told his associates that Frye's letter was the most important one ever to cross his desk.

Until now, the Ford Motor Company had dominated aviation in the United States. During the last years of the 1920s, the market was so saturated with commercial transports that no one was breaking even on them. Ford produced 200 trimotors, at prices ranging from $55,000 to $68,000, but he lost close to an estimated $3 million, although Ford never revealed the exact figure. He could carry the loss because of huge personal reserves from his automobile business. At the start of 1932, it was evident that even Ford was disillusioned with the aviation business, and would soon get out.

Douglas knew the time was ripe for his company to get into the commercial transport field. His decision was reinforced when Harold E. Talbott, Jr., chairman of North American Aviation, Inc., which owned 89,000 shares of Douglas stock, came to see him. Talbott was also a director of Transcontinental and Western Air, which was flying coast-to-coast in Ford and Fokker trimotors. He pointed out that Ford was expected soon to drop out of the commercial transport business, that Boeing's 247 would give United Air Lines an edge over TWA, and that it was time for Douglas to seriously consider entering the commercial field. Douglas also learned from Talbott that General Aviation Manufacturing Corporation, which had taken over the Fokker Aircraft Corporation in the United States, would soon become part of North American Aviation and was expected to submit a trimotor design to TWA.

Douglas pointed out that he had no interest in a trimotor design because he considered such a transport less efficient aerodynamically than a plane with two engines. He said previous two-engine airplanes designed by the company had proved that an airplane could fly safely on one engine during emergency operations. He explained that he had not entered the commercial field earlier because the public had been oversold on three-engine safety, which he knew was a false premise, one that led to inefficient airliners.

Talbott had such respect for Douglas that he did not dispute his claim about two-engine transports. In leaving, he stressed again the importance he and TWA attached to Douglas's entry into the commercial field.

While the Douglas engineering staff studied the requirements and how they could be met, particularly the gross weight of 14,200 lbs and the 2,300-lb payload, they carefully checked TWA's route system because one of the requirements was for a transport that could take off from any airport on two of its three proposed engines.

In a meeting to discuss the matter, Douglas told his engineers, "When you consider the weights and payload TWA wants, this will be quite a challenge. Still, I think we should take a crack at it. We can't go on building military airplanes exclusively, particularly with the peacetime budget Congress has approved."

Meetings were held constantly for a week with Chief Engineer Dutch Kindelberger and his number two man Arthur Raymond. Senior designers Fred Herman, Ed Burton, and Lee Atwood joined top management under Harry Wetzel and they were unanimous that the company should make a bid. Douglas agreed. "The time is ripe to get into the transport field." He paused and looked at them seriously. "I suggest we think about the matter for a couple of days before we get together again."

Next morning, Douglas wrote Frye, "We are interested in submitting a proposal in answer to your bid invitation for the design of a new transport plane. When will it be convenient for some of our engineers to get together with your technical people and present our views?"

A few days later, Douglas opened a meeting by saying, "Well, what do you all think?"

Kindelberger spoke first. "I believe we should forget about three engines. Why build a plane that even looks remotely like a Ford or Fokker? Besides, the nose engine interferes with the pilot's vision and adds to cockpit noise."

They raised quizzical eyes but Kindelberger continued to argue persuasively. "With the more powerful engine coming along, a pair of 'em will pull the load, especially if we wrap them in the new NACA cowling to take advantage of its streamlining and cut air resistance about 50 percent."

"How about availability of such engines?" Douglas said.

"Both Pratt & Whitney and Wright-Aeronautical have promising new engines in test runs. They say they'll be available in time for our airplane. They've got lots of horses and I'm confident they'll have more power in two engines than any three now in use."

Douglas nodded. He had seen the preliminary specs from the engine manufacturers.

Raymond, who had been listening intently, spoke up. "The Boeing design has one bad feature." He walked over to a cutaway drawing of the 247 on the wall. "Notice how the wing spar cuts through the cabin and almost divides it?" Raymond went on, "The cabin isn't high enough, either. A tall person would have to stoop to walk up and down the aisle."

"If we're going to build this thing," Kindelberger said, "let's make it big enough so a guy can walk around without banging his head on the ceiling."

"I agree," Douglas said. Then, to all of them, "Any time any of you have suggestions, don't keep them on ice, or let them burn you up. Tell me about them in your own words. We'll need all the suggestions we can get."

Raymond had another idea. "Why not adopt some of the features of Jack Northrop's tapered wing? This would give us the desired lift and still not present too much wing area. The wing's airfoil characteristics are good, and we can vary the sweepback to give us some latitude with the center of gravity."

He also mentioned that Northrop had developed special angles for his Delta and Gamma airplanes, which permitted easy attachment of the outer wing sections to the center section. He said

Northrop had sent the drawings to Santa Monica for use as desired. Douglas immediately recognized their value and ordered them used on all early DC airplanes.

Raymond said, "We could build the wing in three sections. A center section integrated with the fuselage so it will be strong enough to support the engines. At the same time, we'll eliminate the need for the main wing spar in the cabin."

Douglas liked their ideas, knowing the internally braced rib and spar and all-aluminum construction would be strong enough to support the engines mounted on a stub center wing on each side of the fuselage.

Lee Atwood spoke up. "We can extend the engine mounts forward of the wing so the propeller thrust over the airfoil will provide more lift.

"It will be no problem to bolt the outer wing sections to the center section, and the stressed aluminum skin will provide sufficient strength."

He paused in thought. "I believe we're all agreed the airplane should have a retractable gear system. We can make room in the engine nacelles to tuck them in by using hydraulic pressure."

"Boeing's got a retractable gear," Douglas said. "We'd better have one, too. Such a system should cut drag by 20 percent."

Ed Burton and Fred Herman both expressed concern about meeting the 65 MPH landing speed Frye mentioned in his letter. Herman told the group some kind of flap would be required to increase wing area and slow the aircraft for landings, and also to help provide more lift for takeoffs.

After days of discussion, they all agreed on a low-wing, all-metal monoplane, using a variation of the Northrop wing design. It would have two engines, instead of the three Frye sought, and the gear would be retractable into the engine nacelles.

Douglas listened intently throughout these meetings, saying little but absorbing everything. These ideas were not new, but he was aware that it was the first time all of them had ever been considered for one airplane.

He looked up. "The whole thing sounds almost too simple. However, we need the order because it will give us something to fall back upon if military contracts fall off." The Depression had deepened, and a reluctant Congress had cut sharply into Army and Navy airplane contracts.

The die was cast and Douglas wrote Frye another letter about the company's interest in bidding on the new airliner. He acted quickly, knowing how important it was because Sikorsky and General Aviation were already working on new designs. He also knew that Curtiss-Wright, which was building Condors for American Airways, would not be far behind.

Pilots liked the Condor, Douglas knew, because cockpit visibility was excellent, far better than the Ford trimotor. It could carry eighteen passengers, but was slow due to its biplane configuration. And, once its two huge wings were coated with ice, it became a pilot's nightmare to keep in the air. Otherwise it was a very stable aircraft.

At the end of their last meeting, Douglas told his staff, "Once the word gets around there's money for a new airplane anything can happen. I'm sure other companies won't sit quietly and let someone else grab off the business."

Boeing was far in the lead in building its new 247s, the first of which would fly sooner than the new Douglas airplane. When Boeing described its 247, it called it a low-wing, ten-passenger transport that was derived from its work on the B-9 bomber. When details were released, the entire industry took note because it was advertised as the airliner that could cut coast-to-coast travel time to nineteen hours.

Bill Boeing said of the 247, "This is the airliner that will put us in the Pullman business."

News reports continually extolled the aircraft's potentialities with one reporter saying, "It will be a long time before anyone builds a better or faster airplane."

Such outright enthusiasm for an existing airplane would have discouraged most industrialists but Donald Douglas and his engineers went quietly to work to prove they could build a better airplane. Douglas frankly admitted later that it was the challenge of the 247 that put his company into the transport business.

6

The DC-1

Raymond and Wetzel spent three weeks in New York working out details with Charles Lindbergh, TWA's technical adviser, and Jack Frye. The latter were enthusiastic about what was now called the DC-1, but they were astute businessmen and insisted on tough guarantees. Before Raymond and Wetzel committed themselves, Raymond called Douglas. "TWA insists the DC-1 must be able to climb on one engine with a full load from takeoff, and maintain level flight and climb on a single engine over any segment of the TWA route." They both thought immediately of the 8,000 feet above Gallup, New Mexico, that the DC-1 would have to climb under such conditions.

Douglas's voice remained calm. "Can we do it, Ray?"

"I sure did some fast slide ruling in Lindbergh's office," he said. Before he committed himself he did some quick thinking about the new formula that Dr. Bailey Oswald and physicists from the California Institute of Technology had come up with for measuring aerodynamic performance, so he felt on reasonably safe ground. "I assured them we could and would meet the requirement."

An anxious note crept into Douglas's voice for the first time. "Are you that sure?"

"I'm 90 percent sure but that other 10 percent is keeping me awake nights."

After they hung up, Douglas called in Dutch Kindelberger and they discussed these latest developments.

Dutch said, "The only way we'll ever find out is to build the plane and try it."

TWA made its decision on September 20, 1932, after studying all proposals submitted by several aircraft firms. The Douglas design won, and there was jubilation in Santa Monica. The price agreed upon was $125,000 for the first airplane, payable in gold coin, and the company would have to stand any additional costs. The contract also called for a one-year option for all or part of sixty additional planes at $58,000 each.

Douglas told Wetzel, "It will cost us twice that much to build the first airplane, but future orders are what count."

Douglas signed the work order and sent it to his shop superintendent George Strompl. Although the preliminary work at Douglas had been kept secret from everyone outside the company, word had gotten out after Frye's letter when the stock was selling for $7.12 a share—now it was up to $16.00.

After negotiations, Lindbergh and Frye told Raymond and Wetzel that when they went to the bankers to arrange financing, they had a hard time getting it.

"Why?" Wetzel said.

"Well," Frye said with a smile, "they found it difficult to believe you could meet the performance specifications."

Raymond later spent ten days in Kansas City with TWA officials, ironing out technical details with the operations staff. Upon his return to Santa Monica, Raymond went to the Douglas home to report. He was still shaken from his first experience flying across country in a Ford trimotor.

"Doug, there's a lot more to this thing than just building an airplane that will meet the performance figures. We've got to build comfort and put wings on it."

"I remember the old days," Douglas said. "Five hours was all you could stand because of the vibration and noise. I'm determined to make the DC-1 a lot better."

"It [the trimotor] was so noisy we had to stuff cotton in our ears. And, we had to shout across the aisle to make ourselves heard. The vibration!" Raymond shuddered at the recollection. "My teeth are still chattering." He talked at length about the necessity of heating the cabin, saying, "When we crossed the mountains, my feet were freezing. And those seats! A buckboard is more comfortable than those wicker chairs. The lavatory was so small, I could barely squeeze through the door.

"To top it off, when we landed, mud, sucked in by cabin vents, splattered everybody. No wonder people take the train!"

Raymond's experience was helpful because they all started thinking about soundproofing, cabin heating, better seats and lavatory facilities. In the Engineering Department, Douglas put up a sign in the DC-1 section that was a constant reminder to spur them to their best efforts. "When you design it, think how you would feel if you had to fly it! Safety first!"

Douglas relied heavily on Jack Northrop's experience in designing the Gamma and Delta all-metal airplanes, even though they were out of competition due to the 1933 CAA directive that all commercial passenger-carrying transports had to have more than one engine or face prohibitive restrictions. Northrop, a strong exponent of stressed-skin aluminum structures, was listened to with respect. Actually, his unique structural designs were major contributions to the development of future transports.

Douglas operated on the basic principle that every forward step in the industry must be based upon what had been done before. As the industry grew in knowledge, that knowledge was shared by all. No one suddenly came up with a bright new idea that had never been considered before. Rather, each new design concept was based upon the work of countless others who contributed to the further understanding of the science of flight. When someone came up with a good idea, Douglas recognized its value and took advantage of it.

In the whole history of aviation, those who made progress in the field were those like Douglas who reviewed past efforts, analyzed those which did not work out, and created an atmosphere where good ideas could be shared and allowed to grow normally. He continually cautioned associates that evolution was possible only with adequate knowledge. He warned of the dangers of patting oneself on the back after something new was developed. He reminded them it was far more important to know when to use scientific information that had already been developed. "Each airplane, although developed by the evolutionary process," he told associates, "is quite different. Take what you can from the past, and go on from there. Let past experience be the basis for further advances."

The Boeing 247 made its first flight on February 8, 1933, so the importance of getting the DC-1 designed took on a renewed urgency. One particular problem developed when the gross weight increased by a thousand pounds after many new features were added. In talking with Arthur Raymond while the airplane slowly took shape, Douglas said, "I'm concerned that the weight has increased to 17,000 pounds."

"We've got an ace in the hole," Raymond said. "I've been talking to Al French at Hamilton Standard. They've perfected new controllable-pitch propellers."

Douglas looked up with interest. He had followed the development of these new propellers for some time but he had not realized one had been perfected. By changing the pitch of the blades, he knew, more efficient operations would be possible, not only on takeoff, but also at cruising speed at high altitudes.

"These new props will bail us out," Raymond said confidently. "And the engine companies are promising more horsepower."

TWA approved the cabin mockup on March 15, 1933, and it had all the comfort features Douglas believed were necessary. He and Ivar L. Shogran, the rotund chief of the power plant section, walked through the factory in the middle of April, noting the high screens between the engine teams from Wright and Pratt & Whitney. With a grin, Shogran pointed to a chalk line separating the rival groups. "They don't even speak to one another. Afraid to give away company secrets."

When TWA signed the contract for the airplane, the engines were not included; until Douglas decided which engine would best meet their requirements, the rivalry became intense.

The decision to use the Wright "Cyclone" engine was kept a company secret for a time because, as Shogran pointed out, "We might get a better engine out of this rivalry." The Wright engine was selected primarily because the company had developed a new cooling fin and a new cylinder design.

When the DC-1 rolled out on June 22 there was a gasp from those who had not seen her in the factory. The fuselage was sixty feet long and oval in shape, with a large square window for each row of seats. The two nine-cylinder Wright engines provided as much power as any of the previous trimotors then in service. Its broad, gleaming wing spanned eighty-five feet as the airplane rested proudly on its main wheels and small tail wheel. Pilots admired the cockpit because the big windows provided such good visibility. All the features Douglas had insisted upon were included, such as a large lavatory in the rear, a small galley, and a soundproofed cabin equipped with heating ducts.

One TWA pilot, standing in front of the DC-1, looked at her with awe. To no one in particular, he said, "It won't fly. It's too big."

By rollout time, costs exceeded even Douglas's estimates—$307,000. Meanwhile, a modified airplane with a stretched fuselage was already in the design stage because both TWA and Douglas realized it was possible to design an even better airplane with more seats.

A light wind blew off the ocean July 1 when the DC-1 taxied up and down Clover Field, the bright sun reflecting off the polished aluminum. The flight was scheduled during lunch hour so the plant's 800 employees could witness the historic event. It had taken 332 days to get the airplane ready for its first flight.

Strompl called Douglas in his office at 11:30. "Come on down. Everything's ready."

Douglas walked over to his chief test pilot, Carl Cover, after he taxied the airplane to the flight line following morning runway tests. "What do you think?"

Cover pushed back his green hat, and his handsome face was wreathed in a smile. "She's born to fly, and belongs up there with the angels."

Cover waved to the crowd and boarded the airplane with Project Engineer Fred Herman. The crowd was silent as Cover taxied the DC-1 to the far end of the runway, ran up the engines, and then came back with a rush. The excitement of the workers was intense as the wheels lifted off the ground at 12:36 P.M., and there was a tremendous roar from the crowd.

Douglas turned to Raymond. "Well, she's up." He kept his face averted to hide the tears cascading down his cheeks. They watched the airplane anxiously as she swung over the ocean and began to turn back towards land. Douglas's straining eyes saw the left engine puff smoke, and then quit. When the plane's nose dipped, his heart began to pound; he feared the worst.

Expertly, Cover added power to the right engine and the plane rose a few hundred feet, but it was obvious to Douglas the remaining engine was under great strain. His heart almost stopped beating when the right engine quit. He fully expected disaster as the airplane nosed down steeply. Unexpectedly, both engines started again and a huge sigh of relief rose from the hundreds on the ground.

When Cover tried to gain altitude, both engines quit again. For several minutes, the maneuver was repeated but each time the DC-1's nose rose higher, the engines quit, and when Cover dropped the nose to maintain flying speed they started up again.

Douglas and Raymond watched with tense emotions, wondering what in the world was going on, marvelling how Cover could keep the airplane in the air.

With great skill Cover managed to get the airplane up to 1,500 feet and make his approach for landing.

They rushed up to him as he soberly came out of the airplane. "It was like climbing up a steep hill," Cover said ruefully. "We seemed to move backward a few feet for every one forward."

"Any idea what's wrong?" Douglas said, concern mirrored in his brown eyes.

"It's beyond me. Every time I'd try to pull power in a climb, the engine would quit. When I'd drop the nose, they'd start again."

"How about control response?" Douglas said.

"Fine. Honest, Doug, I don't think there's anything wrong with the airplane. I just don't understand it."

There were no newspapermen in attendance at Clover Field to report the first flight. They were at Mines Field where the Thirteenth Annual National Air Races were being held. Roscoe Turner had flown in from the east setting a new record of eleven hours and forty minutes, and Italo Balbo had led a formation of Italian seaplanes in the first mass flight across the Atlantic.

Douglas walked back with Raymond, saying only, "Once we get the bugs ironed out, I believe we've got a design that will almost equal the speed of Turner's plane."

The engines were removed from the DC-1 and placed on ground test beds where they were run for several days without failing once.

Douglas engineers later found the source of the trouble. The carburetors had been installed backwards, with floats hinged in the rear and with fuel lines feeding in the same direction. Each time the nose of the airplane went up, the fuel supply was shut off. Once the carburetors were reversed, the problem disappeared.

While the DC-1's engines were being worked on, the airplane sat on the ramp looking somewhat forlorn in its stripped condition. A few days after its first flight, Harry Wetzel was standing beside the airplane when a small biplane roared across the runway, and, just a few feet above him rolled over on its back. Wetzel was livid with rage as the pilot time after time swept across the area in his brightly colored airplane, stunting above the DC-1.

When the biplane landed and taxied close to the Douglas transport Wetzel rushed up to the grinning pilot and roared, "I'll have you grounded!"

His concern was understandable because if something had happened to the small plane during its wild maneuvers the DC-1 could have been destroyed.

Wetzel calmed down when the learned the pilot was Colonel Ernst Udet, famous German ace of World War I, and one of the greatest stunt pilots of all time. Udet explained apologetically that he was just putting on a little show for the Douglas people, saying he had flown in to see the DC-1 at the company's invitation while attending the National Air Races.

Udet inspected the DC-1 with interest, saying, "She's got anything beat that Junkers or Dornier ever built. I'll recommend that Lufthansa buy some."

Douglas was on hand when Cover flew the DC-1 again after the problem with the engines was resolved. This time there was no reoccurrence of what happened before, but another problem developed. Upon his return from the flight he told Douglas, "She fishtails."

Gene Root, who rode along on the flight as a design engineer, said, "She behaves like a crack-the-whip machine at a carnival."

"What do you think should be done, Gene?" Douglas said anxiously.

"We can stop the fishtailing by adding more rudder surface, and by changing the airfoil on the horizontal."

Later, when the airplane was taken to Mines Field for landing tests, a tragedy was narrowly averted. Edmund T. "Eddie" Allen flew the airplane with TWA's Tomlinson as copilot while Dr. W.

Bailey Oswald of engineering and Frank H. Collbohm, chief flight-test engineer, took calibrations. The cabin door had been removed so Oswald could lie on the floor with his head out to observe the landing gear, while Collbohm in the pilot's compartment actuated the gear each time they came in for a landing. The arrangement worked perfectly until Collbohm replaced Oswald at the door and Oswald went up to the pilot's compartment.

Neither pilot noticed the change and failed to tell Oswald to lower the gear during the next time around. Collbohm, with his head out the door, was watching the tail wheel, noting that Allen's perfect three-point landings made the tail wheel touch first.

In another second, he was splattered with tar and gravel. He knew immediately what had happened. The main gear was still up and the propellers were chewing into the runway. He withdrew hastily from the door and yelled at Allen, who frantically climbed out of danger. Fortunately, there was little structural damage except for bent props. Later, reviewing the report with Kindelberger, Douglas shook his head, grateful the damage had been no worse.

Kindelberger said, "There's never been an airplane built that wasn't full of bugs. You gotta pick 'em out one at a time. It's like hunting fleas on a St. Bernard."

The airplane was returned to the factory, and it was not until the middle of August that it was ready to fly again. They took advantage of this situation to modify the tail surfaces and, when Allen took her up again, he reported that the fishtailing was almost gone. Allen was one of the greatest scientific pilots of all time. Later, he went to Boeing and lost his life in the crash of the second B-29 Superfortress.

Daily DC-1 flights were made from then on, and one day Allen took the plane to a height of more than 21,000 feet. He told Kindelberger, "The engine superchargers made the difference. She was born to fly high." A design consultant from Cal Tech, Dr. A. L. Klein, had gone along with acoustics expert Dr. Stephen J. Zand to observe how the airplane performed at high altitudes. Their reports were enthusiastic, but Klein passed out at 14,000 feet because of the rarefied atmosphere. Zand's report was especially encouraging because he reported the cabin was extremely quiet.

Douglas gave Zand full credit for this condition, saying, "If it hadn't been for you, passengers would still be flying with cotton stuffed in their ears."

D. W. "Tommy" Tomlinson, TWA's experimental test pilot, reported with a grin, "She's too quiet. I kept thinking the engines weren't pulling full power."

These high-altitude tests brought another problem to the fore—reaction of passengers to such heights. Even though oxygen masks would have to be used, they all knew this was not the ideal answer.

Tomlinson told Douglas, "We should build a pressurized cabin so the pressure can be kept to normal."

"I agree," Douglas said. "Right now it's not possible. Someday we'll do it."

Northrop, a Douglas subsidiary, was building a single-engine airplane with a pressurized cabin so Tomlinson could make high-altitude tests. They all were aware, however, that pressurizing a large commercial transport would take new ideas and possibly years of concentrated effort to make such an airplane safe.

On August 24, sand bags were loaded on the DC-1 to raise her gross weight to 17,500 lbs, and company and TWA officials stood on the flight line to watch the heavily laden plane take off. The takeoff was clean, the wheels leaving the ground after a run of only a thousand feet.

Flight tests proceeded routinely now with the airplane flying at various speeds and altitudes, achieving a top speed of 227 MPH. One day Frye brought along one of TWA's top pilots—a man by the name of Smith. They stood anxiously on the flight line while the DC-1 returned from a flight with Cover at the controls. The fun-loving, handsome Cover was a veteran, seat-of-the-pants army pilot. He looked at them with a grin. They were so anxious to fly the DC-1 that desire was written all over their faces.

"She's ready," Cover said. "Take her up."

Ivar Shogran went along as Smith and Frye flew the airplane for an hour, reporting back later that Frye had said, "She's the sweetest thing I've ever flown."

Word quickly spread among airline officials that the Douglas company had designed and built a great new commercial transport, and queries poured in from other airlines.

During flight tests, there had been the usual debugging and the airplane had performed well. One great hurdle remained and that was to make a single-engine takeoff with a maximum load. Eddie Allen, with Tomlinson in the right-hand seat, took the airplane to

Winslow, Arizona, where it was loaded up to 18,000 lbs gross weight. The Winslow airport was 4,500 feet above sea level, the highest of any on TWA's routes.

Collbohm was with them as they made their plans. Conscious of the importance of the flight to the future of the company, the Douglas crew worked out a flight plan with meticulous care, setting a mark halfway down the runway where Tomlinson could throttle back the right engine to half power while Collbohm worked the gear up slowly as the airplane became airborne. Then, according to the plan, if the airplane responded well on this takeoff, during a second run the right engine would be cut off entirely. The idea of doing it this way was to achieve maximum safety for the plane and its crew. At the almost mile-high Winslow airport, with its thinner atmosphere, the lift would be less and the strain on one engine would be great at maximum weight.

When they were all set for the flight, Allen pushed the throttles forward and the DC-1 slowly gathered speed. It seemed an endlessly long time before the wing began to lift the DC-1 from the runway and Collbohm started to pump the gear up. Then, not according to plan, Tomlinson reached over and cut the switch on the right engine!

Allen gave him a startled glance, but relaxed when the airplane climbed normally away from the field, reaching a height of 8,000 feet on one engine. Once Allen was over his fright, he glared at Tomlinson who sat in the copilot's seat with a smug look on his face.

Tomlinson turned to Allen. "Look at it this way. You work for Douglas. I work for TWA. I just wanted to see for myself if she's as good as you guys say she is."

Allen refused to be mollified. "Next time, let me in on the gag. You're risking my neck, too, you know."

The airplane flew back to Albuquerque on one engine and really proved itself by beating a TWA Ford trimotor into the city by fifteen minutes despite the fact it had taken off before the DC-1.

Dr. Oswald, who graduated as an aeronautical engineer from Cal Tech during the early months of the DC-1's design, conducted wind-tunnel research following his graduation. He had been intrigued by a problem suggested by Douglas's assistant chief engineer Arthur Raymond during one of his weekly lectures to graduate students.

Raymond told them that it was his belief that pilots were not getting the maximum performance from their aircraft because accurate performance charts had never been devised. He said he believed charts should be prepared that would systematically tell the pilot what power settings and altitudes would give him the most efficient cruise speeds to reduce fuel consumption, and thereby increase his aircraft's range. He said he also believed that higher speeds could be attained with less fuel. He then suggested that someone at Cal Tech should explore cruising techniques as a benefit to the industry. Oswald was excited by the idea and, during a year and a half of research, he came up with charts that revolutionized the industry's ideas on predicting aircraft performance.

Raymond and Douglas were so grateful for Oswald's pioneering work that they offered him a job in Engineering Research, which Oswald accepted.

Eddie Allen had flown many high-altitude flights while flying the mail in the mid-1920s. Originally a pilot for Northrop, he was not only a superb pilot, but he had attended M.I.T. for two years, where he had studied aeronautical engineering. Several years before, he had told Northrop officials he was convinced that commercial airlines could reduce their operating costs if they flew at higher altitudes. He said the basic problem of determining an engine's horsepower was lack of a reliable instrument. He and other early pilots had been forced to rely upon a tachometer, which only recorded the propeller's revolutions per minute; hardly an adequate guideline for determining horsepower because it could not register variations in air pressure and lower oxygen levels encountered at high altitudes.

Pilots in those days routinely throttled back at high altitudes because they were familiar with an engine's tendency to increase its revolutions per minute the higher one flew. Allen disagreed with the practice, saying that he had proved that the RPM should be increased. He was almost alone in such a procedure, and he was subject to considerable ridicule.

The simultaneous work in the air by Allen, and by Dr. Oswald at Cal Tech, brought them together almost as partners. When Douglas decided to enter the transport field with the DC-1 in 1932,

Allen was hired as a consultant. He had done considerable work for the company in accomplishing high-speed pullouts in dives under high G conditions.

Before the DC-1 made its first flight, Oswald had convinced Douglas and Raymond that the transport's flight tests should be made with the idea of creating a complete set of performance charts to determine how the airplane could be flown most economically. Douglas agreed, and personally assigned Franklin W. Collbohm to the project as flight-research engineer.

After 200 flights, the DC-1 was not only approved for service, but airlines were given precise directions for determining the power setting for the engines under all speed and altitude conditions, along with proof that if these settings were used the airplanes would fly twenty miles an hour faster under cruise conditions, with a substantial savings in costs per mile. These performance charts proved beyond the shadow of a doubt that atmospheric pressures had to be given serious consideration. At low altitudes with the pressures normally high, the charts recommended low RPM settings with the reverse true at high altitudes. The charts also indicated optimum cruising altitudes should be used for greatest fuel economy and engine efficiency. For the DC-1, this altitude was set at 16,000 feet, or 2,000 feet higher than the height established by the Department of Commerce.

There were many considerations that went into the final calculations including propeller pitch, or angle, because a propeller with a low angle turned more easily than one with a larger pitch. Oswald and Allen quickly learned with the DC-1 that, with its propellers set at low pitch, the airplane could take off at full-rated horsepower even though the throttles were not fully advanced. They also learned that the DC-1 operated most efficiently as it flew higher if the propeller pitch was increased to take a bigger bite of the thinner air. Now, they said, if the pilot opens the throttles wider, the plane will fly faster.

Airline officials were enthusiastic because this new method promised to reduce operational costs. Any method that saved money by cutting fuel costs and increasing speeds was greeted with enthusiasm. Such charts soon became standard throughout the industry, even though old-time pilots resisted the change in flying methods.

Douglas credited Dr. Robert A. Millikan, chairman of the California Institute of Technology, as one of those who contributed most to the success of the DC-1 and its direct successors. In July 1932 Millikan set up one of the world's most modern aeronautical departments, along with an up-to-date wind tunnel, after receiving a grant of $350,000 from the Guggenheim Foundation. Millikan worked closely with Douglas, and it was through their association that Arthur Raymond was selected to make his weekly lectures to graduate students.

Douglas's close relationship with Dr. Millikan and Cal Tech scientists paid big dividends. Through Millikan's efforts, and those of Dr. Arthur L. Klein, the Douglas Company was saved from a costly mistake made by previous designers of low-wing monoplanes. Their research revealed that the DC-1's center of gravity should be much farther forward than normal. Klein had learned that the curvature of the fairings between the fuselage and wing should be increased as it went to the rear of the airplane to reduce drag. His calculations proved so accurate that the drag of the plane's fuselage and wing was the lowest of any airplane ever designed.

Douglas also gave credit to the National Advisory Committee for Aeronautics. It had developed a new engine cowling, a formula for properly placing engine nacelles at the correct distance from the wing, and had recommended the precise cross section for the DC-1's wing.

Although the United States was bogged down in the Great Depression, the aeronautical industry was one of the few that were expanding. Militarily, the nation ranked in fourth place in numbers of combat aircraft behind France, England, and Italy. It was generally conceded, however, that American airplanes were far superior in quality to their foreign counterparts. From the time when Douglas formed his company in California until 1934, 1,200 planes were built at a cost of $24 million. He sold the planes for $3 million more than their cost, which left him with a fair profit for fourteen years of activity. Most other aircraft businesses were losing money at the time.

The first generation of aircraft manufacturers—the Lockheed brothers, the Wrights, Boeing, Curtiss, and Martin—not only designed and built airplanes, but actually flew them during their testing phases, and later demonstrated their products to prospective customers.

Douglas had never learned to fly because he had been too busy. He was part of the next generation of aeronautical engineers, and actually had no interest in piloting an airplane. He often did fly in the early days when his pilots reported a particular problem, at times taking the controls briefly to get the feel of a problem. From the first, Douglas established a precedent of attending the first flight of each new airplane.

The DC-1, on loan from TWA to the National Aeronautical Association, broke five world records between May 16 and 19, 1935, and set two records in new categories. The Douglas plane helped the United States come within a point of the world lead by establishing thirty-nine world records compared to France's forty. The United States's jump from third place to almost the top spot was phenomenal.

Although conservative by nature, Douglas had risked the company's future when he gave the go-ahead for the DC-1. He also knew there had been no alternative, with military appropriations being whittled to the bone, but the gamble had been well worth the risk. Only one DC-1 was built but it fulfilled its mission; fostering a whole new generation of commercial transports.

Years later, after fruitful service with TWA, the DC-1 was sold to Howard Hughes who, for a time, considered using it for a projected around-the-world flight, but he selected another airplane instead. Hughes sold it to Viscount Forbes in England, who planned a trans-Atlantic flight that never materialized. The DC-1 next served the Republican forces during the Spanish Civil War where it was used as a personal airplane and troop carrier.

After the war, Iberia Air Lines of Spain used it until it was destroyed on takeoff in 1940 when an engine failed. True to its long record of carrying people safely to their destinations, all passengers and crew members emerged unscathed from the wreckage of the sturdy transport. It was beyond repair so the airline cannibalized every useful part. When they were finished, little more than the fuselage remained. Monks from the cathedral at Malaga took pieces of metal from her cabin and fashioned an Andas, or metal carrier, which, on church festival days, is used to carry the Blessed Virgin Mary through the streets.

Douglas ordered a six-meter boat called *Gallant* from a firm in Norway. It was constructed with a heavy frame to withstand the strong westerly winds off the coast of California, and he used it to compete in the 1933 Olympic Games in Los Angeles. He was successful in qualifying for the American boating team and proudly marched in his Olympic uniform in the opening ceremonies at the Los Angeles Coliseum.

Charlotte and the children went out on the seventy-five-foot *Endymion,* with their guests, to watch the races in Los Angeles Harbor. During the races there was an unusual calm, and foggy weather persisted. The *Gallant* was too heavy for such calm weather so Douglas lost any hope of picking up a gold medal. He did win a silver medal, and he was proud of it. He wore his Olympic beret and sweater at sea for years afterward.

7

Optimism Pays Off

T he DC-1 was officially accepted by TWA in December 1933, and immediately placed in service. It had more than met its performance goals. The cruising speed was close to 180 MPH, and passenger payload was up 20 percent over the original TWA specifications. Although the DC-1 had proved itself, everyone was aware that additional seats would add to the economic viability of the airplane. Instead of building more DC-1s, it was agreed that a DC-2 should be designed by adding three feet to the cabin's length to raise the total seating capacity to fourteen. Wright had managed to get more horsepower out of the original engines so the higher gross weight was no problem.

There were other changes, including a duplicate instrument panel in the cockpit, an automatic landing gear system to replace the hand pump, power brakes, which the pilot could use by pressing the tops of the rudder pedals, and an automatic pilot.

Douglas, who had been concerned about the initial contract, decided to fly back to New York in November to talk to TWA President Dick Robbins when the DC-1 went on a coast-to-coast demonstration flight with Cover and Tomlinson at the controls. Douglas believed that the contract should be declared null and void because it stipulated payment in gold coin. Now that President Roosevelt had taken the country off the gold standard, the original contract, he believed, should be adjusted to reflect the lessened value of the dollar.

It was two o'clock in the morning when they took off from Clover Field for Newark, New Jersey. It was Douglas's first flight in the

DC-1, and he enjoyed every minute of it, telling Cover and Tomlinson he felt as much at home as on his yacht.

The DC-1's first flight across country was uneventful until they got to Albuquerque. Suddenly, one engine quit, and Douglas peered out the window as the propeller slowed and was feathered. He was anxious at first,but the airplane flew back to Albuquerque on one engine without incident. Repairs were made quickly, and they finished the trip to Newark.

In New York, Douglas had long, serious talks with Robbins and other TWA officials, frankly disclosing that the DC-1 and the engineering studies on the DC-2s had already cost the company more than $300,000. They argued the matter for some time until Robbins agreed that adjustments should be made to the original contract. A new contract was signed calling for twenty-five DC-2s with TWA agreeing to pay $1,625,000. This was an increase of approximately $7,000 per airplane.

Anthony H. G. "Tony" Fokker came to see Douglas in 1933. One of the world's greatest designers, Fokker was enthralled after a flight in the DC-1. The two men quickly became close friends, and Douglas, who needed more sales to break even with the DC-2, made a deal with Fokker for him to market his planes in Europe. Douglas considered Fokker an inventive genius. Fokker bought one DC-2, and obtained the manufacturing and sales rights for the European market.

Douglas was in his office with company officials on February 9, 1934, when word came that President Franklin D. Roosevelt had instructed Postmaster General James A. Farley to cancel all domestic airmail contracts, and to order the United States Army to fly the mail, effective February 19. At first they were stunned. Douglas, his soft voice betraying no emotion, said, "We may lose some of our customers. Without airmail money, some airlines will go out of business."

His calm appraisal of the situation had a sobering influence. He said with a sigh, "Maybe it's a good thing. The airlines have to grow up someday. I've been telling them lately they've got to find ways to make money carrying passengers. They can't exist forever on airmail subsidies."

They looked at him expectantly. "Frye and Lindbergh believe TWA can make money with the DC-2. I do, too."

"Rickenbacker says the same thing," Kindelberger said.

Major General Benjamin D. Foulois, chief of the Army Air Corps, accepted the challenge to replace the airlines carrying the mail. He believed it would be valuable training for his peacetime air force. He told the postmaster that the army would maintain fourteen routes connecting eleven major cities, and make daily runs of 41,000 miles. He said it was his belief that the job would take 500 officers and 148 airplanes. Although Foulois did not admit it, he was disturbed that he had only ten days to prepare for the huge task of delivering the mail.

TWA's Jack Frye fought back. At 10:00 P.M. on February 18, two hours before airmail contracts would be officially canceled, he left Burbank Air Terminal in California in a DC-1 filled with mail sacks. With Eddie Rickenbacker as copilot, the DC-1 headed for Newark on a well-publicized flight. This was TWA's way of proving to the government that new airplanes such as the DC-1 could do a better job than army planes.

Despite adverse weather conditions, including a blizzard over the Alleghenies, the DC-1 made it to Newark, with one refueling stop at Kansas City, in eleven hours and five minutes. The fast trip was made possible by a tail wind at 19,000 feet that boosted the DC-1's ground speed to 225 MPH.

Roosevelt's action made the flight front-page news, and the DC-1 received wide attention in the nation's press. One newspaper said, "The DC-1 has made all other transport equipment obsolete."

Military pilots performed well, but they lacked the training and the proper aircraft to take on the huge job of delivering the nation's airmail. Due to bad weather, and failure of equipment, ten army pilots were killed by March 10, and Foulois temporarily halted the program.

With better weather, army flights were resumed on March 19, but by May, public uproar over further losses became so intense that Farley was forced to call off army flights. Although the postmaster bore the brunt of the criticism, he had never believed in the presidential order. Now, in an attempt to save face, he specified that no airline would be considered for a new contract if it had been involved in the so-called "spoils conference" of 1930 when most airmail contracts were grabbed by the three largest carriers. Airlines merely changed their corporate names slightly and refiled for contracts. In the process, American Airways became American Airlines, Eastern Air Transport assumed the name of Eastern Airlines, and Transcontinental and Western Air put in their bid as TWA, Inc.

The DC-1's cross-country flight proved a point and the government never again considered letting the Army Air Corps take over delivering the nation's mail. Although the takeover lasted only a few months, it was years before airlines recovered financially from cancellation of airmail contracts.

TWA got its first DC-2 on May 14, 1934, after it had been tested by Bureau of Air Commerce inspectors, who gave it a blue ticket to serve as a common carrier. There were minor bugs in the airplane, and the autopilot had to be reworked. The power brakes took some getting used to because pilots had to learn to use them carefully or the airplane would come to a screeching halt up on its nose.

In tooling up for production of the DC-2, costs began to mount until they reached 59,000 man-hours per airplane. When Douglas saw the reports, he called in his shop superintendent George Strompl. Douglas sat back in his chair as Strompl's heavy-set figure appeared at the doorway. He motioned him to a seat, and pointed to the budget director's report.

Strompl recognized it immediately. He remained silent until Douglas spoke. "We've got to do better than that. If we don't, we'll have the sheriff at the door."

"It's like this, Doug. The parts of the first airplane were made mostly by hand. I'm waiting now to get some big hydraulic presses. Then we'll stamp out parts just like they do in an automobile factory."

"Hope you're right. Our estimates indicate we can barely make a profit at 38,000 man-hours."

The big presses were the answer to the problem and manufacturing costs dropped to 32,000 hours. Still, on TWA's first twenty-five airplanes, Douglas lost $266,000, which was offset later because other airlines purchased the airplane. People were hired daily as DC-2s were produced at the rate of one every two weeks, and one of the biggest problems was finding experienced aircraft workers.

The original North American Aviation was incorporated as a holding company in December 1928. An aviation investor named Clement M. Keys headed it and, with $4.5 million, invested in airlines. It soon owned all of Eastern Air Transport, which had evolved out of Pitcairn Aircraft, 27 percent of Transcontinental Air Transport, and 5 percent of Western Air Express. It also invested in Sperry Gyroscope, Ford Instruments, Intercontinental Aviation, Berliner-Joyce Aircraft Company, and the Douglas Company. In the late 1920s, its original investment in Douglas amounted to $299,000.

In 1933, General Motors Corporation invested in North American Aviation by purchasing 30 percent of its stock, and one of its executives, Ernest R. Breech, became North American's board chairman. After General Motors took control, Breech moved to consolidate aircraft manufacturing operations. North American Aviation had purchased a majority interest in Berliner-Joyce in 1930 after General Motors had purchased a 40 percent interest in the Fokker Corporation of America in 1929. Fokker was now renamed General Aviation Manufacturing Corporation, and was merged with Berliner-Joyce. The combined companies became the General Aviation Corporation.

The Air Mail Act of 1934, which made it illegal for a company to engage in aircraft manufacturing and also own an airplane, appeared to pose a difficult problem for Breech. He intimated at first that he was interested in a merger with Douglas, which he had no intention of doing, and then suddenly acted to dispose of several aircraft and airline holdings. Among the assets he disposed of was the original investment in the Douglas Company, which now amounted to a quarter interest.

Next, Breech sought an experienced executive to head up General Aviation Corporation, which became part of the Berliner-Joyce Aircraft factory in Maryland. By this time, however, the new company was in bad shape. Its employment was down to 200 from a premerger total in both companies of 1,300 people. Breech offered Dutch Kindelberger, vice-president of engineering at Douglas, the job of president and general manager of Berliner-Joyce.

Kindelberger accepted the job on July 6, 1934, and brought along

John L. "Lee" Atwood, who was Kindelberger's chief of advanced design at Douglas. A meticulous perfectionist, Atwood complemented the bold and innovative Kindelberger. They were a superb team.

When they arrived at the plant in Maryland, they were appalled by conditions. "Things couldn't have been worse," Kindelberger reported to Breech. He immediately recommended substantial changes. In October, Kindelberger signed a new contract and, when North American was dissolved as a holding company on January 1, 1935, North American Aviation, Inc., became an active aircraft manufacturing operation with Kindelberger as president, and Atwood as vice-president and chief engineer. General Motors, as the largest single stockholder, was represented on North American's board of directors to provide counsel and advice until it disposed of its interests in 1948.

In a parallel action, Board Chairman Breech appointed World War I fighter ace Eddie Rickenbacker to head Eastern Air Lines, which in 1938 became a separate corporation.

Erik Nelson left the army in 1924 to become vice-president of sales for the Boeing Airline Company. He accepted a small salary and took the rest of his compensation in Boeing stock. He and Bill Boeing retired as millionaires from the sale of their stock.

United Airplane and Transport Company, Boeing's parent company, was cited in 1935 under provisions of the Sherman Anti-Trust Act for vertical integration, in which it was claimed that there was no competition between the manufacturing company and its consumer company. Therefore, United Airplane and Transport was dissolved, and out of it evolved United Airlines, United Aircraft, the Boeing Airplane Company, and several smaller companies.

Douglas DC-2s went into transcontinental service August 1, 1934. TWA's Sky Chief left Newark at 4 P.M. and, with the time differential, arrived in Los Angeles the following morning at 7 A.M. Stops were made at Chicago, Kansas City, and Albuquerque. TWA broke the transcontinental record between New York and Chicago four times during the DC-2's first eight days of service.

Shortly after DC-2s were placed in service, Douglas's father and mother decided to fly from Los Angeles to New York in one of their son's airplanes. Douglas tried to convince them they should not try to make the trip all at once and recommended they spend the night in St. Louis. William Douglas was adamant. They would make the trip in one day. Upon their return, William told his son, "It was a great ride, but my back felt as if it were broken for two days afterwards."

Douglas was invited to speak at the twenty-third Wilbur Wright Memorial Lecture in London in May 1935, so he took his wife and children on a tour of Europe. They left Clover Field in Santa Monica on May 7 and were joined by Mr. and Mrs. William Douglas in New York after they had decided to go with them. They sailed for England on the fashionable North German Lloyd Line's *Bremen,* arriving in London on May 16.

While Charlotte and the children toured the usual sites, Douglas met with Lord Beaverbrook and Lt. Col. J. T. C. Moore-Brabazon. The latter was president of the Royal Aeronautical Society. At their meeting, Moore-Brabazon showed Douglas a cable from Orville Wright. "Greetings to the council and members assembled for the Twenty-Third Wilbur Wright Memorial Lecture. Development of the airliner has been an outstanding feature in American aviation. Mr. Douglas's part in this has been second to none. We are proud of him."

At the Dorchester Hotel, Douglas saw a company advertisement in an English aviation publication, extolling the merits of the DC-2. Although he had approved the advertising copy long before, it still intrigued him to read about his company in a foreign publication. He had almost forgotten that 100 DC-2s had been delivered to twelve of the world's leading airlines.

In his lecture to members of the Royal Aeronautical Society, Douglas expanded on a theme that he would frequently return to in the years ahead. He believed that airplanes would "shrink" distances around the world, and bring people closer together. It was a viewpoint that Harry F. Guggenheim had expressed in 1930.

Douglas took his family to Scotland after the lecture. There, after several visits to castles where suits of armor were of particular interest, Charlotte put her foot down or he would have acquired more suits of armor than he would ever have any use for. During his teen years his great-uncle James Wills had owned such a suit, and he had often dreamed of the time when it would become his own. His great-uncle bequeathed the suit to someone else, much to his dismay.

After a week in Scotland, he took the family to Holland, where he hired a boat to tour the canals. Adding to his joy of the trip was a meeting with old friend Tony Fokker. The famous Dutch builder had been so intrigued with the DC-1 after flying it, that Douglas gave Fokker European sales and manufacturing rights to the DC-2. Since then, Fokker had proved to be an outstanding Douglas sales representative on the continent. Douglas was particularly intrigued by the Fokker plant, which was then building a low-wing monoplane that was called the fastest fighter in the world with a speed of 274 miles an hour.

Charlotte and Barbara Jean went to Berlin for several days while Douglas took Donald, Jr., and William on a barge trip through the canals of Belgium and Holland. Barbara Jean was fascinated by her trip to Germany, but horrified by the Hitler youth who were then marching through the streets of Berlin.

Douglas decided not to visit Hitler's Germany because he was afraid he would not be permitted to leave the country. Whether Hitler would have dared to order his retention is doubtful, but Douglas decided that such a trip by one of the United States's leading military procurement producers was not worth the risk. While his family saw the sights in each country, Douglas surveyed aviation in England, Holland, France, and Italy. After noting their progress, he was convinced that his country was forging ahead in the field.

The Douglas Company certainly was helping the United States to excel. Company employees now totaled 3,200, and among the new executives were Frederick W. "Ted" Conant, and Jacob O. Moxness, who started out as a test pilot and later transferred to the sales department. Douglas met Ted Conant at Catalina while sailing. For years Conant operated a successful construction business but by 1933 the Depression wiped him out. Sailing was a strong bond between Douglas and Conant, each was tight-fisted when it came to handling money, both were friendly to associates, and they dearly loved a good joke.

Cyrus R. Smith, who had started in the airline business as treasurer of Texas Air Transport, always believed that an airline could make money carrying passengers, despite the experiences of other airlines that airmail contracts were necessary to subsidize passenger operations.

He had merged Texas Air Transport with Southern Air Transport, and later remerged it with the Aviation Corporation. The latter was a holding company that also owned American Airways. Smith applauded when the Black-McKellar Bill, designed to eliminate the power of such holding companies, was passed in June. When American Airways was forced to separate from its holding company, it became American Airlines with Smith as president. Although Smith's American Airlines had a lucrative postal contract, he did not have a modern airplane—one that could compete with the DC-2. His airline was saddled with outmoded Condors and Fokkers.

After TWA's Jack Frye took delivery of his first DC-2, Smith received a southern coast-to-coast airmail contract from the United States Post Office, increasing the long-haul carriers to three with the existing TWA and United.

So successful was the DC-2 in service that orders began to pour in from Eastern, Western, KLM Royal Dutch Airlines, and the Swedish line AB Aero Transport.

There had been some in the Douglas Company during the past few years who had tried to convince the "old man" to do as other companies and set up his own airline. He would have none of it, believing strongly the two should be separate. His opinions were justified when Congress passed the Black-McKellar Airmail Act of 1934, which specifically outlawed such a relationship.

C. R. Smith was a new breed in the airline business, a businessman who started out as president by learning every phase of the airline's operations. It was not long before he realized that American's collection of transports could not possibly compete with TWA's DC-2s and United's Boeing 247s. He and his chief engineer, William "Bill" Littlewood discussed their many problems. They were in agreement that American needed a sleeper plane where passengers could get into pullman-sized berths and sleep on their way across the United States at night. An early experiment with the Curtiss Condor proved the feasibility of the idea, but they needed a larger airplane.

Although American did not have any DC-2s, Smith and Littlewood knew the airplane well, and thought it would be ideal for their use if made into a sleeper. And, they knew the company would be one up on TWA and United in passenger service.

At American's headquarters in Chicago Smith put in a call to Douglas. When he had him on the line he asked Douglas if his company would be interested in making a sleeper for American. "I believe a sleeper version of the DC-2 would be ideal for us because it's the best way to compete with United and TWA. Can you design one?"

Douglas did not like the idea because he felt the commercial market was near the saturation point, and the company would be lucky to break even on such an airplane. He told Smith, "We can't even keep up with orders for the DC-2."

Douglas tried to get his thoughts across to Smith but the head of American persisted and the call dragged on and on, costing hundreds of dollars. Finally, to shut him up, Douglas told Smith he would talk it over with his people after Smith promised to buy twenty of the new type if Douglas would build them.

"Good," Smith said. "May I send Littlewood out there to work with your engineers?"

Somewhat reluctantly, feeling he was being rushed into something about which he had grave doubts, Douglas agreed. He decided to go ahead with the DST—Douglas Sleeper Transport, which would stretch the DC-2's basic fuselage in length and width.

Once Smith had Douglas committed, he had to raise the money to buy new aircraft. He got in touch with his old Texas friend Jesse Jones, whom President Roosevelt had placed in charge of the Reconstruction Finance Corporation. Smith was frank with Jones that his airline would go bankrupt unless he got a loan for new aircraft. Jones agreed to loan him $4.5 million, and American Airlines was back in business.

Douglas helped to design a thirty-five-foot sloop in 1934 for Don and Will, and daughter Barbara became a permanent member of the racing crew of the *Altamar* during daily races. The father went along the first year of competition to teach them the tricks he had learned through the years. Barbara loved being "one of the boys," and after Don brought some of his buddies from Stanford University to help crew the boat, they won many races.

As was his habit, when Don, Will, and Barbara went into the library on Friday nights to get money to go to the movies, Douglas would ask the cost. In those days a ticket cost fifty cents. If he did not have the correct change he reminded them he expected it back the following morning. Sometimes he would tell them to buy gum or candy, but if he gave them extra money, he expected to receive any change that was left over. They were constantly reminded that frugality was part of the bargain in seeking money to go to the movies.

After the twins were born in 1931, the closeness of the family began to break down. Charlotte's time was necessarily aimed at taking care of the young boys in her usual selfless manner, and the company was growing so fast that Douglas found less and less time to devote to his family.

From 1935 on, family vacations together were rare. Charlotte, daughter Barbara, and the twin boys took their vacations together, though, and during the Christmas holidays Barbara, Don, and Will were almost always at Sun Valley.

Now they saw their father mostly at dinnertime. Infrequently, Barbara, a boyfriend, and her father would take a boat trip to Catalina, but these trips practically ended after she entered college in 1939.

Through the usual growing pains of developing a new transport, the DC-2 continued on the line at a high production rate. After the first DST flew December 17, 1935, Douglas was as ecstatic as Smith about the airplane. It looked beautiful taking off and Carl Cover said it performed magnificently in all flight tests.

American Skysleeper service commenced on September 18, 1936, with sleeping accommodations for fourteen people. The DST now provided 200-mile-an-hour flights across the country at night with only two refueling stops. Its payload was one-third greater than that of any previous airliner.

Although Douglas was proud of the DST as a commercial transport, he did not believe night sleeper service would attract a sizable clientele, even though popular movie stars such as Shirley Temple used it. He told Arthur Raymond, "Night sleeper flying will be about as popular as silent movies." Again, he was proved correct.

Another market materialized when Sunflight Corporation bought a DC-2 for use as an executive airplane, completely furnished as a flying office. Other companies quickly followed suit, and tailor-made executive airplanes joined the assembly lines.

The first great accolade for the DC-2 came after a KLM airplane won first place in the handicap division and second prize in speed during the MacRobertson International Air Derby. Twenty airplanes finished; most were specially built racing planes. Christened *Univer,* the DC-2 flew the 12,300 miles from London to Melbourne, Australia, along KLM's regular route, in seventy-one hours and twenty-eight minutes. There were three passengers on board, plus mail, and the DC-2 averaged 160 MPH. The flight gained worldwide attention because it lost out in the speed category to a specially designed racing plane built by DeHavilland. The Boeing and Lockheed entries were so outclassed that the DC-2 became the world's most outstanding commercial transport.

While DC-2s and DSTs rolled down the assembly lines, Douglas engineers were busy adapting the DST to regular passenger service with twenty-one seats. It was easy to fit the DST with fourteen seats on the left side and seven seats on the right. This new version was named the DC-3, and its development costs exceeded $400,000.

Although the DC-2 had been a great success, the DC-3's performance through the years would far eclipse it because its payload was a third more than any other commercial transport, and its 25,000 lb gross weight was half again that of other transports. Once the DC-3 went into regular service, its economy was such that its operating costs were half those of previous transports, and the cabin was the quietest of any transport flying. American's Bill Littlewood told Douglas, "We've got a marketable product, and one that can operate at a profit." C. R. Smith's confidence in the airplane was such that he bought them for years at $110,000 apiece.

When the DC-3 was shown publicly for the first time at the Pan-Pacific Auditorium in Los Angeles on June 10, 1936, it attracted much attention and a few laughs. Raymond met Douglas walking away from the exhibit, and seeing the set look on his face that appeared only when he was really mad, hurried to the exhibit to see what was wrong. At first, everything seemed in proper order. Then, he looked at the company placard in front of the airplane. With a start, he read, DOUGLAS DC-3, 14 BIRTHS OR 21 SEATS!

So successful was the DC-3 that the DC-2 went out of production.

The company had built 191 of all versions of the DC-2s, certainly far more than Douglas himself had thought possible. He had anticipated a total sale not to exceed fifty, and the company broke even on the program at the seventy-fifth aircraft.

The decision to build the tools to make the DC-3 had been a tough one, and Douglas had hesitated about signing the order to build tools for just twenty-five airplanes. When the DC-3 started to sell better, these original production tools built 350 airplanes before additional sets were authorized. Douglas was always a man who was slow to take risks and he knew unneeded tools could prove financially disastrous to the company. His decision paid off, however, because 803 DC-3s were eventually built, as well as 10,323 Air Force versions, plus some for the United States Navy. In all, the DC-3 and its derivatives amounted to a billion dollars worth of business.

As Douglas said later, the DC-3 converted millions of ground lubbers to air travel as a safe and practical means of transportation. It quickly gained worldwide attention, and the production lines at Santa Monica were humming as never before.

The DC-3's inherent stability, with its low stalling speed, provided a pilot with full control response at all speeds. Pilots learned to appreciate it even more when they had to fly on instruments. Once a crippled Chinese Airway's DC-3 flew back to its home base following an accident in the back country where a DC-3 wing was not available. Despite the shorter DC-2 wing, the DC-2 1/2, as it was known, flew normally with only minor trimming necessary to compensate for the three-foot shorter wing section.

Recognition of the earlier DC-2's merits came that year when Douglas was awarded the Collier Trophy, aviation's highest award, for development of the airplane. President Franklin D. Roosevelt personally presented the trophy at the White House on July 1, 1936, three years to the day since the DC-1 had made its first flight to start the series.

Roosevelt read the citation. "This airplane, by reason of its high speed, economy, and quiet passenger comfort, has been generally adopted by transport lines throughout the United States. Its merit has been further recognized by its adoption abroad, and its influence on foreign design is already apparent.

"In making this award, recognition is given to the technical and production personnel of the Douglas organization."

Douglas humbly accepted the award on behalf of his company. It was a proud day for him and the company because the DC-2 was called the "outstanding twin-engined commercial transport plane."

Douglas was sincere when he told the president, "I accept the Collier Trophy, not for myself, but for the thousands of employees and executives at Douglas.

"There is nothing revolutionary in the airplane business. It is just a matter of development," he said. "What we've got today is the Wright brothers' airplane developed and refined. But the basic principles are just what they always were."

Upon his return to Santa Monica, Douglas learned that an American Airlines DC-3 had flown that day from Newark to Chicago nonstop and return, a distance of almost 1,500 miles, in eight hours and five minutes. American also revealed they would use their DC-3 flagships for nonstop service between these two cities in the near future.

The company again expanded, particularly after it received an order for a twenty-three-passenger DC-3.

The DC-3 was a winner from the start, cutting coast-to-coast travel time in half compared to all rival transports.

Brig. Gen. Henry H. "Hap" Arnold, assistant chief of the Army Air Corps, came to the plant in 1936 to inspect the production lines where military versions of the DC-2 were being built as C-33 and C-39 transports.

In Douglas's office he said, "I can foresee the day when fleets of planes will link Air Corps bases all over the United States and overseas."

Douglas agreed.

Arnold shook his head sadly, "I only wish Congress would give us the money, but they think the idea is ridiculous."

8

"Are You Just Looking or Buying?"

D uring the 1930s Douglas continued to build military aircraft. Army aircraft were not produced in quantity, but several different observation aircraft were produced, some of which were sent to China. When the carrier *Lexington* went to sea for the first time in 1928, it had on board the T2D1 torpedo bomber. The navy was changing its requirements as aerial tactics changed, and navy officials were more and more interested in aircraft that could fulfill several types of missions such as scouting, horizontal bombing, and observation. Torpedo warfare still had a prominent role in aerial warfare, however, and the XTBD-1 Devastator was built to carry a pilot, a bombardier, and a rear gunner. It was designed to dash to a target, release its torpedoes, and get away fast.

Meanwhile, Douglas flying boats were built for navy service over the Atlantic and Pacific oceans. The P-2D1 came out in 1933. A twin-engine biplane, it was equipped with both floats and wheels, but it was primarily for use on long patrol missions over the oceans.

A much larger aircraft, the P-3D1, was built during 1935 and 1936. A high-wing metal monoplane, it was powered by two 1,000-horsepower Wright Cyclone engines mounted on top of the wing.

Sales for amphibious aircraft during the 1930s were difficult, as more than one company learned to its sorrow. One of the few to buck the trend successfully was the Douglas Dolphin, which started out as strictly a commercial airplane but proved so successful that the U.S. Navy, Army and Coast Guard purchased them in quantity.

Douglas did not build fighter planes in the early years, but in 1933 the all-metal XFT-1, a two-seater with an enclosed cockpit and a fixed landing gear, was designed for the U.S. Navy. Two guns fired through the propeller, and another flexible machine gun was mounted on a rail around the rear cockpit. This fighter was advanced for its time with a top speed of 204 MPH, but the production contract was awarded to Grumman.

Through the years the navy had relied upon biplane fighters because they had lower landing and takeoff speeds—two factors of prime importance for service aboard carriers. The XFT was a low-wing monoplane that could have met carrier requirements, but the navy's decision against its production was due, in large part, to their insistence upon a biplane configuration.

Ed Heinemann was named chief engineer of the Northrop Division in 1936 and immediately reorganized the Engineering Department. One important change was to assign one man as a project engineer—an innovation in the industry. In the past, a project book containing all of an airplane's manufacturing drawings was used for reference when something did not fit correctly during the manufacturing process. The engineer involved simply made new notes and diagrams on a page, tore that page out, and pinned it to the shop drawing. These books soon became so messed up that drawings were impossible to keep current. The project engineer was able to keep drawings up-to-date because only one man was responsible for the design of the entire airplane.

Despite failure of the XFT to sell, a new XFT-3A design was built. It had welded aluminum fuel tanks, but the pilot had to transfer fuel from one tank to another.

After the first 3-A and its pilot were lost at sea, investigation indicated that the crash may have been due to failure of the pilot to transfer fuel properly. Heinemann told Jack Northrop that the crash site was at the point where fuel transfer would have been mandatory. Inasmuch as the 3-A was at a low altitude, a successful ditching would have been difficult, if not impossible.

The press picked up the story of the plane's crash, sensationalizing it by reporting that the Japanese somehow had spirited the airplane away. Douglas scoffed at such rumors, but they died hard.

Later, when Northrop became discouraged with the possibilities for sale of the 3-A to the United States Navy, he sold the blueprints to Chance Vought and they used them to improve the quality of their entry in the navy competition.

Rumors about Japan stealing the 3-A's secrets refused to go away, and some journalists speculated that it became the model for the Japanese Zero. However, the Japanese fighter was well along in its own independent cycle by this time, and the 3-A definitely made no contribution to its later success.

The Northrop subsidiary was next approached by the U.S. Navy to take part in bidding for a new dive-bomber, one that had to achieve stable, "zero-lift" dives at speeds not to exceed 250 knots. When Heinemann discussed the proposal with Jack Northrop, he had no illusions about the difficulty of meeting the navy's specs. Such a dive bomber had to operate from carriers, withstand 9-G pullouts, carry a 1,000 lb bomb, and incorporate a displacement system so the bomb could be ejected safely away from the propeller.

Heinemann told Northrop that dive brakes were his greatest concern. He said the German Stuka used slats as dive brakes that folded out from under the wing, but the Stuka made its dive-bombing runs at less than a forty-five-degree angle, and not vertically. They decided to bid on the project, and determined that the airplane would have to approach a target at 20,000 feet, extend its brakes, and dive straight down with a pullout at 3,000 feet.

The division had some background for design of the new dive-bomber because it had developed the A-17 attack bomber for the Army Air Corps and was producing it in quantity. The new aircraft, identified as the XBT-1, had a shape similar to the A-17, but its wing was six feet shorter. It had a partially retractable landing gear and an observer-gunner's seat to the rear of the pilot. Heinemann personally designed new trailing-edge flaps that would be extended during dives.

Test Pilot Vance Breese reported a serious tail flutter after the airplane's first flight. Douglas and Heinemann, who witnessed the first flight, questioned Breese when he returned. Heinemann decided to go along on the next flight to see the problem firsthand. When the tail flutter grew violent, it scared the hell out of him.

Later he called Charles Helm at the National Advisory Committee for Aeronautics (NACA) and described the condition. Helm agreed to visit the plant. After checking the drawings and going over the flutter problem, he recommended cutting holes in the trailing-edge flaps. Such a procedure did not appeal to Heinemann at first, who thought the flaps would look like pieces of Swiss cheese. To his amazement the idea worked, particularly after rows of holes were cut all along the flap. The flutter not only disappeared, but the 250-knot dive speed was attained while the bomber proved remarkably stable in all attitudes.

In March 1936 navy competition narrowed to Douglas and Chance Vought. Both entries used the Pratt & Whitney 1534 engine. Jack Northrop and Heinemann were relieved when the navy awarded contracts to both companies. The first of fifty-four BTs was delivered by the Northrop Division to the navy in the spring of 1938.

An improved model, the XBT-2 was designed with a fully retractable landing gear and other changes, including installation of the Wright R-1820 engine. This model had better armament, controls, and control surfaces. By agreement with the navy the division designed and built the new version outside normal development cycles due to the rise of Nazism in Germany, and Adolf Hitler's threat to the free world.

During one of Douglas's periodic visits to El Segundo, he was told by Heinemann that the BT-2 could fly faster with its new engine and, "with flaps or speed brakes you can make a zero-lift dive. Earlier dive-bombers, such as the Berliner-Joyce and the Great Lakes, were biplanes with fabric-covered wings, so their diving was limited. The BT-2 works!" he said.

It was a far better dive-bomber than the German Stuka, which had a fixed landing gear and speed brakes. If the Stuka tried to make a vertical dive, he told Douglas, it would never come out of it. He emphasized that all American airplanes of the period could dive vertically, but not all the way to the target and pull out successfully.

"You can auger this airplane around until you get right on the target, hold her there until you're ready to release, and then pull out around 5,000 feet. You can actually pull out as low as 3,000 feet," he told his boss, "and still have a thousand-foot clearance while pulling 9-Gs. It's the only plane in the world that can do that." Actually, this plane and its successors remain the only airplanes to this day that can complete such a classic maneuver and pull out safely.

In April 1937 Northrop decided to leave Douglas and form his own company. The plant was renamed the Douglas El Segundo Division.

The BT-2 was refined again, giving it a flying range of 1,000 miles. It was renamed the SBD (Scout Bomber Douglas) Dauntless. This great airplane, which provided the margin of victory in most early battles in World War II in the Pacific, was the only naval carrier plane ready for operations at the start of the war that continued in use throughout the war.

After the Battle of Midway in which four Japanese carriers were sunk, largely by SBDs, Adm. Chester W. Nimitz wrote Douglas and credited the Dauntless with stopping the Japanese. Until the SBDs arrived on the scene, he said, Midway was a Japanese triumph.

It was true that early versions were underpowered and underarmed. Pilots and gunners found their cockpits noisy and drafty. But crews loved the airplane because it was tough and could withstand incredible punishment and still bring them home. It provided the necessary backbone for the navy's carrier divisions during those first two critical years of the war.

Despite his protests, Douglas insisted that the SBD patent be issued in Heinemann's name. "You did the drawings," Douglas said. "It's an entirely different airplane. You've got to take credit for it."

From time to time Heinemann called Douglas during the prewar period to say, "We've got a mockup over here. I'd like to show it to you."

"Sure," Douglas invariably replied. He would pick a time and date from his busy schedule and appear at El Segundo promptly.

Unlike some other bosses Heinemann had known, Douglas always came to his office first. Ed liked this because some bosses would stop and talk to his supervisors before they got to him, hoping to learn something that would catch him off base. Douglas never did that.

One day Douglas walked in and said, "Well, what are you doing?" He sat down with a smile on his face. He never engaged in wisecracks, and was always casual and pleasant.

Ed said, "I want to show you something we're interested in." He took Douglas next door to show him some new drawings, and Douglas commented favorably on their concept.

Heinemann then invited him to the shop where a mockup was

being built for a new aircraft. The day was hot, and while they walked through the shop, Douglas took off his coat and put his arm around Ed. Heinemann had known many bosses but Douglas was the only one who showed his appreciation in such a friendly fashion. The gesture meant a lot to him.

While they walked around the mockup, Ed said, "Climb up into the cockpit."

Douglas chuckled, and there was a twinkle in his eyes. "Sure it will hold me?" He laid his coat aside and climbed in.

Heinemann knew how to fly, but did not profess to be a first-class pilot. He left that job to those with special expertise. His mind was too filled with design ideas, and he knew he had to concentrate on one or the other. He and Douglas were aware that pilots had to fly regularly if they were to develop their skills. Many early aircraft designers tested their own airplanes, but Douglas and Heinemann thought that was wrong. They knew that to be a good pilot instead of a mediocre one took much more time than either could spare.

In August 1934, the Army Air Corps' Materiel Division at Wright Field sent out a circular to all aircraft firms to announce they were interested in a new bomber. Specifications were strict because the aircraft would have to carry a ton of bombs, with a radius of action of over a thousand miles, and fly at a speed in excess of 200 MPH.

When Douglas read the circular, noting that the Air Corps wanted as many as 220 new bombers, his interest heightened. After the DC-1 proved successful, he had thought of recommending its conversion to a bomber. The Air Corps was seeking such an aircraft, but he noted that a flying prototype had to be delivered within a year. With his production lines filled, he wondered how it could be done. Still, he knew, a proper balance between military and commercial production was mandatory if the company was to be kept in sound financial condition.

The year's deadline to produce such a new aircraft seemed almost insurmountable so he decided to delay committing his company to enter the competition. Days later, still mulling over the decision, he called in Carl Cover, his chief test pilot, who also acted as military sales manager. They discussed the circular at length. Finally Douglas said bluntly, "What do you think we should do?"

Cover didn't hesitate. "Let's take a crack at it. I'm sure Martin will submit a version of its B-10, and I hear Boeing has a four-engine design."

"Four engines?" Douglas said with a lift to his eyebrows. "That's out for us. It would be too costly to design a bomber with four engines. We'd have to start from scratch."

Douglas sat thoughtfully for a few minutes. "What do you think our chances would be?"

Cover had been to Wright Field before the circular was issued, to discuss a bomber version of the DC-1 or DC-2. "If we can meet the deadline, I think we can win."

Douglas called in Arthur Raymond, who had replaced Kindelberger as chief engineer when Dutch left the company the month before to join North American Aviation. During a session with Raymond's top design engineers and Carl Cover, numerous helpful suggestions were made. Raymond turned to Douglas. "We can use the basic DC-1 wing, stretch it again to save time and money for new tooling."

One obvious change was that the bomber's wing would have to be raised to the middle of the fuselage because of the bomb bays. It was decided the DC-2 tail configuration could be used, but extensive modifications would be necessary for the bombardier's compartment.

As details of the design were worked out, it was necessary to strengthen many areas because of the higher gross weight. One designer told Douglas, "She'll look like a DC-2, only a little bit pregnant."

The company went ahead, calling their airplane the DB-1. In other words, it was the first Douglas bomber airplane. The Air Corps selected its own designation, referring to it as the XB-18 competition.

In one of the most intensive programs in the company's history, the airplane was delivered to Wright Field a month ahead of time in July 1935. It was a rugged airplane, bristling with gun turrets and blessed with the proven aerodynamic characteristics of its commercial cousin. Weighing in at 25,000 pounds, the XB-18 was almost twice the weight of the Martin entry. And, she had a top speed of 217 miles an hour, could carry a bomb load of 4,400 lbs, and fly 2,400 miles.

Clairmont "Claire" Egtvedt, Boeing's president since Bill Boeing sold his stock in the company and left the business, was desperately trying to counter Douglas's dominance of the commercial transport market. The 247 had been overwhelmed by the DC-2 and the DC-3. It was a good airplane, but it just was not large enough.

In 1934 Egtvedt scrapped a proposed two-engine successor to the 247 and accepted his engineers' suggestion for designing a four-engine commercial transport to be called the Model 300. Shortly afterwards the army asked Boeing to enter the competition for a multi-engined bomber. Egtvedt replied that he was ready to do so if the army was interested in a four-engine bomber that would be the military derivative of its Model 300. Maj. Jan Howard, engineering head at Wright Field, Dayton, Ohio, responded that the army was interested.

Boeing unveiled its entry as Model 299, a four-engine bomber that later became known as the B-17 Flying Fortress. When it arrived at Wright the Douglas crew believed they had lost because the 299 was so huge, with reported performance characteristics so superior to any other contestant that they thought she would win the competition hands down.

During flight evaluation tests, the 299 crashed, so the decision was delayed until almost the end of the year. When the announcement came, the big contract for 103 B-18As, an improved version of the original bomber, went to Douglas. Boeing remained as a future contender with a contract to build thirteen YB-17s.

Another bomber, the B-23, was produced also prior to the war. Like the B-18, it carried forward many of the basic design features of the DC-3.

Douglas was jubilant when the B-18A went into production. By the time it was phased out in 1939, Douglas had built 500 of them. Nicknamed "Bolo" the B-18A was used only in a limited way by the time World War II started, but she served a useful purpose in hunting Nazi submarines for the British and in guarding the Atlantic lifeline along the shores of the United States.

W. E. "Pat" Patterson, formerly with Boeing Air Transport, a subsidiary of the Boeing Airplane Company, became head of United Air Lines (UAL) when it was split away by government decree.

UAL's Boeing 247s proved no match for TWA's and American's Douglas DC-3s so when UAL achieved its independence, Patterson came to see Douglas. He found it difficult because Douglas officials considered Patterson practically a spy for Boeing.

He finally met Douglas at a luncheon of the Aviation Committee of the Santa Monica Chamber of Commerce. Patterson leaned over to him and told Douglas how hard a time he had had in getting to see him. He said, somewhat plaintively, "All I want to see you about is to buy some airplanes."

Douglas said he had not known and expressed his regrets.

Patterson told Douglas, and Wetzel who was sitting next to him, "I'm trying to get someone interested in a four-engine transport. I believe the time has come when bigger airplanes are needed to fly across the country without refueling."

"How about some DC-3s?" Wetzel said.

"We'll need some. While I'm here, I'd like to take a ride."

Wetzel was embarrassed. "Have to borrow one," he said apologetically. "Don't have any demonstrators. Costs too much to run them."

At first, Patterson was startled, but he soon learned such candor and honesty was typical of Douglas and his officials.

His feelings at the time, strengthened later through years of association, were to play an important part in Douglas's history because this meeting welded a respect that remained undiminished throughout both of their business careers. For Douglas, Patterson's respect for his integrity and forthrightness was to play an important part years later when Douglas sorely needed friends.

Patterson was enthusiastic about the DC-3 after Wetzel found him an airplane in which to fly. Most important, UAL bought a quantity of them. Patterson, meanwhile, called in his sales and operations people to get their views on United's future transport needs. Now that he had DC-3s in operation, he was ready to talk seriously about a four-engine commercial transport, which he believed was the next logical step. Jack Herlihy, vice-president in charge of operations, and his assistant W. G. "Bill" Mentzer, both graduates of M.I.T., agreed with Patterson's view that a four-engine airliner was needed for safety, speed, and profitable operations. Specifications were drawn up for an airliner that would carry at least forty passengers, which was almost twice the DC-3 load, and which would fly at 230 MPH.

Patterson had gone originally to Boeing with his proposal but they were not interested. They were building a four-engine flying boat for Pan American World Airways to carry passengers across the Atlantic and Pacific oceans. When Patterson approached Douglas, he explained that he knew exactly what he wanted, and that he had asked United Aircraft Company in Hartford to help on power plants. He told Douglas that United's head, Frederick B. Rentschler, had called in his chief engineer George J. Mean, and Comdr. Jerome C. Hunsaker, M.I.T.'s aeronautical genius and Douglas's old friend, to help with power plant and wing designs.

Douglas's interest quickened when he learned Hunsaker had done some preliminary studies for United, and he called in Arthur Raymond. After much discussion, Raymond put the matter bluntly to Patterson. "Such an airplane will be costly, about $600,000 to build an experimental model. Are you just looking or buying?"

Patterson turned to Douglas. "I'm not bluffing. If you'll go ahead, I'll guarantee $300,000 towards the engineering costs."

Douglas looked at Patterson thoughtfully. The costs for such a project might be astronomical. Orders had to be sufficient from other carriers to make the whole project worthwhile and he told Patterson so.

Patterson explained that he had already called a meeting with executives from TWA, American, Eastern, and Pan American and that all of them believed such a plane was needed. He said frankly, "We decided that we'd all go broke if each tried to finance a new airplane. So, we've agreed not to spend any money on another airplane until yours is evaluated. United we fly, divided we lose money."

Douglas looked at him with surprise. He already had learned that Patterson was an astute businessman, but to get these highly competitive airlines to pool their resources on one airplane was astonishing. Not that he doubted Patterson, but he gained a new respect for him.

Douglas agreed to go ahead and the DC-4E was born, with the best engineering talents among the airlines working closely with Douglas engineers.

Behind canvas curtains, the DC-4E slowly took shape. It took 500,000 hours to design the plane, and another 100,000 hours of ground and laboratory tests over an eighteen-month period. The initial cost before she flew was high—over $1.6 million.

The airplane was far ahead of its time because its sheer size forced engineers to use power-boosted controls. She had a wing span of 138 feet, a cabin length of 97 feet, and weighed 65,000 pounds.

There were seats for forty-two passengers.

Patterson visited the plant often, only once disagreeing with Douglas when he complained the galley should be moved from the rear to the middle of the aircraft. He told Douglas and Raymond, "The pretty stewardesses will run their legs off serving forty passengers on a short flight." His point was well taken, and the change was made.

Meanwhile, Boeing's president Egtvedt ordered his engineers to revise the original Model 300 commercial transport, which had provided the basis for the B-17 Flying Fortress. The new version, the Model 307, used the wing and tail surfaces of the B-17, and Egtvedt hoped that it would be a strong competitor to the Douglas plane. When TWA ordered six of the thirty-three-seat Stratoliners, and Pan American ordered three more, Egtvedt believed he had a head start over Douglas in the four-engine transport field.

After arguing the matter for weeks, the DC-4E was fitted with a tricycle landing gear so it would be level with the ground for ease of servicing, and to improve landing and takeoff performance.

Carl Cover flew her for the first time on June 7, 1938, reporting later to Douglas, "She flies herself."

Using the lush phrases of his director of public relations, A. M. "Rock" Rochlen, Douglas released a statement after the flight that said, "The story of the DC-4E is the story of the organization that made it possible. It is a symbol—a goal achieved and a task fulfilled.

"Here in our plants where other wings of commerce and defense have taken shape to spread over the world's skyways, engineering and craftsmanship find their highest expression.

"Scientist and mechanic alike have a heritage and tradition with which there can be no compromise. Together they work, together they plan ahead and look ahead.

"The DC-4E is a tribute to the men who designed and built it. The ship is our token of a job well done and the promise of progress to come."

Benny Howard, a United pilot on loan to Douglas, was also enthusiastic about it, saying, "Flying the DC-4E is about as exciting as a game of solitaire."

At first, Jack Herlihy, United's vice-president of operations, spoke highly of the airplane. He told Douglas, "That's the plane for us."

Ted Conant was more sensible. He told Douglas, "The results were predictable. Not an airline in the bunch wants the damn thing."

The DC-4E did not perform all that well. For one thing, the control surfaces were unsatisfactory. The triple rudders were redesigned five times. Despite increases in their sizes, the DC-4E still lacked stability. Its payload was 20,000 lbs; it was faster than any transport then flying, with a top speed of 240 MPH, and it could cruise at 22,900 feet for a maximum range of 2,200 miles.

The airlines had participated in the design of the airplane and, despite their early favorable comments, the plane's shortcomings became increasingly evident. They were due, in part, to the committee approach to resolving design problems.

The initial euphoria over the merits of the new airplane settled into serious doubts among airline officials that it would be a successful airplane for them. They had confidence enough in Douglas that the DC-4E would eventually meet her speed and comfort requirements. So many modifications were demanded by each of the airlines, however, that Douglas doubted a successful standard airplane could be developed for all airlines. Actually, only United and American agreed to purchase production models of the airplane, and they talked only of twenty each, which would not have recovered the plane's high development costs.

Harry Strangman, Douglas's old sailing partner, who had been persuaded to join the company as comptroller, now lent his weight to a go-slow policy. With the company's production lines jammed with DC-3s, tax problems were an increasing headache. Strangman had left New England as a young man, and had sought his fortune around the world, working as a mucker in a copper mine, and later managing a trading post in the Alaska bush. Douglas had great respect for the courtly Strangman because he had both feet planted firmly on the ground, and always made decisions on the basis of cold facts.

Although the DC-4E proved the feasibility of large commercial transports, it had so many new ideas that some were beyond the state-of-the-art. They were sound ideas that later would be adopted as standard in all commercial aircraft. The innovations included a retractable tricycle landing gear, complete climate control for the passenger cabin, and under-wing refueling.

After the company had invested $3 million in building and flight-testing the DC-4E, Douglas met with his staff and they discussed the situation. Should the airplane be this large? The consensus of opinion was that it should be smaller.

Raymond said, "Should we scrap the 4E?"

It was a difficult decision, and only Douglas could make it. He said nothing for a few moments, then turning to them, he said, "Let's start with a clean piece of paper."

It was agreed that a more practical DC-4 should be designed; one that could be produced without stretching technology to the breaking point. As Douglas told them, "Our progress must come by orderly evolution of sound, well-developed principles." This was his creed; one he had kept inviolate throughout his life, and one with which they had no quarrel.

The DC-4 was designed for growth, as were all previous commercial models. The triple rudders of the E were abandoned as unnecessary, and the airplane went into production. In reality, the DC-4 created a revolution in aeronautical thinking, and airlines were quick to place orders totaling forty for delivery in 1942.

The one DC-4E that was built was sold to the Japanese in 1939, and Jake Moxness agreed to deliver it to Japan and train Japanese pilots to fly it. The plane was disassembled, crated, and shipped to Japan from Oakland, and Moxness and his crew went along with it.

After docking near Tokyo, the Douglas crew was met by a military escort and taken to Haneda airfield. Moxness took one look at the field and saw it was barely adequate to fly a large airplane like the DC-4E. The runways were only 2,600 feet long.

Resigned to his fate, he started to train the Japanese crews. Not one man spoke English, which complicated Jake's problems, but he was even more concerned by the Japanese propensity for high living each night, returning to Haneda the next morning in no shape to fly a complicated airplane.

Due to the shortness of the runways, each landing and takeoff was a challenge to the Douglas crew. When the Japanese insisted on making three-engine landings, with one propeller feathered, Jake put his foot down. The field was just too small.

Moxness and his men had one respite from the operation when they went to the American Club in Tokyo to hear Ambassador Joseph C. Grew speak. Moxness was shocked by the frankness of the

American ambassador, who told the Japanese gathered there that the war they were planning against the United States was one they could not win. Furthermore, he said, "You won't like the price of trying."

Moxness, who had wondered why they were confined to Haneda with a constant military escort, now understood. The coldness of the military men with whom he had come in contact now was understandable. Fortunately, during their stay in Japan, civilians were very friendly.

He was happy when they completed their training of the Japanese crews and could head for home. While in Honolulu, en route back to California, he was not surprised to learn that the Japanese had crashed the DC-4E, killing all its occupants. The Japanese Navy used the DC-4E's basic design in building its own four-engine Shinzan bomber.

While Jack Northrop was still with Douglas, engineering work had begun on the 7-A attack bomber. It was a two-engine airplane, with a crew of three. The French, faced with a war in Europe against the Germans, had expressed a strong interest in the airplane. In early 1939, they asked President Roosevelt for permission to witness a demonstration flight. He did so, but insisted that no French pilots be on board the airplane, and that the demonstration be closed to the American press.

After members of the French Air Commission inspected the newest version, the 7-B, test pilot John Cable took the plane off from Mines Field. After he was airborne, Douglas and Heinemann noted excited chatter among the French delegation, and asked the spokesman what was the problem. He told them that an engineering member of their party, Captain Chemidlin, had disappeared and they suspected he had hidden himself aboard the aircraft. Douglas was perturbed because the president had specifically ordered that no member of the French delegation should fly on the 7-B.

Cable brought the bomber over the field at 500 feet, so their concern about the French engineer momentarily was forgotten. When Cable feathered one of the craft's two engines, Douglas and Heinemann drew in their breaths. This was counter to their specific orders. Johnny did so to demonstrate control of yaw with the tail swinging back and forth. It soon became apparent that the yawing was getting out of control and then, to their horror, the 7-B spun to the left and Cable quickly ejected, believing he was the only one on board. He was too close to the ground, however, and his parachute did not open. All winced as his body crunched into the earth in a tortured lump. The airplane, meanwhile, crashed into the ground and the aft section broke free of the fuselage before it exploded. Incredibly, Chemidlin was still alive and Heinemann and some others pulled him out.

The crash could not be kept from the press, an uproar ensued, and Douglas was charged with taking sides with the French government despite the isolationist policy of the United States. Congress demanded an investigation, and President Roosevelt stepped in, saying he had personally authorized the demonstration.

Despite the crash, a few weeks later the French Air Force bought 480 of a later version known as the DB-7C. When this model flew the following August, the DB-7 went into production and France received the first of them in February 1940 at Casablanca. They were used in May, but after France fell to the Nazis in June, the remaining bombers on order were accepted by Great Britain.

A still later version, the A-20 Havoc, was purchased on June 24, 1939, by the United States Army Air Corps and the British Royal Air Force. The United States eventually purchased 2,000 A-20s, and the British another 1,800. After Soviet Russia became an ally following the German invasion of her homeland, she received 3,600 under the lend-lease program.

Carl Cover was excited about the prospects for converting the A-20 into a small, commercial transport. During the design cycle, the commercial version kept growing in size. When Nat Paschall's sales department got into the act, he wanted to make a twenty-one-passenger transport, so the plane ended up as an entirely different airplane than the one originally conceived.

At the close of 1938, KLM Royal Dutch Airlines' officials approached Douglas about a twin-engine transport to replace the DC-3. They suggested it should have its wing on top of the fuselage instead of underneath like in the DC-3. Such an arrangement, they said, would permit shorter landings and takeoffs, particularly on dirt strips for flights on KLM's East Indian Service.

The transport that had started out as a commercial A-20 now bore no relationship to that original concept. It was designated the DC-5, although it flew before the DC-4E. It was designed and produced at El Segundo at the plant Douglas and Jack Northrop had founded in 1933 as the Northrop Corporation. Under the management of E. R. "Ed" Doak, the plane was designed by Ed Heinemann's engineering team headed by Leo J. Devlin.

The plane flew in February 1939, with Cover and Jake Moxness at the controls. Later Moxness reported, "She was a great airplane after we got her gentled down. Until we did, she sure was horsey. Once, while flying at cruise altitude, I began to feel like I was in a saddle. It felt just like bobbing up and down on a horse."

The pilots talked to Heinemann after the first flight. Ed decided to go along on the next flight, but the DC-5 behaved perfectly while he was on board. Later, the stability problem reoccurred and Chief Designer Devlin went to work to solve the problem. It was learned that at certain attitudes the air flowing back from the engines against the horizontal tail surfaces caused the tail to fluctuate up and down. The problem was solved by changing the engine housings and relocating the tail surfaces.

Harry Wetzel died in July 1938. Douglas was shocked when he heard of his untimely death. He had been his right-hand man since the start of the company.

Carl Cover succeeded Wetzel at first, but then Douglas made Ted Conant his top aide. The Douglas-Conant-Raymond team proved to be an ideal combination. They all had extensive engineering backgrounds, and they complemented one another.

Harry Strangman told associates that Douglas ran his company like a Scottish fiefdom. When the company was small, he said, Douglas treated his employees as friends, not just paid help.

When associates came to him to tell him a costly design change was necessary, his first question invariably was whether the change would improve the aircraft's design. Despite the cost, and some design changes ran into millions of dollars, he always said, "If that's what it takes, let's do it."

With such a man at the top of the organization, it is not

surprising that his people were more devoted to him personally than was the case with most other leaders in the business world. They knew that excellence was his byword, and lesser efforts would not be tolerated.

At home, Charlotte assumed responsibility for training the children in the social graces, with Barbara Jean receiving special attention. She was introduced to tennis and golf, and Charlotte made certain that her daughter and sons became members of several prominent clubs. She had a profound influence on the children, particularly after her husband became preoccupied with running his expanding company.

The late 1930s were busy ones for Douglas, but he still found time to spend with Don and Will in his workshop. The two boys, each different, with Don the extroverted one, grew up in a normal competitive environment. Like brothers the world over, they fought frequently, with Will often waiting until he believed the time was right to tackle Don, while his brother wanted to resolve a growing conflict at once.

Don and Will had long pressed their dad to help them design a metal hydroplane that could be raced to Catalina Island. Before they began, Douglas insisted that methodical drawings be prepared and they decided it would be powered by a Johnson Seahorse motor.

Douglas refused to let them race the boat until he had checked it out using remote controls from another power boat. He selected Cherry Cove for the run, and decided to clock the boat's speed with a stop watch. With the boys keyed up for the event, Douglas got the hydroplane under way and up to full speed. In checking his stopwatch, he unintentionally knocked his hand against the controls and the hydroplane spun out of control and was wrecked. The two sons were inconsolable for a long time, and Douglas felt bad that he had been the cause of the mishap.

During their early teenage years Don and Will never realized their father was a famous man. Once they started to travel with him, however, noting the deference given their father by others, they began to realize he was no ordinary dad.

Douglas always tried to be patient with his children, exposing them to new conditions and different people during their travels, but never pushing them. If new thoughts and opportunities proved uninteresting, he was tolerant and never forced the issue.

Don Douglas, Jr., went to Stanford University in 1934 to study mechanical engineering. After he failed to complete the engineering course he enrolled at the Curtiss-Wright Technical Institute in Glendale in 1938. Completing this short course, he married Molly McIntosh on May 1, 1938. His father considered the marriage ill-advised, and was so furious that he all but disowned his son, refusing to let him work for the Douglas Company.

Curtiss-Wright Institute, owned by a family friend C. C. Moseley, offered Don a job teaching stress analysis and drafting. He quickly learned his students' biggest problem was their inability to read blueprints. Douglas made visual aid models, which he carved out of wood, to describe orthographic projections that a draftsman would be using. These proved highly innovative, and were extremely helpful. His father's early insistence on learning to use tools helped him at a critical time in his teaching career.

Don liked his job, but the $40-a-week pay was not enough to support him and his wife. He decided to try and get a better job at the Douglas Company, but the estrangement between him and his father prevented a direct approach. Instead he went to the employment office headed by C. Tom Reid and applied for a job.

Although Don never learned, he was sure Reid called his father to tell him his son was applying for a job, and certainly would not have considered hiring him if his father objected. Evidently his father offered no recommendation one way or the other because Don was hired.

He was given no special privileges and, like all new employees, he had to participate in a training program to introduce him to the policies and practices of the Douglas Company. After completing introductory training, he was assigned to the power plant section in the Engineering Department, where he reported to Supervisor Rudy Loeckner, who was responsible for the C-54's engines. This U.S. Air Corps transport was the military version of the DC-4. Rudy was also a test pilot and, shortly afterward, was killed while diving the SBD Dauntless.

After Loeckner's death, the young Douglas was the only man in the department familiar with the C-54's engines. The Air Corps had established a high priority to get the C-54 operational, so he had to work long overtime hours, which, as an hourly employee, entitled him to extra pay.

His new supervisor, noting the large paychecks Douglas was getting each week, called him in. "We're going to have to put you on a green badge." At Douglas, green badgers were on salary, and therefore not entitled to overtime pay. It was the first step an employee had to take if he was interested in supervisory positions. Many hourly employees refused salary offers because most green badgers made less than hourly employees on overtime.

Don was not sure he liked the idea of a drastic reduction in take-home pay, so for the first time in three years he went in to see his father. Despite the lack of contact, his father had followed his progress within the company, but Don was not aware of it. All he could think of was that a green badge was a lousy idea that would cost him money.

He asked his father, "Should I accept this stupid thing?"

"It's the only way to get ahead," his father said calmly. "You have to make that step some day."

Don reluctantly accepted his father's advice.

A man who later played a key role in the fate of the Douglas Company graduated in 1921 with an aeronautical degree and later served as a pilot with the Army Air Services. James McDonnell designed a monoplane in 1927 called the Doodle Bug in hopes of winning the Guggenheim Safe Aircraft Competition. The plane's tail structure failed while McDonnell was flying it and, in the resulting crash, he was seriously injured. The third lumbar disc in his spine had to be surgically removed.

He worked briefly for Glenn L. Martin as a chief project engineer before founding his own company in July 1939 in St. Louis. He managed to put together $165,000 of his own funds and those of family and friends.

A year later, Douglas's Ted Conant received a copy of a letter James McDonnell addressed to Colonel Schneeburger at Wright Field. Attached was a note from the colonel to Ted, "Please examine this list of aircraft manufacturing facilities submitted by the McDonnell Aircraft Company as to the equipment required to fulfill its subcontract with you to produce airplane parts in connection with our order to Douglas Aircraft for A-20 attack bombers."

Douglas generously told Conant to give the fledgling company all the subcontracts possible to keep them in business. At the time, McDonnell had none of its own aircraft in production.

Douglas flight operations, now headed by Jake Moxness, grew monthly, reaching a total of 128 pilots before the end of World War II. It was a far cry from 1934 when Moxness and George Cerveny were the only test pilots working for Carl Cover. John Martin joined the department in 1940. A former barnstormer, rum runner, pilot for the United States Weather Bureau, and, in 1936, a United Air Lines pilot, Martin was later to achieve international renown for flying supersonic experimental aircraft after the war.

In his workshop at home, Douglas was continually tinkering with new things, many of which were completely beyond the scope of the aircraft industry. In conjunction with the Douglas laboratories, he developed a prototype for an electronic stethoscope, and another for a phono-cardiograph that screened and classified a half dozen of the most common heart murmurs. He was an early advocate of pacemakers. Not wishing to produce these items because he did not want to make money out of their manufacture, he gave the rights away.

While Douglas was proceeding with the DC-4, Howard Hughes took TWA's Jack Frye to Lockheed in 1939 to discuss the design of a four-engine, forty- to forty-five-passenger commercial transport that would fly at 300 MPH. Lockheed's Chairman, Robert Gross, promised to start work on such a transport. The Model O-49 Constellation proved to be way ahead of anything Douglas or Boeing had in production. It could carry sixty-nine passengers and cruise at 270 MPH. Although the airplane was canceled during World War II, fifteen were delivered to the United States Army Air Corps as C-69 military transports.

9

No Task Is Too Great

I solationism was strong in 1940 and the aircraft industry was under attack. Rochlen wrote a fancy statement for Douglas, which despite its flowery phrases accurately reflected his views. "I know no formulae by which to tell a defense airplane from one used in offense. Our tables deal with mathematics, not motives. In a world so full of conflict and confusion, the greatest discoveries and gifts of science become slaves and servants, not always on the side of justice and right. The laws of gravity and aerodynamics recognize no distinctions between aggressor and victim. The dictator and the defendee share alike in the triumphs of science."

Perhaps the most provocative airplane of all was started in the spring of 1937—the B-19. Basically it was designed as a flying laboratory for the development and testing of airplane ideas for the future. For its time it was the largest, most powerful airplane ever built, and it cost $3 million.

The B-19's four Wright Duplex Cyclone engines had to be specifically developed. They were capable of generating 8,000 horsepower, or the power equivalent of the enormous steam turbines of a 10,000-ton ocean liner.

The B-19 was designed to fly 7,750 miles, more than three times the distance World War I destroyers could travel. Fully loaded it weighed 164,000 lbs, three times the weight of the DC-4, and it could carry a bomb load of 18 tons. If the B-19 had been a passenger transport it could have carried 125 passengers and a crew nonstop from coast-to-coast.

It had approximately ten miles of electrical wiring, three million rivets, a fire-alarm system, and many other innovations that truly made it one of the nation's major engineering triumphs.

June 27, 1941, as thousands of Douglas workers cheered, the B-19 took off from Clover Field. Its huge 212-foot wing cast a giant shadow as it left the ground and headed for March Field near Riverside.

Maj. Gen. George H. Brett, vice chief of the United States Army Air Corps, said of the B-19, "There are forces in the minds of men— in the minds of many men—that permit them to triumph over mere matter. Such a triumph is exemplified in the B-19, the dream that has now come true. It was the dream of many men, and that it comes true gives credit to as many men, and to hundreds, yes, thousands more, who translated that dream to the B-19."

His final words were prophetic. "It will become the experimental model from which will come the great transcontinental and transoceanic land planes of the future; the airplanes that will conquer any distance to any place on the surface of the globe."

It truly was a triumph for all who took part in its conception because it paved the way for the bombers of World War II, and the great ocean-spanning commercial transports of the postwar era.

Douglas was well-entrenched in the airplane business by the summer of 1939, having delivered 1,503 military aircraft to the U.S. Army, another 300 or so to the U.S. Navy and the Coast Guard, and almost a thousand commercial transports to the world's airlines. The company's commercial transports were carrying 92 percent of the world's passenger traffic, and more than 400 DC-3s had been built.

July 6, 1939, marked Douglas's twenty-fifth anniversary in the aviation field, so it was decided to honor the event with something special. The DC-4 was selected as the platform for a party in the skies above the city he had brought to prominence in the aviation world. With Carl Cover and Jake Moxness at the controls, about forty prominent people, including his father, joined Douglas for a unique birthday celebration with a seventy-five-pound cake topped by a globe with airplanes circling it while bagpipes played. The DC-4 circled the cities of Santa Monica and Los Angeles where the Douglas

Company had grown and prospered. High in the sky, Douglas and Nick Ball sang a song about his boat, the *Endymion,* which was broadcast over a California radio network.

The gala affair not only had many of the original members of the company in attendance, men such as Bill Henry, David Davis, Eric Springer, George Strompl, and Henry Guerin but also people such as Harry Chandler, publisher of the *Los Angeles Times,* who had helped to give Douglas his first start.

Afterwards, messages poured in from well-wishers across the country. Karl T. Compton, president of Massachusetts Institute of Technology, reminded Douglas how twenty-five years before he had graduated from M.I.T. and was appointed to the staff to assist in teaching new graduate courses in aeronautical engineering. "In the twenty-five years that have elapsed since this auspicious beginning of your professional career, you have continued to pioneer and to play an outstanding part in the development of American aviation."

Air Corps Chief of Staff Major General Arnold wired that the corps was greatly indebted to his genius, which had contributed so largely to his company's recognized position in the world of aeronautical achievements, ranging from its pioneer flight around the world to the company's latest bombers.

Rear Admiral John H. Towers, chief of the United States Navy's Bureau of Aeronautics, wrote, "Your efforts have greatly influenced the development of commercial aviation throughout the world, and have contributed materially to plans for national defense."

Douglas's senior vice-president and general manager Carl Cover spoke for all employees when he said, "Doug is a kind and capable leader, a constructive critic, a kindly, thoughtful associate. It has been truly said that often a great institution is only the lengthened shadow of a man. Such a man and institution are Don Douglas and the organization he built."

In the previous five years the company's growth had been phenomenal. The number of employees had grown ten times, to a total of 9,000. Tony Fokker wrote that the fact Douglas planes then were circling the globe was the greatest reward a man such as Douglas could receive.

That December Douglas was shocked to learn that Tony Fokker was dead. He had died in New York after a short illness at the age of forty-nine. Douglas was heartbroken. In memory of his friend, he wrote, "When death took Tony Fokker, it cut short a career that inspired our times." He called him an aviation pioneer, one who had grown with the industry and helped to shape its destiny. Fokker and Douglas had shared much in common. They both loved to sail and fish. Fokker's death was a deep personal loss to Douglas.

Douglas's talents as a creative engineer were recognized again in January 1940 when the Institute of the Aeronautical Sciences presented him with the Daniel Guggenheim Gold Medal for "outstanding contributions to design and construction of military and transport planes."

Foreign representatives of the Institute met at the Biltmore Hotel in New York at the annual dinner on honors night. Dr. Jerome C. Hunsaker, the man who had given Douglas his start more than a quarter century ago, made the presentation as chairman of the award's board. He told the gathering that Douglas had created the air transport industry by means of a vehicle that was "safe, fast, and economical, just as he was fundamentally responsible for the first world flight."

With thunderous applause ringing in his ears, Douglas said, "I stand before you tonight humbly grateful for the high honor you have conferred upon me, and keenly aware that I can accept it only as a custodian for the countless brave and able men whose endless efforts, vision and courage have made aviation what it is today."

He gave tribute to the Wright brothers, calling them pioneers who first made manned, powered flight possible. "That inspiring journey of aviation to its present position in our lives and destinies has not been made without sacrifice. Triumphs and tragedies, rewards and ruin, success and failure, are some of the milestones in its upward swing.

"We still have far to go and much to do. Ours is a task that never ends."

Refusing to prophesy about the future, he referred to himself as an engineer and not a philosopher.

With Douglas's greatest challenge—to help arm the free world—

now facing him, he continued to run the company as he had in the past. While most large corporations no longer were headed by their founders, Douglas remained an exception. His personal control was recognized and unchallenged. He said once, "It would be impossible for any banker to tell me how to run this aircraft business. If any person tried, and I found myself in a position where others could dominate company policy, I would certainly get out. It just wouldn't work."

He had never forgotten what had happened in World War I when the aircraft industry was set up by businessmen with no interest in airplanes, but only in the profit they might make from them. The result was chaos.

Although the Army Air Corps had a great need for cargo aircraft, and it had bought some C-33 and C-39 transports based upon the DC-2, funding for a large fleet of military DC-3s was almost impossible to get approved.

Arthur Raymond and Douglas spent many hours at Wright Field talking to Maj. Frank Carroll, chief of the engineering division, and Maj. K. B. Wolfe, chief of the production division, both of whom were personally enthusiastic about the possibilities of adapting the DC-3 for military use. These officers insisted, however, that more payload was needed, which meant larger engines and more fuel capacity.

Raymond and Douglas agreed these things could be done but the officers cautioned that funding would be a problem. They reminded Douglas that congressional appropriations went primarily for bombers, fighters, and trainers.

"We understand," Douglas said.

Carroll said, "We like your ideas. I'm hopeful we can buy some. But, it's up to K. B. to find the money."

Wolfe chuckled. "We could buy them as generals' personal airplanes," he said. "There's a fund for them, oddly enough. Then, we can use 'em as cargo carriers."

Since the days when Hap Arnold had been assistant chief of the Army Air Corps, he had pushed strongly within the Corps for more and better transports. He talked several times in the next few years with Douglas personally about conversion of the DC-3 to a military transport, and he was convinced such an airplane made sense.

There actually were a few generals' planes delivered as C-51s and C-53s, but the majority were fitted with bucket seats along the sides of the cabin to carry troops.

New urgency for transport planes developed after Hitler's invasion of Poland on September 1, 1939. So many varying requests for transports came in that Arnold personally had to intervene so a standard airplane configuration could be ordered for mass production.

The original decision to buy a military version of the DC-3 was one of historic significance because Air Corps C-47s and Navy R4Ds contributed greatly to the success of the Air Transport Command and the Naval Air Transport Service.

After the Germans smashed Poland's defenses, the British ordered DC-3s, which they called Dakotas, under Roosevelt's Lend-Lease program.

Douglas sold one DC-3 to a Soviet Russian airline, and the Russians started to build the airplane under a license agreement. Thousands were built, just how many the Russians never revealed. They called their version the Ilushin-2.

Japan, too, acquired a license to produce the DC-3. Nakajima Hiroki completed its first DC-3 September 30, 1938, and built seventy-one. The Japanese Imperial Navy authorized Show Hiroki to produce the airplane as L2D2s. A total of 416 were built for the Japanese Navy and were popularly called the Zero transports. The L2D2s were twin-engined personnel and cargo transports and were constructed of metal, except for fabric-covered control surfaces.

The Allies called the Japanese version TABBY, and these Japanese-built DC-3s were used throughout the Pacific theater of operations. Their use frequently led to tragic recognition errors on the part of the Americans.

Nakajima also had acquired permission in 1935 to build the DC-2 under license to Douglas, but this option was never exercised because of the availability of the DC-3.

In the fall of 1940, Douglas and his director of public relations, Rocky Rochlen, listened to President Roosevelt as he spoke in Chicago. His "quarantine the aggressor" speech called for the production of 50,000 planes a year. They looked at one another in amazement. "What do you think, Doug?"

"We can do it," he said without hesitation.

Rochlen wrote out a statement for release to the press, quoting Douglas as saying, "No task is too great and no accomplishment impossible for a nation united in love of country and its institutions."

Immediately after Roosevelt's speech, the phone rang and Rocky picked it up. He listened for a moment, then turned to Douglas. "It's a reporter from the Associated Press. Wants to know what you think of Roosevelt's request for 50,000 airplanes a year."

Douglas backed off. "What'll I say? You're my public relations man. You tell him."

Rocky handed him the statement he had just written.

When Douglas open the *Los Angeles Times* next morning and saw the headline **DOUGLAS SAYS WE CAN DO IT!** it scared him for a moment. Then, knowing the strength and incredible vigor of the industry, he was positive it could be done.

The high-flown rhetoric in the Douglas statement was vintage Rochlen, born in the days when he worked for the Hearst newspapers. Douglas did not talk like that, but it accurately reflected his views. By war's end, the United States had built almost 300,000 aircraft—exceeding Roosevelt's goal.

The Department of Defense in 1940 ordered that only limited expansion would be permitted West Coast defense plants, and that all new aircraft production plants must be built in the Midwest. Government officials were concerned about the vulnerability of plants on the coast.

Douglas insisted that the War Department permit him to build a new plant in the Los Angeles area to utilize trained personnel now working at Santa Monica and El Segundo. His proposal pointed out that the Los Angeles area already was a source of aircraft parts, materials, and services that would be needed to build up plant capacity quickly to meet the president's production goal. He argued that another West Coast plant would produce more aircraft in less time. His arguments were so convincing that the War Department authorized him to proceed with plans for such a plant.

Douglas had started consideration of such a new plant in January 1940, and various sites had been under consideration. In August, Douglas announced that Long Beach had been chosen for the plant, and he called the decision to build there one of the first

major steps in the implementation of President Roosevelt's "Arsenal
of Democracy." The plant site was adjacent to Long Beach Municipal
Airport, which would simplify flight testing and delivery of aircraft
to the armed forces.

In his initial announcement, Douglas said the new plant would
be primarily an aircraft assembly and fly-away location. Other
Douglas plants and supporting subcontractors throughout the United
States would send components to Long Beach where aircraft would
be assembled, flight-tested, and delivered to the U.S. Army Air
Corps. It was a unique program, and one that called for production
of large assemblies for wings and fuselages from cities all over the
country for assembly in Long Beach. Never before had such extensive
subcontracting been considered on such a large scale. And it was
being done while the United States was still at peace.

In the summer of 1940, the Army Air Corps requested Douglas
to provide engineering, tooling, and production plans for an initial
order for 999 A-20B attack bombers and 545 C-47s. Another order
for observation planes subsequently was canceled. Actually, the
C-47s became the plant's major production effort, and were built at
a rate of eleven per day in 1944.

A two-story house just south of the Santa Monica plant was
established on July 15, 1940, to serve as planning headquarters and
within two weeks flow charts and production plans were supplied to
the Air Corps. It was decided to disperse the buildings to reduce
damage from possible enemy bombing attacks, and buildings were
designed without windows for the same reason. The Long Beach
plant was the first large aircraft plant to be so built.

President Roosevelt authorized funds to start constructing the
Long Beach plant November 13. When it was completed it covered
242 acres. Only a few automobiles owned by executives were permitted
within the plant, while the main parking lot was established across
the street. This action was taken to avoid a possible bomb-laden car
from blowing up part of the plant's facilities.

To finance the plant, Douglas formed a wholly owned subsidiary
called the Western Land and Improvement Company, authorized by
the government under an Emergency Plant Facilities contract. This
was a quick way to meet national defense needs. The first contract
was for $13 million, which was later expanded to $27 million to
provide additional production areas to build the B-17 Flying Fortress

under license to the Boeing Airplane Company. In later decades of high cost overruns involving plant acquisition or expansion, it is interesting to note that the original estimate of $27 million was exceeded by slightly less than $2 million by the end of the war.

Douglas turned the first shovelful of dirt to officially start construction of the plant on November 22 with many business and military leaders in attendance. He told the gathering the plant would be a significant contribution towards the nation's goal of making itself invulnerable to attack. "America aroused is America united," he said. "America united is America invincible."

Douglas received a call later from Hap Arnold who told him, "Don, you're going to Tulsa to run a plant."

"The hell I am!"

"The hell you aren't. You're there now."

The disgruntled Douglas went to Tulsa to make arrangements for a new plant. After landing at the Oklahoma City airport, before going on to Tulsa, he was asked by a reporter what he thought of Oklahoma City's plans for its new $25 million airport.

Douglas was blunt. "If you really want to know, I think you're crazy."

That year the Douglas Company had a backlog of $69 million in orders with about 8,000 employees. The following year, after war was declared, the company expanded at a phenomenal rate reaching, by 1943, 160,000 workers in six plants.

During the war, 87 percent of the workers at the Long Beach plant were women. In fact, this plant had the highest percentage of women employees of any in the United States. At Long Beach, and all over the nation, women served their country, liberating themselves in the process. Many became supervisors during the war, and a large number stayed in the business after the war.

Major plants also were established in Oklahoma City and Chicago. The fact the company could expand at such a rate was due to Douglas Aircraft's knowledge of how to build airplanes economically, and the fact that Douglas had a knack for picking good top men to run his plants, and then leaving them alone as long as they proved capable of doing the job. He was a hard-headed businessman with an engineer's passion for precision. He believed in dreams, but in his fertile brain there was no room for nonsense.

Late in the war he was asked by a reporter what he would do with the Long Beach plant when the war ended. "I'll shut the damn shop up!"

Carl Cover brought General Arnold to Heinemann's office at El Segundo early in 1941. While on a plant tour Arnold put his arm around Heinemann. "Ed, I hate like hell to do this to you, but we can't go ahead with the DC-5. We've got to build the C-47 and go balls out to build them, and you've got to stop this airplane."

Heinemann was disturbed by this decision, but he understood the reason for it. He knew the C-47, military version of the DC-3, was so far along that cancellation of the DC-5 was realistic.

Only thirteen were produced, and one of the navy versions was lost on a test flight. KLM bought four, Bill Boeing one, while seven were purchased by the U.S. Marines and the Navy as R3Ds. Military crews liked the airplane because it was so easy to exit by parachute in an emergency.

The DC-5's empty weight actually was less than the DC-3, and it matched that transport's seat-mile costs. The DC-5 had less wing area, but still had higher lift due to its special flap system.

Heinemann did not like the high wing, but Carl Cover, who had promoted the airplane from its original concept of a commercial A-20, insisted because passengers would have a better view than in a low-wing airplane. Cover was one of Heinemann's top bosses, so he had to go along with the concept.

All customers liked the airplane, and it was a great success in the navy, whose pilots appreciated its tricycle landing gear. It was used daily to carry high-priority mail to the West Indies when President Roosevelt vacationed at Roosevelt Roads in Puerto Rico.

On December 7, 1941, Douglas, Hap Arnold, and several others went out to shoot ducks at the company's lodge and hunting preserve in the remote Simi Valley, northwest of the San Fernando Valley. They had roamed far from the lodge since early morning, and returned late that afternoon.

The caretaker was excited when Douglas and Arnold walked up, saying he had heard on the radio hours before that the Japanese had attacked Pearl Harbor.

The Army Air Corp's chief of staff was particularly irate because he had not been notified immediately, and he was sure Gen. George C. Marshall was furious because he had not been able to locate him.

Douglas demanded to know why the caretaker had not come out and told them about the attack. Somewhat sheepishly, he said, "I didn't know how to do it."

Arnold left immediately for Hawaii to assess the damage caused by the Japanese sneak attack. Upon his return to Santa Monica he joined the Douglas family for dinner and described what had happened at Pearl Harbor. He said he was taken around Hickam Field by its commander, who pointed to destroyed airplanes littering the field.

"What the hell were the airplanes there for? Why weren't they up in the air?" he asked.

"No guns on them," the escorting general replied.

"Where the hell were the guns?"

"Over there in that bunker."

"Where was the ammunition?"

"In the ammunition bunker."

"Why in hell weren't the guns and ammunition in the airplanes?"

"Those were our orders, general."

"Whose orders were they?" Arnold said belligerently.

"Yours, general."

Arnold laughed somewhat ruefully.

He told another one on himself. He said he found the Tactical Air Force was not using the Douglas A-24s because the Air Force did not know how to use them as dive-bombers. "Why in hell don't you use them?" he asked the general in charge.

"We've got orders there'll be no more single-engine bombers used in combat."

"Who issued those orders?"

"You did, general."

The Long Beach plant was officially occupied and the entire factory was completed in August 1942. Without windows, it was necessary to air condition all manufacturing areas during the hot months. The plant was well lighted and one of the most modern in the nation, but the mercury vapor fluorescent lights produced a blue effect, which accentuated blemishes on the faces of employees, and distorted facial makeup in a most unflattering way.

One of the principal problems in the start-up of production was the lack of good managers, most of whom had to be trained from scratch. George Strompl, the plant's first manager and a longtime Douglas associate, had the experience but lacked the sensitivity to handle management personnel who had been transferred from other plants largely because they could be spared, and not because of their abilities. Once George Huggins was put in as general manager in September 1942 most problems were resolved. A big event that month was Roosevelt's visit to the plant.

The major problem confronting Long Beach officials was the addition of the high-priority B-17 Flying Fortress to the production effort. It was a Boeing design and that company's engineering drawings, production plans, and tooling were unfamiliar to Douglas employees. At the time, Boeing's manufacturing methods were not as advanced as those at Douglas. Initially, attempts were made to learn the Boeing system through special training and handling, but when such efforts did not work, Douglas officials replanned and retooled the B-17 to match its own production methods.

The problem was not isolated to Douglas, so it was necessary to form a committee representing the three companies building the B-17 to resolve problems for this priority warplane. It was called BDV Committee, and was made up of Boeing, Douglas, and Lockheed-Vega and was located at Boeing headquarters in Seattle where it handled interpretations and coordinated changes between the three companies. After a slow start at Long Beach, the problems were resolved and the plant built 3,000 Flying Fortresses.

Although few American warplanes were built in time for the start of World War II, the United States was producing at the rate of 50,000 per year by the end of the war so it had proved its ability to tool up quickly for mass production of combat airplanes. The Douglas Long Beach plant turned out one-sixth of the total of all United States planes, as measured in pounds, that were delivered during the war. Employee turnover became a problem by 1943 when many new employees left the company, some without even completing their training program, because nearby shipyards paid $1.13 an hour, with more overtime, than the average Douglas wage of $1.00 an hour.

That year the United Auto Workers-CIO and the International Association of Machinists-AFL started to organize workers to join their unions. The National Labor Relations Board held an election in early 1944 but no clear majority was evident, so a runoff election was scheduled a week later. The UAW won the runoff. Plant officials were disturbed by the communist propaganda activity engaged in by a few workers at the plant, and a struggle for power between the two unions further disrupted production.

Employment dropped from 41,602 to 29,000 by the end of 1943. With a smaller work force, and better-trained supervision, many of the early start-up problems were behind them.

Ed Heinemann frequently got a call from Charlotte Douglas saying Douglas's father, William Douglas wanted to take her and her sister, along with Ed and his wife, to Earl Carroll's, the number one entertainment spot in Hollywood. Heinemann liked Doug's father because he was easygoing and fun.

Heinemann particularly appreciated Charlotte's kindness to his wife Lillian who was having serious health problems at the time. She often called her, saying, "Let's have dinner today at Perino's." This was the finest eating place in Los Angeles. In those days Perino often served the main course himself.

During the war years, Charlotte frequently called Ed on a Thursday to ask, "Who's in town this weekend?"

At any one time there were representatives from various companies throughout the world, and they were invited to the Douglas home for a Sunday afternoon dinner. At first, Doug would show up for these affairs, but then his absences became more and more frequent. Eventually he did not show up at all. On those occasions, Charlotte asked Ed to sit at the head of the table to substitute for Douglas as host. Heinemann found this embarrassing, but figured Douglas did not enjoy socializing, and preferred to be out on his boat. He learned later that Charlotte and Doug were drifting apart, particularly after Marguerite C. "Peggy" Tucker joined the company as a courier driver just prior to World War II.

Charlotte delighted in using their home and gardens for numerous charity events such as "Bundles for Britain" teas with Basil Rathbone and Nigel Bruce acting as greeters. Barbara and her mother handled all the flowers and food.

St. Monica's Catholic Church in Santa Monica was often given permission to use the Douglas residential facilities, with their extensive grounds, for charity parties and fashion luncheons. The movie "Going My Way" was about the church's pastor Monsignor Connelly. Daughter Barbara and the twins attended his parochial school during their seventh and eighth grade years. During these church parties Charlotte and Barbara helped to set up the chairs and tables, and then placed them back in order after 300 visitors had attended. Charlotte often chided Monsignor Connelly that, "You work the women of the parish too much, and charge too little for these nice luncheon parties." The Monsignor always explained that the Depression was still on, and that $1.25 was all most people could afford.

Charlotte's rose garden was famous. If a friend was having a dinner, Charlotte would gather about three dozen roses from her garden, carefully remove all the thorns, and deliver them to that person's house.

Charlotte worked hard throughout the war years, always avoiding the limelight, and was generous with her time and money for worthy causes. She often took families of foreign airline officials to the beach, and the youngest children absolutely adored her. Military men, temporarily attached to the company, could always count on Charlotte to help move their families in and out of houses, get medical assistance, and help their wives and children when the men were out of town. In those days, when military pay was low, frequent discreet help with money from Charlotte was a boon to many a hard-pressed military family. Many of these people became Charlotte's lifelong friends.

Charlotte made up for Doug's lack of compatibility with strangers by her outgoing, selfless style. You never could open a door for her, even in later years when she was restricted to the use of crutches or a wheelchair.

The Douglas family. Clockwise from lower left, Donald, Harold (his brother), William (his father), Dorothy (his mother), and an unidentified woman.

Midshipman Douglas in Norway.

Douglas with Glenn Martin in Cleveland.
From left, Larry Bell, Glenn Martin, Eric
Springer, and Donald Douglas.

Douglas, center foreground, checks a Martin
Type R airplane prior to flight.

1920

1920

1921

192

1922

1940

SANTA MONICA

EL SEGUNDO SM17564

*Douglas offices and plants from the 1920s
through the 1940s.*

128

Logos of Douglas-owned companies.

Douglas, in rear cockpit, checks progress of the Cloudster.

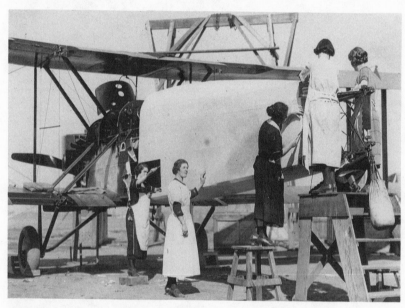

Women workers sew fabric onto the Cloudster.

Sons Will and Donald, Jr., pose by one of the wheels of the Cloudster.

World Cruiser ready for around-the-world flight.

The Dolphin in 1931.

Douglas in his Franklin roadster.

The only DC-1 ever built.

NC-30,000, the company DC-3.

DC-2. This KLM airplane was flown in the England-to-Melbourne race in 1934, carrying passengers and mail. It made every scheduled stop, turned back to Allahabad, India, to collect a missing passenger, and still came in second against a DeHavilland Comet. Douglas, third from left, stands with crew that made the flight.

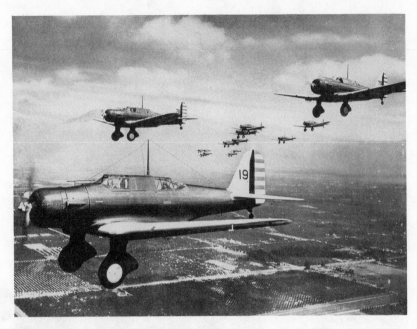

*A-17 attack aircraft produced by the El
Segundo Division in the mid-1930s.*

*A B-19 overflies the dedication ceremonies at
the Long Beach plant on October 17, 1941.*

The 2,000th C-47, covered with workers'
autographs, prior to delivery.

Old Reliable. The DC-4 was converted for war use as the C-54.

The A-20, known as the Havoc.

The A-26, known later as the B-26 Invader.

On September 13, 1944, these gentlemen bought 93 DC-4s. From left, Eddie Rickenbacker (president of Eastern), W. A. Patterson (president of United), A. N. Kemp (president of American), Douglas, and Harold J. Roig (president of Panagra).

General of the U.S. Air Force, "Hap" Arnold often visited the Douglas plants. Here he meets with Douglas, Jr., and his father.

A jovial moment with Ed Heinemann in 1947. Heinemann, chief engineer of the El Segundo Division, led the design team that built the Skystreak.

The DC-6 was the finest propeller-driven transport ever built.

Lord Hamilton arrives at the plant, met by Douglas, who gave him a Scottish salute.

The Globemaster. Sturdy and dependable,
446 C-124s were produced at Long Beach.

Dr. Jerome Hunsaker visits his old friend
Douglas four decades after they made the
wind tunnel studies at M.I.T.

Douglas and "Bar."

D-558-2, the Skyrocket, was first to fly over twice the speed of sound.

The Skyray, record holder for speed and altitude. The company made over 400 for the U.S. Navy.

Creators of the DC-3, the world's most famous aircraft. They had a reunion in 1958. From left, Arthur Raymond, Lee Atwood, George Strompl, Bailey Oswald, J. H. Kindelberger, Donald Douglas, Ed Burton, Frank Collbohm, and Jake Moxness.

The DC-8 was the first Douglas transport to fly with jet-powered engines.

*The DC-8 team. Seated from left, Ed Burton,
Donald Douglas, Arthur Raymond, and Nat
Paschall. Standing, left, Schuyler Kleinhans,
Jake Moxness, Harold Adams, Jim Clyne,
and Ivar Shogran.*

*In November 1963, the Douglas space facility
was dedicated at Huntington Beach,
California. Douglas and his son escorted
dignitaries around the facility prior to the
ceremony. From left, Donald Douglas,
Donald Douglas, Jr., Vice-president Lyndon
Johnson, Governor Pat Brown of California,
Congressman Richard Hanna, Mayor
Lambert, and facility head Charles Able.*

In a relaxed mood. Douglas's office was simply furnished, and he resisted any attempts to "pretty it up."

Rollout of the DC-9 in 1964.

Blast-off of Discoverer by Thor from Vandenberg Air Force Base.

"He Builds Them Like We Do Automobiles"

F ortune Magazine said in 1941, "The development of the airplane in the days between the wars is the greatest engineering story there ever was, and in the heart of it is Donald Douglas." Shortly after the Japanese attacked Pearl Harbor the government commandeered the majority of the airlines' transports, most of which were DC-3s. Still in their airline markings, they were quickly put to use ferrying troops and supplies to bases in Alaska, the Caribbean, and South and Central America.

Orders for the C-47 continued to come in and thousands were produced at the government-built plants in Oklahoma City and Long Beach operated by the Douglas Company. Production was maintained on an around-the-clock basis. The peak rate at Oklahoma City reached 306 C-47s during one month, while Long Beach produced 267 one month.

Immediately after war was declared the War Department sent Douglas a telegram ordering him to stop production of the DC-4. He was incensed at their lack of foresight because he knew such four-motored transports, capable of flying long distances over the oceans, would be vitally needed.

In a special message to Secretary of War Henry L. Stimson, he urged him to rescind the order, pointing out that such an airplane could be used throughout the world, and would be far safer than ships, which were the constant prey of enemy submarines.

Much to Douglas's chagrin, the secretary refused to change the decision. Douglas was so confident they would eventually see the light that he continued to produce the airplane on his own. His courage and vision were vindicated three months later when another telegram ordered him to proceed with the airplane for the air force as the C-54.

Lt. Gen. William S. Knudsen, boss of the Air Technical Service Command, came out to the Douglas plants to inspect the production lines with General Arnold. His eyes popped when he saw the long lines of C-54s going down final assembly. He had been head of General Motors before he was "drafted" for duty in the Pentagon. He turned to Arnold. "Yaah, this Douglas, he builds them like we do automobiles. He just took the 3 and puffed it up, bigger wing, bigger body, more power. We do the same thing. We make the Chev. and then the Pontiac, then the Olds, then the Buick, and finally it grows into the Cadillac, but it is all the same." It was not quite that easy, as Douglas well knew, but there was much truth in Knudsen's comments.

Allied shipping losses on the Atlantic in early 1942 became so catastrophic that consideration was given to alternate forms of transportation to deliver men and supplies from the United States to Great Britain.

Henry J. Kaiser, noted builder of Liberty ships, told government officials that U-boat attacks against surface ships could be circumvented by building huge flying boats mostly out of wood, which could fly over the oceans in comparative safety. Such flying boats, he said, should be of a size and design never before contemplated, and 5,000 would be needed to take over the job of surface ships.

President Roosevelt was intrigued by the idea and he told Donald Nelson, chairman of the War Production Board, to set up a meeting presided over by Donald Douglas to discuss the matter. Industry and military representatives met with Kaiser and Douglas in the company's dining room in Santa Monica.

After Kaiser made his proposal, the idea was greeted negatively by Douglas and most industry members, who considered the proposal impractical and beyond the capabilities of the period's technology. It was pointed out that obtaining sufficient plywood would not be a problem, but super alloys for the huge aircraft's eight engines were critically short. Douglas pointed out that all systems would have to be made of metal. It was quickly apparent to everyone but Kaiser that a great amount of extremely critical metals, vitally needed in the war effort, would have to be allocated.

Douglas said the proposed Wright 3350 engines, with two banks of nine cylinders each, would need a great amount of molybdenum and other scarce alloys. He told the gathering that metals were so scarce that although the whole industry was producing combat planes at a high rate, they could not be delivered because of a shortage of engines. They were being rationed, he said, while airplanes were being stored for lack of power plants.

Although Douglas did not condemn the proposal outright, his private thoughts were that if you could not get sufficient engines for other airplanes, why build this wooden monster? He made it clear that his thoughts on the subject were completely negative. All military representatives joined him in recommending that the airplane not be built.

Kaiser remained convinced of the project's feasibility. His first proposal involved a twin-hulled flying boat that could land on water, or be beached on shore. Some government officials and the nation's press were intrigued by the idea, particularly when Kaiser said a prototype could be built within ten months of the signing of a contract. Furthermore, this man, who had revolutionized the fast building of ships, claimed that he could build 500 such flying boats a year. While there were scoffers, many people took Kaiser seriously because he had built surface ships in only six working days. This was an incredible achievement because most new ships took months, even years, to build.

Most government officials did not share Kaiser's optimism for his flying boat, pointing out that he had no experience designing or producing aircraft of any kind.

Kaiser persisted until he got some response from aircraft designer and builder Howard Hughes, who at first was not receptive to the idea. The shipbuilder was so persuasive, however, that he finally convinced Hughes to join him in a partnership to design and build 500 flying cargo aircraft.

Kaiser's design amounted to little more than an artist's concept with proposed capabilities and capacities, so Hughes decided to start from scratch. He soon abandoned the twin-hulled Kaiser concept for a more conventional single-hull seaplane with various engine configurations.

The Kaiser-Hughes Corporation submitted a tentative design for a huge eight-engine flying boat to the government in September 1942. Despite refusal of the military services to invest in the cargo plane, Kaiser talked Jesse Jones's Reconstruction Finance Corporation into financing a contract for the design, construction, and testing of three airplanes. The initial $18 million contract, signed November 16, went to Hughes to design, build, and test a prototype. If the plane proved itself, Kaiser would go into full production.

Although Kaiser continued to maintain that the prototype could be designed and built within ten months, Hughes knew better. Privately, he told associates the project would not be completed in less than two years.

Hughes insisted on approving every detail of the design personally. It was soon apparent that the first order of business was to construct an 859-foot-long, 250-foot-wide hangar, rising to 100 feet, to accommodate the huge airplane.

With aluminum in extremely short supply, Hughes decided to use the duramold process, which involved laminated wood with a continuous seamless construction. He had used this process to build the Hughes H-1 racer, which set a number of world speed records, so he was working with familiar materials.

Kaiser lost interest in the project when a year went by and there was no physical evidence that the prototype was about to take shape. It was still in the design stage.

Once the submarine menace was reduced by the joint use of Allied escort carriers, destroyers, and destroyer escorts, and with government interest at a low ebb, Kaiser's enthusiasm waned even more, although he still had confidence in Hughes's design. Kaiser's interest had always been in the mass production of such airplanes and when such a possibility became even more remote, he decided to withdraw from the venture.

Howard Hughes stubbornly continued the project even though the Reconstruction Finance Corporation wanted to cancel it. President Roosevelt's intervention kept the project alive throughout the rest of the war, but the world's largest airplane still was not ready to be flight-tested.

A Senate committee was formed in early 1947 to investigate $6 billion worth of undelivered wartime contracts, including the Hughes Hercules flying boat. Most of the committee's attention was focused on the Hughes project. When he was subpoenaed to appear at a hearing, he defended himself vigorously against attacks that became quite personal when Senator Owen Brewster accused him of wasteful expenditure of taxpayer dollars. In a heated exchange Hughes said, "If the flying boat doesn't fly, I'll leave the country and never return." Eventually Hughes was exonerated from any wrongdoing, and some members of the committee praised his efforts.

The Hughes flying boat made its first, and last, flight on November 1, 1947, in Long Beach harbor when it seemed to float off the water and rise 50 feet into the air. When the right wing began to dip down, Hughes brought the Hercules back to a smooth landing. Development continued for several years, but the Hercules never flew again.

Donald Douglas's rejection of the project was more than justified by the airplane's history.

General Arnold talked to Douglas in early 1941 about the army's need for gliders that could be filled with troops and landed behind enemy lines. Heinemann received a call from his boss, who described the type of glider needed and explained that the Santa Monica plant was so jammed with production orders that it was impossible to take on a new project. "Can you build them?"

Heinemann had no interest whatsoever in gliders but, knowing he was one of the few design engineers in the company with experience in working with wood in airplanes, he reluctantly agreed to take on the assignment. The first two, the XCG-7 and XCG-8, were completed long after the war started. Later, much to Heinemann's relief, Douglas dropped out of further competition, although the company's efforts were noteworthy and contributed substantially to knowledge in this specialized field.

Douglas factory officials such as George Huggins, Henry Guerin, and Arch Wallen helped to develop high-speed assembly lines so mass production methods could be adopted for making parts for aircraft assemblies. The company's streamlined production methods were unique, and certainly contributed to the successful prosecution of the war effort. The moving line was just one of many innovative ideas.

Former French auto mechanic Henry Guerin had developed a process in 1935 that proved crucial to quantity production of aircraft during World War II. He designed inexpensive dies that could shape sheet metal into parts in minutes rather than hours.

New methods of fabrication, routing of materials, and plant layouts for maximum efficiency proved so intriguing to automobile manufacturers that they sent experts to Douglas to learn how things were done. Most of them adapted these new techniques to the manufacture of parts and assemblies in their own plants, which had been converted from automobile production to defense work.

Douglas, who inspired and pioneered the formation of the government's Aircraft War Production Council, also served as one of its presidents. The council's work was vital in unifying joint efforts by all companies and in the interchange of facilities for maximum effectiveness.

By 1943, Douglas's life had settled into a busy routine. He got up each morning at 7:30, awaking without benefit of an alarm clock. Thirty minutes later he invariably had an egg, one piece of white toast, and a cup of black coffee before getting into his 1941 black Lincoln Zephyr to make the ten-minute drive to work.

There, in his walnut-paneled office he sat down to a desk covered with letters and engineering reports neatly arranged for his perusal. Within reach was an array of pipes, which he smoked throughout the day with an occasional cigarette in between. On the front of his desk was the Douglas coat of arms with its inscription, *Jamais arriere* (never behind).

Most visitors knew his routine, whether they were vice-presidents or friends in the industry. He would greet each person warmly, snap off the desk lamp, and remove his spectacles. The discussion continued until he picked up his glasses and turned the desk light back on, and knowledgeable visitors would realize the meeting was over, whether or not they had reported everything they came to say. They took the hint, and beat a hasty retreat.

His private dining room was across Ocean Park Boulevard. At exactly 12:10, a routine that only an emergency would alter, he left his office and walked across the street. His lunch seldom varied—a hamburger, black coffee, and a chocolate sundae.

Back in his office he worked steadily to reduce the pile of correspondence and reports, with an approving "D" or "Tell him nuts."

He was ready to return to his $150,000 white-brick Spanish-style home in Santa Monica at 5:30 P.M. and Charlotte knew he wanted his dinner at 6:30 sharp, with the inevitable chocolate sundae for dessert.

While his wife and daughter listened to the radio upstairs, something he absolutely refused to do, Douglas settled himself in his favorite chair near the library's fireplace. Over the mantel was a painting of the *Endymion,* which he often glanced at fondly while he read his yachting books. These books were for his own use, and, when he was not reading them, he hid them in a secret panel.

Charlotte had long ago given up trying to get him to go out for social events. He would rather stay home. Prior to the war, however, he was out on his yacht with a few friends each weekend. Now such excursions were few because of wartime restrictions.

When he had learned to play the bagpipe, he practiced methodically until he became adept. Before the war he had organized an employee band, which he outfitted with kilts. They regularly cruised to Catalina, and Douglas led his bagpipers up and down the hills playing familiar Scottish melodies.

In 1943, Douglas owned only 1 percent of the 600,000 shares of stock in the corporation, compared to the 200,000 he was given when the company was incorporated in 1928. He collected $120,000 a year in salary and, despite the fact the company had never lost money since it was founded, dividends were still small. The company had had its best year in 1941 when it earned net profits of more than $18 million after taxes on a gross of almost $42 million. The percentage of profit to gross was below 3 percent in 1943, at a time when the company's annual business volume was $1 billion with a $2.5 billion backlog. It was the fourth largest in the nation.

At its peak in 1944, sales of military equipment exceeded $1 billion, and the company employed more than 160,000 in six plants around the United States. This was a far cry from the $130,840 achieved in 1922 when the company had sixty-eight employees.

Despite six years of intensive efforts by unions to organize his company, only 15 percent of the more than 160,000 employees were members of a union. The Douglas Company in 1943 had one of the largest open shops in the country. Through the efforts of its industrial relations head Rocky Rochlen, unions were constantly kept off balance, and he and Douglas stayed a step or two ahead of union leaders by granting wage increases. Wartime labor turnover was high, of course, frustrating union efforts to organize employees.

A special DC-4 had been delivered to the air force in 1942 for use as the first personal plane for the president of the United States. The press dubbed it "The Sacred Cow," a name Roosevelt detested. He only used it twice but it was used on numerous diplomatic missions and became known throughout the world. It ended up in the Smithsonian Institution after the war ended.

General Arnold and Bill Knudsen called a meeting of all aircraft manufacturers during the early part of 1944 in Los Angeles. Each company brought along its key engineering and production men, and the 400 people gathered at the meeting listened silently as Arnold and Knudsen set them new goals.

Later, Arnold spoke to Douglas privately, saying, "I want 400 extra C-47s."

As Douglas was about to speak, he interrupted. "I mean in addition to those you're already building. This is something special. We want them faster than you've ever built them before!"

Arnold stressed secrecy as he told Douglas of the changes needed for these C-47s. He said he wanted the interiors stripped and special attachments made for the fuselage and wings so that jeeps, guns, ammunition, spare parts for tanks, and a host of other military hardware could be carried. He added that some C-47s should be equipped to tow gliders. It was not until June 6, 1944, D-Day, that the reason for these changes became clear.

In the days following the landing, C-47s carried more than 60,000 paratroopers and their equipment to the coast of France. It was an awe-inspiring sight. Douglas knew that the men and women of his company had worked unstintingly for long hours to help make the invasion a success. Looking back, he also knew that the men of the air force such as Hap Arnold, who had long fought for air power, were even more responsible. Without their courage and determination, often against great odds, he knew that what had now occurred never would have been possible.

While these airplanes were being built Douglas engineers designed an experimental airplane whose engines were housed in the fuselage and drove counter-rotating tail propellers. The XB-42 had a large bomb capacity but it and its jet-propelled successor the XB-43 were never placed into production.

Douglas scientists had been doing highly secret work on missiles before the war and by 1940 the Roc I, a 1,000-pound air-to-surface rocket was developed for use on a guided beam to home in on ground targets. A tactical version, Roc II, went into production too late for use against the Axis, but it was the forerunner of many guided missiles.

Roosevelt's call for 50,000 warplanes a year had, at first, sounded too visionary but once the production pace was established the industry did its part and Douglas was in the forefront. At the El Segundo Division, the company built 5,396 SBD Dauntless aircraft during the war, including those with the army's A-24 designation.

The SBD had no bugs, no streaks of temperament, a thoroughly honest aircraft, navy fliers said. It could take a frightful beating and stagger home on wings that often looked like nutmeg graters. Its loss ratio was the lowest of all United States carrier aircraft in the Pacific.

In totaling production among all divisions and the 240 built by Boeing, various versions of the A-20, including the BD-1, the BD-2, the P-70 night fighter, and photoreconnaissance models, reached the impressive figure of 7,478. By March of 1944, the rate was 322 aircraft per month. At the Long Beach Division alone, 4,285 C-47s were produced, along with 3,000 Boeing B-17 Flying Fortresses. Such a phenomenal rate has never been equalled.

Another new attack bomber, the A-26B, reached a production peak of 108 per month. It had been developed in early 1940 to carry heavy loads just above the ground at high speeds. General Arnold personally sought such an airplane. The A-20 was considered for the role, but it quickly was evident that it was impossible to install a 75-mm cannon in the nose. Heinemann had also pointed out that the Havoc could not be redesigned to carry heavy cannons, and he recommended consideration of an entirely new airplane. The A-26 Invader did not fly until 1943, and it saw only limited service in World War II. It served with the Ninth Air Force in Europe from November 1944 until the end of the war. Years later it served with distinction in the Korean War.

After the Tulsa, Oklahoma, plant was finished in 1942 Douglas produced the Consolidated B-24 bomber. Although not its own design, Douglas manufactured 962 Liberators. Plants in Oklahoma City and Chicago also played important roles in the war effort by building C-47s, C-117s, and C-54s.

Benny Howard, who worked directly for Douglas without a specific assignment, was a frequent visitor to the El Segundo Division in 1943, where he prowled around design and test areas without Heinemann's knowledge. He had been a company pilot, but after a serious accident left him in great pain, he was no longer permitted to fly, but was given various assignments by Douglas.

Each time after Howard had been around talking to Heinemann's engineers, he'd get a call from Douglas. "Benny says, such and such. How about it?"

Ed would say, "Doug, I haven't heard that. Who did he talk to?"

Douglas would name the engineer.

Heinemann would call in the engineer and confront him. "What have you been telling Benny?"

Inevitably his reply would be completely different from what Douglas had told him.

"That's not what he told Doug," Ed would say. "He's got it all wrong."

Douglas did not condone such tactics, and certainly he did not ask Howard to spy on Heinemann's activities, but he finally got exasperated. He called Ed. "I'm so damn tired of getting two different stories. Benny says one thing. You say another. I've decided to end this whole damn thing. I'm putting one guy in who will be responsible for all flight tests. And Junior is that guy."

Heinemann did not appreciate the younger Douglas taking over an operation his department had always handled, but he had to agree. After Don became director of flight-test operations, Howard left to work for Convair.

That same year the United States Navy knew it had to have a better torpedo bomber than the ones in use. The navy authorized Douglas's El Segundo Division in October to build two prototypes of what became known as the XTB2D1 Skypirate. The largest engine then available, the Pratt & Whitney R-4360, capable of 3,000 horsepower, was selected by Heinemann's engineers to power the torpedo bomber. Two Curtiss-electric, counter-rotating propellers were selected to help achieve a 300-knot speed. The Skypirate was a complex aircraft, and it encountered numerous propeller control problems during flight tests, which were delayed until 1945.

Ivar Shogran was the company's expert on engines. During one of the bomber's tests he flew with Carl Cover while he checked the temperatures of the engine at different altitudes. Once the tests were completed, Cover called, "Ivar, we've got altitude for a terminal velocity test dive."

Shogran, who was longing for a return to the safety of the ground, was not keen about the idea. He shook his head, and pointed down. They were at 12,000 feet over the Pacific Ocean, with Playa del Rey off to the right.

"How about it?" Cover insisted.

"I'm an engineer, not a test pilot."

"Ready?" Cover persisted.

"Hell no! I don't have a parachute."

Shogran's normally red face turned crimson as Cover headed toward the blue Pacific. As the plane's speed built up, Shogran prayed the plane would hold together. This was the first time it had been tested at terminal velocity. That was all he remembered for a few minutes as his body succumbed to the unaccustomed G forces and he blacked out. When he came to, Cover was laughing as he climbed the airplane. "How'd you like that?" he yelled.

Shogran tried to express appreciation, but his heart was not in it. "Great," he said. He remembered that his boss Arthur Raymond had once said Cover was one of the world's greatest pilots, but "I wish he wouldn't take such a lighthearted view of flying."

Shogran could not agree more with Raymond's assessment as Cover said, "Good. We'll do it again." With the plane picking up speed every second as it plummeted towards the ocean, Shogran blacked out again.

Carl Cover returned to active duty with the air force in 1944, and was killed during a landing accident at Wright Field. The fun-loving Cover had long been a Douglas favorite, and was sorely missed.

During the war the navy asked manufacturers to come up with a successor to the SBD Dauntless. The Douglas dive-bomber had served valiantly, but was an old design and a new one was desperately needed. To Heinemann's consternation Curtiss-Wright won the competition with its SB2C Helldiver even though it was more expensive than the SBD, heavier, and not all that great an improvement.

The Douglas El Segundo Division later got a contract to build a successor to the SBD and the Helldiver. It was called the XSB2D-1. It was not a good airplane, Heinemann conceded to Douglas, and he agreed with navy officials when the airplane was officially canceled in June 1944.

Heinemann tried to salvage some of their efforts by redesigning the airplane and calling it the XBTD-1 Destroyer.

During an evaluation meeting in Washington, Heinemann realized the Destroyer had not proven itself in flight tests, and that drastic action was necessary if anything was to be salvaged from the two programs. Rear Adm. Lawrence B. Richardson, assistant chief of the navy's Bureau of Aeronautics, listened intently as Heinemann recommended that the BTD program be scrapped. He went on to say that his division wanted to design a completely new single-engine attack airplane, using the funds still available from the BTD program. He said it would take his engineering department about thirty days to prepare the new design.

Richardson nodded, but said, "You'll have to have a design for us by 0900 tomorrow. And, you'll have to use the new R-3350 engine."

Although Heinemann was pleased his company had been granted a reprieve to stay in the competition, he was shocked by the time limit imposed by Richardson. Aloud, he agreed to the terms. Back in his hotel Heinemann called Douglas and Arthur Raymond to explain the situation, and they supported his action. He, Leo Devlin, and several other engineers worked on the design until exhaustion forced them to quit at 3:00 A.M. Four hours later Heinemann took their preliminary drawings out to get blueprints made.

With trepidation he presented their design concept for a new dive-bomber to Bureau of Aeronautics officials promptly at 9:00 A.M. Henry Kaiser's Fleetwing and a Martin entry appeared to be Douglas's strongest competition. Ed was relieved when Adm. Richardson agreed to continue the competition, making it clear the navy was interested in only the best product regardless of the manufacturer.

Heinemann called his staff together upon his return to El Segundo. He reminded them that the El Segundo Division desperately needed a new program now that the SBD was out of production. He told them the new airplane had to be lighter than the other entries, carry a heavier load of bombs and weapons than the other entries, and provide for better performance. "We only have six months," he said, "so we must work fast."

The new aircraft was designated the BT-2D. Perhaps its later success was due to the all-hands effort to keep the gross weight as low as possible.

The airplane made its first flight on March 18, 1945, and the United States Navy placed an additional order for 500 after its successful flight-test program. It was renamed the AD Skyraider and through the years 3,180 were built in several versions. It was the workhorse of the fleet during the Korean War, and was still around during the Vietnam War.

This experience provided a reminder of something Douglas had told Heinemann early in his career with the company. In the 1920s Douglas had said, "The navy operates in the dynamic, hard-hitting environment of the aircraft carrier. They ask more from their pilots and their planes. Therefore the designer must give more of himself if he wants the navy's business."

Ed never forgot that advice. Jack Northrop had said much the same thing; it was far more difficult to build aircraft for the United States Navy than the army because their airplanes had to be better built to withstand the rugged punishment they took operating from carriers.

Of all the Douglas-designed airplanes the A-20 and its A-26 derivatives, the SBD, the C-47, and the C-54, were most acclaimed by airmen. Crewmen admired their toughness, their ability to withstand incredible punishment and bring them home safely.

Throughout the early years of the war the SBD Dauntless fought in every major battle in the Pacific, earning accolades such as Rear Adm. John S. McCain's comment that "the SBD has sunk more enemy combatant tonnage than all other branches of the service." As chief of the Bureau of Aeronautics he was in a position to know, and no one disputed him.

Douglas's affection for the C-47 was expressed when he said, "It is certainly the best-loved airplane we ever produced. But the circumstances that made it great just happened. They were not of our making. I doubt whether any airplane will have the same impact, or the same opportunity again."

In all, the Douglas Aircraft Company produced 29,385 aircraft during World War II, approximately 16 percent of the entire industry's output when measured on a pound-for-pound basis. More than 10,000 C-47s were built, and they were familiar sights in the far corners of the world. Gen. Dwight D. Eisenhower said it was one of four weapons that did most to win the war, along with the bulldozer, the two-and-a-half-ton truck, and the amphibious "duck."

The C-54—canceled by the War Department after Pearl Harbor, but later reinstated—made almost 100,000 ocean crossings. It was used to carry President Roosevelt, Winston Churchill, and other Allied leaders to important conferences, and, at the end of the war, it ferried Gen. Douglas MacArthur and two divisions of troops to Tokyo to accept the Japanese surrender.

Douglas served several times as president of the National Aircraft War Production Council during the war. For his contributions to Allied victory he was awarded the Certificate of Merit by the president of the United States.

Arch C. Wallen was appointed general manager of the Long Beach plant in 1945 prior to negotiations with the Congress of Industrial Organizations for unionization of the plant. Once negotiations were completed a meeting with Douglas and union officials was scheduled in Santa Monica. Although Wallen had attended meetings with Douglas, he had never met the man, because

Douglas had not been to Long Beach since President Roosevelt visited the plant. Wallen felt awkward going to Santa Monica to preside over a signing ceremony between the top union official and Douglas, when he had not even met his boss. He worried what he would do if there was an impasse and Douglas would not know with whom to discuss the problem.

In a Santa Monica conference room while they completed last minute details before Douglas was called in, Wallen admitted with embarrassment that he had never met Douglas, even though he was head of one of the company's major plants. Once they were in complete agreement, and only Douglas's signature was required to finalize the contract, Wallen sent word to Douglas's office.

Douglas walked in, strode up to Wallen, and said, "Arch, how are you? Good to see you."

Wallen felt weak with relief. He realized now, as had so many other managers before him, that Douglas may not have met them, but there was not much he did not know about them.

Douglas signed the contract first and Guy Cox, representing the union, picked up Douglas's pen and scrawled his name on the document. Without thinking, he put the pen in his coat pocket. Douglas reached over, without saying a word, and plucked his pen out of Cox's pocket, put it into his own, and walked out.

The U.S. Army Air Forces, the navy's Bureau of Aeronautics, and the National Advisory Committee for Aeronautics had held a conference in early 1944 about development of research aircraft for exploration into the transonic speed ranges.

Once the war was over these organizations sponsored a visit to Europe by aerodynamicists to study German air technology. The party included A. M. O. Smith and Gene Root of Douglas, and Dr. Clark Millikan of Cal Tech. After studying jet airplane developments in England and Germany, it was apparent these nations were far ahead of the United States. Upon their return they urged government officials to provide funds for research programs on an emergency basis. They pointed out that the United States, as the arsenal of democracy, had fallen behind in jet-age technology.

General Arnold was aware of the implications for the United States, and he knew it would become a second-rate air power unless something was done immediately. He called in his staff the day after

VJ-Day. He had recently suffered a severe heart attack and was only partially recovered. In some ways, however, he was in better shape than his staff members who were suffering withdrawal symptoms from overindulgence and celebration the night before.

"The United States has just won a war with a lot of heroes flying around in obsolete airplanes," he said. "The next war may well be fought by airplanes with no men in them at all. There's no doubt in my mind that such a war will be fought with airplanes so superior to those we've known that there will be no comparison. In the future, the heroes will be on the ground designing, building, and perhaps directing them."

In conclusion, Arnold cautioned that it would be necessary to discard most of what they had learned about airplanes, and get on to aircraft of the future. "They will be different from anything the world has ever seen."

On VJ-Day a Western Union boy brought Douglas a telegram that canceled immediately all government orders. The complex organization that had been so ingeniously put together for war production disintegrated almost overnight as 90,000 workers were laid off within a week.

Douglas had been preparing for just such an eventuality, but he now faced the worst crisis in the company's history. He believed the thousands of military transports that had been built would almost preclude the sale of commercial transports for several years if the military sold them cheaply for adaptation to civilian use.

The Douglas Company had produced an astonishing number of military aircraft during the war, but it was not wealthy. Profits were only 1.5 percent of total sales. Douglas tightened up the company, watching expenses even more than usual. As one old-timer said, "He still has his eyes on the stars, his feet on the ground, and one hand in his pocket keeping track of dimes."

Douglas faced 1946 glumly, despite his confidence in the company's future, saying to intimates, "The future is as dark as the inside of a boot." His pessimism seemed warranted as three of his plants were closed, and employment dropped to 27,000—a far cry from the 160,000 men and women who had been with him during the war years.

Douglas told his staff to look at other products to build. Diversification plans considered production of boats, buses, and prefabricated houses. Some aluminum boats were made, and a few houses actually were constructed, but plants for airplanes proved too costly to operate, and those projects were shelved.

In all of 1946 the company produced only 127 airplanes. The AD-1 Skyraider remained in production, fortunately, and it was the one bright hope for the future.

Douglas had never been one to fret and fume about misfortune, and he did not do so now. He told executives that they must produce a radically new kind of passenger transport, even at the risk of their financial resources. This hardly seemed the time to take such a bold step but they were all for the idea of designing a pressurized passenger plane that could operate at high altitudes, where higher speeds and more economical operations were possible in the thinner atmosphere.

Engineers set to work, knowing they had to surmount difficult design problems such as a cabin structure that could withstand pressures of at least eight pounds per square inch, and locate systems that could operate at temperatures possibly -100°F outside the cabin, while maintaining a living room atmosphere inside. And so the DC-6 was born. It was a dramatic attempt to press forward into realms for passenger flight that had hitherto not been explored.

Lockheed was fortunate when its air force order for C-69s, military version of the O-49 commercial transport, was canceled in 1944 permitting the company to convert the remaining 20 C-69s into commercial transports.

William Allen, who had taken over as Boeing's new president that same year, also began to think of the postwar commercial market. He decided his company had its best opportunity to enter the competition with a commercial version of the C-97 military transport and converted it into a commercial airplane called the Stratocruiser.

After the war ended the race was on to get the first new commercial transports into production. At the start of 1946, with the Douglas Company still six months away from delivering its first DC-4s to American Airlines and the first flight of the DC-6 several months in the future, Lockheed was ready to deliver its Constellations to TWA. These airplanes, with their pressurized cabins, were far in advance of the competition. Boeing's Stratocruiser was still on the drawing boards, and in a poor third position.

John Martin flew Douglas to Washington in February 1946 to attend a conference at the Pentagon. After several days, and no word from his boss as to when he would be ready to fly home, Martin called him. Douglas told him to meet him in the lobby of their hotel in twenty minutes. "We're going to Minneapolis."

"Boss, I've got to get home," Johnnie said. "The DC-6 is about ready for her maiden flight. Besides, it's twenty degrees below zero in Minneapolis. Why do we have to go there?"

"I'll tell you on the way. If it's that cold in Minneapolis, you'd better reserve a hangar for the plane."

Martin quickly assembled his crew and met Douglas in the lobby. While they took a taxi to the airport Douglas told him that an army officer in Minneapolis had a vizsla bitch who had whelped a litter of pups, and that he had been promised three of them. He explained that vizsla resembled weimaraners, a breed of hound that made excellent hunting dogs. Martin wanted to protest, but he knew anything he said about dogs would get him nowhere with his boss.

After arriving in Minneapolis and driving fifty miles to get the pups, they returned to the airplane. Martin sniffed the air inside the cabin, wondering about a peculiarly pungent odor. He found it came from three sacks of oysters that Douglas had bought in Washington and which, after a day in the closed airplane, had taken on an odor the likes of which John had never known. He quickly turned on the air conditioning, so the odor would not be so noticeable.

Martin picked up the puppies and started to put them in the baggage compartment. An irate Douglas yelled, "What do you think you're doing with those pups?"

"I'm putting them in the baggage compartment."

"Why?"

"So they won't mess up the cabin's rug. It's only been laid a week, and it's expensive."

Douglas refused to let Johnnie put his prize puppies below decks. "Don't worry about the rug. We can get it cleaned. Let 'em run. I want to see the little rascals play."

Martin was resigned and carried the puppies into the cabin where they immediately roamed from one end to the other of the DC-3, occasionally squatting to relieve themselves while Douglas roared with laughter. During the flight home the puppies kept nibbling at Martin's heels while he flew the airplane. He wanted to kick them, but Douglas's eyes were on him and he did not dare.

An Instinct for Teamwork

D ouglas spelled out what he looked for in an executive in 1945. Actually, his thoughts applied to anyone with whom he came in contact.

"Primarily what I seek is a warm, balanced human being. Successful leaders in business or industry need other characteristics, too. They must be friendly, well-adjusted, with sympathetic understanding of human motives, limitations, weaknesses, and strengths. They must have a lust for life, inherent enthusiasm, impersonal curiosity in things and people, and a faith in the men and women they direct. Good executives must have judgment, self-confidence, a sense of justice tempered with kindness, an instinct for teamwork, a sense of fair play, and a talent for helping and teaching their associates."

In particular, Douglas always wanted people around him who worked well together.

With the war over, General Arnold was more aware than ever that the peacetime United States Army Air Forces would have to work closely with the scientific community if it was to retain its world leadership. He knew that, for the most part, active duty personnel would need professional guidance as nuclear weapons were developed and jet and rocket vehicles of the future were designed. He talked at length with Douglas about the air forces' problems and in 1946 the two agreed Project Rand should be created to study the science of intercontinental warfare, particularly as it related to air warfare.

With an initial sum of $10 million, and with the Douglas Company acting as manager of the project, a start was made to develop techniques for recommendation to the U.S. Air Force. Douglas reluctantly agreed to let his company serve as initial manager, despite serious concern about a conflict of interest.

One of the early Rand studies in 1946 called for a Globe Circling Space Ship or satellite. At the time, Gen. Dwight D. Eisenhower was army chief of staff. Douglas went along with Raymond to make a proposal that the army fund such a project. Eisenhower reviewed the project, but was not impressed. "Of what possible use is that?" he said. Even after the Russians launched their first Sputnik, Eisenhower remained unconvinced of the value of space exploration.

The Rand Corporation was well enough established in 1948 that Douglas decided to withdraw his company's managerial support. Frank Collbohm, who had been with Douglas for many years, was elected by Rand directors to serve as its first independent president. He had served as Raymond's assistant and was a good choice. He believed strongly that the Rand Corporation should be permitted to choose its own research programs, and he was remarkably successful in maintaining its freedom to do so.

The navy's project officer for lighter-than-air programs came to Ed Heinemann in 1948 hoping to convince the Douglas Company it should bid on new navy blimps. Heinemann was negative on the subject, knowing the Douglas Company had no interest in getting into a field about which it knew nothing. The officer pressed the issue, saying he was tired of being pushed around by Goodyear, and that he wanted another company to bid against Goodyear if only to get its price down. Ed continued to protest. "The answer is no! By the time we learned how to design such a vehicle, and got through the learning process, the program wouldn't be worthwhile for Douglas." The project officer continued to insist, and Heinemann reluctantly agreed to submit a design.

He, Leo Devlin, and Clinton Stevenson went to the Marine Corps Air Station at El Toro to study the Goodyear blimps in service there. Back at El Segundo, a design team was ordered to get to work. Ed cautioned that if they were to submit a design, it had to be far superior to anything Goodyear had come up with in the past. The

Douglas design proved so good, and the anticipated performance so much greater than present Goodyear blimps, that the company won the competition and the navy insisted Douglas build its new blimps.

Heinemann was in a quandary. He had no interest in getting into the blimp business, and he had submitted a design only in hopes of helping the navy to get Goodyear to reduce its prices.

Douglas received a call from P. W. Litchfield, president of Goodyear, after the award's announcement. He asked for a meeting with him, and a date was set. Douglas had been generally aware of the design work Heinemann had been doing for the navy, but he wanted no part of a production contract. "Now what do I do?" he asked Heinemann.

"I'll come over on that date and fill you in. We don't want to build them, but we did bid on them, and we won the competition."

When Heinemann met with Douglas, he explained the situation, telling Douglas how the navy official had said it would only use Douglas to drive Litchfield's price down. The deal was, Ed explained, that if the Douglas threat of competition managed to drive Goodyear's price down, "We would bow out, and the navy would pay us to reimburse the company for costs in design and other monies we have expended."

When Litchfield arrived at Douglas's office he said he was afraid Douglas would get into the blimp business. He said he was scared that Douglas, being on the West Coast, would develop blimp service to Hawaii.

Douglas assured him that his company was not interested in establishing such service, or in producing blimps. "We don't have a loft, and everything else it would take to build blimps. If you'll get your price down, I believe you'll be able to continue doing business with the navy."

Litchfield was relieved to hear this, and went home to order his cost analysts to lower their bid price and resubmit it to the navy. Their lower bid was accepted, Douglas was paid for its efforts, and many of its innovations were used in the Goodyear design. Goodyear's earlier design had strung three cars below their blimps' bags and, in flight, they tended to sway independently of each other, causing a disturbing articulation. The Douglas design called for double-decked cars that would not sway.

In the 1930s, commercial aviation had grown rapidly, primarily due to the success of the DC-3, which, in the words of C. R. Smith, head of American Airlines, "was the first airplane that could make money by hauling passengers." Perhaps one of the greatest tributes ever paid to the DC-3 was the action by the Civil Aeronautics Board that decreed it would no longer issue certificates of airworthiness to DC-3s as commercial passenger carriers after 1947 because they were no longer needed. The deadline was extended until 1953 when the board declared that henceforth the DC-3 would be rated airworthy indefinitely. Douglas said he did not suppose any airplane would ever dominate aviation again the same as the DC-3 had done.

With performance improvements over the DC-4 and a strengthened world economy, the DC-6 was an immediate success after United Air Lines and American received their first airplanes November 24, 1946. With its fully pressurized cabin, the DC-6 set a new standard of excellence in passenger service by flying high at a cruising speed of 300 miles an hour while carrying up to eighty passengers in perfect comfort. Without a doubt it was the outstanding achievement in commercial aviation during the late 1940s. The DC-6 had double windows to prevent any possibility of pressure blowout, and the wing's leading edge was heated to prevent formation of ice at high altitudes.

Lockheed and Douglas now were engaged in the fiercest competition in the history of commercial transportation. The contest in Europe was particularly strong because at least 40 percent of all transport orders were from overseas. Often these orders made the difference between profit and loss for a company.

Once, in Madrid, Lockheed officials hired the most famous Spanish gourmet chef to cater a luncheon for European airline officials. Lockheed was famous for its lavish use of entertainment funds, which the more parsimonious Douglas refused to match. At times Douglas sales officials were put to a decided disadvantage in the competition to entertain airline hosts. This time Mike Oliveau, Douglas's international sales manager in Europe, recalled that the chef Lockheed had hired was well known for his liberal use of strong spices. He decided to use this knowledge to his company's advantage.

He sent out for a large supply of antacid tablets from a nearby Spanish *farmacia*. When Lockheed's airline guests started to emerge from their long luncheon meeting, he and Nat Paschall, Douglas's general sales manager, noted that most of them were in various stages of acute gastric distress. They moved among them, commiserating with them, while they handed out the antacid tablets. They did not criticize Lockheed or its planes, merely reminding them that the economy and integrity of Douglas airplanes offered the greatest relief for headaches and upset stomachs caused by maintenance and repair problems. Oliveau had neatly turned the tables on Lockheed, and airline officials enjoyed the joke immensely. The frugal Douglas team accomplished its purpose at a cost of only $4.32—far below the thousands of dollars Lockheed had paid for its lavish luncheon.

Douglas loved to tease his sales people, and they never knew what to expect of him. On important sales junkets, he always went along. Even Nat Paschall agreed that Douglas almost single-handedly made all the important sales.

While in New York negotiating with Pan American for an order, Paschall told Douglas that he would like him to talk to Canadian Defense Minister C. D. Howe, because a sale to the Canadian government was a strong possibility. Douglas put off a call to the minister until they concluded their talks with Pan American, and invited the sales team up to his suite for a few drinks before dinner. Paschall, telling Douglas that his intervention with the Canadian official could well be crucial in solidifying a big sale, kept pressing him to make the call. After the call, he said, he would go to Ottawa the next day and complete the details. Douglas procrastinated, saying they should have dinner first. After dinner, he still avoided making the call. Finally, to shut Paschall up, Douglas went into his bedroom by himself and picked up the phone.

He called Paschall in the other room, "I'll call Howe for you."

Paschall smiled, happy that he had finally talked his boss into making the call. He heard Douglas say, "The Honorable Mr. Howe, please. This is Don Douglas calling."

While Paschall waited expectantly, he heard Douglas say, "Mr. Howe? This is Mr. Donald W. Douglas."

Paschall was surprised by Douglas's formality because he knew Howe well.

Paschall was stunned to hear Douglas, evidently replying to a question from Howe, "Hell no! I don't have time to go chasing around the country after every bastard who wants to buy an airplane. That's what I have salesmen for."

Paschall anxiously peered in at his boss, wondering if he had had too much to drink. This was not like Douglas at all.

He heard Douglas say, "Howe, where you buy your airplanes is a matter of such complete indifference to me that I would as leave talk about your weather, except that it's rarely a fit subject for anybody but savages."

Paschall sank into a chair and groaned. Suddenly, he grabbed the extension phone in the sitting room as a thought struck him. Douglas slammed down his receiver as he did so.

Douglas walked out of his bedroom, saying innocently as he noted the phone in Paschall's hand, "Did you want to make a call?"

By now Glenn Snyder and Ed Burton were in hysterics, and Paschall ruefully realized his boss had been talking into a dead phone with one of his fingers holding the buttons down.

The DC-6 went into service in April 1947 and the Lockheed Connie quickly lost its label as queen of the airlines. After the Burbank-based company came up with the 649 Connie, however, Lockheed again had a temporary lead with its commercial transport, which Eastern's Eddie Rickenbacker called the world's most advanced airliner.

Boeing's Stratocruiser proved to be twenty miles an hour slower than the DC-6, but a little faster than the Connie. It cost $1,000 an hour to fly the Stratocruiser, compared to $375.00 for the DC-6. Although passengers liked the deck lounge below the passenger cabin, the plane was too costly to fly. Once again it was clear that it was almost impossible to take a military design and make a commercial aircraft from it. Boeing's Bill Allen temporarily decided to abandon the commercial business to Lockheed and Douglas.

After Douglas developed the DC-6B, and a Navy military version called the R6D, Lockheed countered with the 1049 Super Constellation but the Lockheed plane's cruising speed of 225 MPH was far below the DC-6B's and Douglas again led the field. The DC-6B undoubtedly was the finest, most economical propeller airplane ever built.

Nat Paschall, Bill Boeing's stepson, had joined Douglas in 1939. He was named manager of domestic sales after the war, and this dynamic individual helped immeasurably to get the airlines in a buying mood. Even Douglas was surprised by the acceptance of the DC-6 and, after a low of only six commercial airplanes delivered in 1946, the production lines began to hum again as other versions improved speed, range, and payload.

The C-118A, with a five-foot longer fuselage, was sold to the U.S. Air Force. One of them, the "Independence," was specially fitted to replace the "Sacred Cow" as the presidential airplane.

Douglas's thriftiness became legendary through the years, and he personally approved expense accounts of his managers. Jackson R. McGowen, who had joined the company in 1939, was on the DC-6 project in 1946. As such he was one of those expected to entertain customer airline officials.

Late one afternoon he invited an official of a foreign airline to bring his wife and join him and his wife, Delores, for dinner at the Beachcomber in Hollywood. The official agreed, and on their way there they began to pick up friends of his until the party totaled eighteen people. Jack was disturbed by the number and began to worry how he would justify such an expenditure to Douglas.

He worried even more when he paid a bill for $350.00.

Next day he hurried over to Douglas's office to explain. Douglas eyed him intently for a moment, noting the nervousness of the handsome young man in front of him, and said, "Don't worry about it. I understand. You had to do it. Just send the bill to me and I'll okay it."

Jack was relieved and hurriedly left the office.

Next day the airline official called Jack and told him he would like to reciprocate and would he and his wife join his party at the Beachcomber again.

Jack readily agreed.

There was quite a gathering and everyone was having a fine time until it came to paying the bill. The airline official signed a check on a foreign bank, but the manager of the fashionable Beachcomber refused to accept it.

Jack, watching the proceedings, cringed in his seat, knowing what was coming as the airline official approached with an apologetic face. He told Jack, "I'm embarrassed, but they won't accept my personal check. Would you guarantee it?"

Jack gulped nervously. "Of course," wondering what he would tell Douglas in the morning. He was even more shocked when he signed the check, noting it was for $400.00.

Next day he went to Douglas's office with trepidation, nervously explaining his predicament. Douglas smiled slightly. "Jack, I trust you. I know you're not like some of the chiselers around here. You did it for the good of the company. Don't worry about it," he said kindly.

After the war airline travel began to climb rapidly as more and more people accepted it as the convenient and safe way to go from one city to another both in the United States and throughout the world. In essence, air transportation came of age, and Douglas was ready with the airplanes to sustain this growth.

For some time, he resisted airline pleas to produce another short-haul transport. He did agree to rebuild some DC-3s with a new wing and tail section, plus a more powerful engine. The fuselage was lengthened and other refinements were made in the Super DC-3. Airline interest proved minimal, and only 106 were completed, and most were bought by the navy as R4D-8s.

Although the DC-6 became one of the safest transports in the world, it was not without its early troubles. In October 1947, a United DC-6 burst into flames high above Bryce Canyon and crashed, killing all fifty-two people on board. Douglas insisted his engineers find out what had happened and why. Piece by piece the wreckage was brought to Santa Monica and scientifically reconstructed. They learned the fire had started in the lower fuselage and warnings were issued to all airlines to be on the alert for fires.

The next accident was not long in coming. An American DC-6 radioed it had a fire over New Mexico. It landed safely at Gallup, and the fire was extinguished. Fortunately there was no loss of life. Douglas ordered the airplanes grounded while a further investigation was made.

Arthur Raymond sent teams of engineers to the scene and a long investigation resulted that kept the DC-6s on the ground for five months. One of the things they learned was that a fuel-tank transfer switch had been left on. Although this was not recommended procedure, it also was not barred by company directives. This was a slight clue, but in tracing the circumstances that led to the fire it was found that when this switch was not turned off during fuel transfer, the wing tank overflowed. Therefore, in certain attitudes, fuel sprayed out of the tanks' fuel vents and flowed back into a heater duct on the bottom of the fuselage. When this happened a fire resulted. The problem was corrected by moving the fuel vents to the outer tips of the wing.

Throughout this agonizing period Douglas laid down a firm rule that everything must be changed that could even remotely become a fire hazard. "I don't care how much it costs," he told Raymond.

Many changes were made to avoid a possible repetition of the disaster.

Right after the war many airlines had bought surplus C-47s and C-54s from the government and Douglas retrofitted many as commercial transports. Hundreds were also converted by other companies. When airline officials asked Douglas if he would stand behind those not converted by his company, even though there was no legal reason to do so, he replied, "We'll back them up. That's true of any airplane with the Douglas name."

Military contracts slowly returned to the company with the introduction of the C-74, but its impact was a long time in having any appreciable effect on the company's operations.

Long Beach Plant Manager Arch Wallen invited Douglas to be present for the first flight of the C-74. For the first time he met Marguerite C. "Peggy" Tucker, Douglas's executive assistant, who drove him down. She had joined the company before the war as a courier driver after playing bit parts in several movies. A tall, beautiful woman, she had attracted Douglas and the two developed a relationship that eventually sent shock waves through the company.

"If It Weren't for the El Segundo Division, We'd Go Under"

Ϙ ne Douglas project that bore fruit was a small contract let in 1945 by the United States Navy in collaboration with the National Advisory Committee for Aeronautics for the D-558 National Research Project. The Skystreak was the result of the first phase of this contract. Thin-winged, powered by a jet engine, it was designed to carry a pilot and 500 pounds of instrumentation. There was only enough fuel—a kerosene-type—in the wing, which had a capacity of 230 gallons, to fly the sleek aircraft for thirty minutes.

The Skystreak pioneered many innovations. It was a rugged airplane, able to withstand 18-G loads—higher than any other aircraft of its time. At high subsonic speeds the airframe heated up, so a cooling system was provided for the pilot and the instruments. At 600 miles an hour the temperature of the aircraft's structure rose 64 degrees above atmospheric temperatures. Without air conditioning the V-shaped cockpit enclosure would have been uninhabitable at 178°F. Even with air conditioning, which held the temperature inside the cockpit to 100°F, it could be a sweatbox.

The Skystreak, with its straight wing and cigar-shaped fuselage, had a tail much like the AD Skyraider. The horizontal stabilizer was placed high on the vertical stabilizer to reduce the influence of the air passing over the wing. Its overall weight was just under 10,000 pounds, it had a twenty-five-foot wing span, and was thirty-five feet long.

It made its first flight on May 28, 1947, with Douglas test pilot Gene May at the controls. The bright red plane streaked down the runway gracefully, but its first flight was brief due to unexpected engine problems, which grounded it until August.

Follow-on flights proved the concept after the Skystreak achieved a speed of 0.85 Mach, which was well into the transonic speed zone. With world attention focused on the dramatic aircraft, Comdr. Turner F. Caldwell, assigned to the fighter-design branch of the navy's Bureau of Aeronautics, reached 640.7 MPH over a 3-km course to set a new world's record. That same week marine Maj. Marion E. Carl from the Patuxent Naval Air Test Center achieved a top speed of 650.8 MPH. Such phenomenal success with a new aircraft was incredible, particularly when it was considered that up to this time the Skystreak had flown only ten hours!

Tragedy struck on May 3, 1948, when NACA pilot Howard Lilly was killed shortly after takeoff when the Skystreak suddenly lost power. The crash was caused by disintegration of the turbine blades in the General Electric TG-180 engine. Despite the loss of the airplane the Skystreak had more than fulfilled its goal of exploring the transonic speed zone. It almost reached the speed of sound, which it was not designed to do, by reaching a speed of Mach 0.99 in a slight dive on October 14, 1947. Its performance was overshadowed, however, by the rocket-powered Bell X-1, which after being released at high altitude from a B-29 was first to penetrate the sound barrier with air force Capt. Charles E. Yeager at the controls.

Not long after starting work on the Skystreak an aircraft that would fly at even higher speeds was proposed to the navy. Heinemann's engineers told navy and NACA officials they believed such an aircraft, with combination rocket and jet engines, could fly at twice the speed of sound.

During a period when most aircraft factories were shut down Douglas received a go-ahead for the second phase of the D-558 research program. A revolutionary aircraft, called the Skyrocket, now began to take shape at El Segundo. It was designed to use rocket power with a Reaction Motors engine to augment a 3,000-lb thrust jet engine. The new contract called for three research vehicles, each with a swept wing and side-mounted air intakes for its jet engines. The wing was conventionally designed, but the tail surfaces were thinner and swept five degrees more than the wing to avoid control problems at high speeds. This concept was unique at the time, but it proved to be an excellent design method and was used on many later aircraft. The first airplane was built before wind tunnel tests were completed, but tests with models were added insurance and gave them confidence in their design concept.

The Skyrocket's early flights were made by taking off with its jet engine, and then using its rocket engine for high-altitude and high-speed runs. Such a procedure was necessary because the rocket engine burned a ton and a half of alcohol and liquid oxygen in a few minutes.

Heinemann told Douglas that he particularly liked the airplane because it could take off normally and be independent, unlike the Bell X-1, which needed a mother plane.

Douglas Chief Test Pilot John P. Martin flew the Skyrocket first on February 4, 1948. It proved sluggish. After Martin completed the initial series of flights, testing was turned over to a pilot who had been hired specifically for the purpose. After his first flight he criticized the airplane, saying everything was wrong with the Skyrocket, and he wanted his salary doubled if he had to continue flying it.

After navy officials saw the report they sent out one of their own pilots to fly it, who said afterwards, "There's nothing wrong with that airplane."

That was not quite true. It was not until a year later, after its rocket engine was installed in the summer of 1949, that the Skyrocket burst through the sound barrier. By now, the contract pilot had quit, and another pilot was hired to make the rest of the flights. In follow-on tests the flights were gradually lowered until the Skyrocket was flying only 100 feet off the ground.

Test pilots are a special breed because theirs is a risky business. In those days, when the unknown was being explored by highly experimental aircraft, a pilot's life expectancy was rather low. Many test pilots demanded and received enormous sums of money for the limited hours they spent in the air, or they would have refused the work. And for those with special skills, particularly as engineering test pilots, the number was incredibly small despite the tens of thousands of military pilots who had fought in World War II. In contrast, however, many military experimental test pilots suffered the same risks, but for far less money.

The experience of flight-testing the Bell X-1 had taught NACA and navy officials that the full potential of the Skyrocket would not be achieved unless it was taken aloft by a B-29 to make high-altitude runs. Former navy patrol-plane pilot William Bridgeman made a number of such flights with the Skyrocket.

Heinemann became disturbed when reports came back that Bridgeman was spouting off in a local bar at night that Douglas engineers were trying to kill him. He sent one of his engineers to listen to what Bridgeman was saying, and the man confirmed the rumors. Further, Donald Douglas, Jr., head of flight-test operations, was being told identical stories by Bridgeman. Heinemann decided to ignore Bridgeman's comments because the pilot obviously did not know what he was talking about. Bridgeman's flights were so successful that he reached an altitude of 74,494 feet in the summer of 1951, before the Skyrocket was turned over to NACA for further tests.

Douglas and Heinemann followed the NACA tests closely, as they probed the unknown realm of supersonic flight. Scott Crossfield flew the Skyrocket at twice the speed of sound in November 1953. A new altitude record of 83,235 feet was established by marine Maj. Marion Carl a few months later. These flights, however, were rocket-powered without the jet engine.

A month later, the Bell X-1A flew two-and-a-quarter times as fast as the speed of sound.

Douglas and Heinemann both considered the D-558 Research Project one of their proudest achievements, and one which benefited the entire industry. Douglas freely admitted that his company had shared its growing knowledge with the aircraft industry in order that research vehicles could more than double the performance of existing planes.

Talk of manned flight to outer space in the early 1950s was often discussed by Douglas and Heinemann. Both knew that a manned flight to the moon was not only feasible, but only awaiting the vast funds that would be necessary. For the most part they kept such thoughts to themselves, knowing all too well they would be subjected to ridicule if they voiced them outside their circle of intimate associates.

Heinemann proposed a third research project after NACA took over responsibility for continuing flight tests of the Skyrocket. He recommended to government officials that his division be given a contract to design a rocket-powered vehicle that would fly to the ionosphere at an altitude of at least 700,000 feet. In returning to the earth's atmosphere, he said, such a vehicle would fly at nine times the speed of sound.

The navy rejected the idea because of its concern for the cost of the project which Heinemann estimated would total $24 million for three research vehicles. In contrast, NACA and the air force liked the idea but the El Segundo Division was a navy plant and it refused to participate.

So keen were air force officials that they talked North American Aviation into designing a similar rocket ship. When former Douglas chief engineer Dutch Kindelberger gave the go-ahead the X-15 was born and became a highly successful program.

Heinemann and Douglas both believed that the navy made a mistake in not going ahead with the program. The Douglas D-558-3 actually could have achieved higher goals than the X-15. The NASA Space Shuttle, developed twenty-five years later, was quite similar to the Douglas concept.

Military business became predominant by the end of the 1940s, in comparison to commercial sales, amounting to 87 percent of all sales. The Long Beach plant was busy turning out the C-124 Globemaster, and this cargo hauler and troop transport became the standard airplane of its type in the United States Air Force; 447 were built.

Again the nation was fortunate that various new airplanes were in production when the Korean War broke out. The AD Skyraider, termed the "workhorse of the Fleet," went through twenty-eight configurations and 3,180 were built. Its main problem centered around the Wright R-3350 engine, the same engine that caused so many problems with the Boeing B-29 Superfortress in World War II. Wright persisted in using cast fins, which had to be placed too close together and, as a result, caused overheating problems. Pratt & Whitney engines used machined fins with far better results.

Heinemann had gone back to Paterson, New Jersey, to talk to the top people at Wright Aeronautical. He literally begged, "Won't you give us machined fins?"

At first, Wright officials were adamantly opposed. Heinemann explained that when a 3350 engine was not in operation oil drained down and fouled the plugs on the bottom cylinders. Such a situation was intolerable, he told them. "Each time you start the engine you're facing the possibility of breaking a cylinder head." To solve the problem, he said, the engine had to be turned over by hand before it was started. Once the bottom cylinders were flooded, the plugs had to be removed, dried out, or replaced by fresh ones. For years Wright officials refused to address the problem, and it eventually cost them most of the postwar engine market.

In 1949, Wright finally agreed to the use of machined fins. Now, their engines overcooled. It was necessary to change the size of the cowl, through which the air entered the engine, to counteract this condition. At last, those Wright 3350 engines performed normally.

In 1945 the United States Navy had sought bids from aircraft manufacturers for its carrier-based nightfighter. The specifications called for a two-engine aircraft that could detect an enemy plane 125 miles away at 40,000 feet while flying at 500 miles an hour.

Douglas won the competition against Grumman, Curtiss, and Fleetwing. Heinemann's engineers at El Segundo found their biggest problem was the size of the airplane and the weight of its radar systems. Heinemann constantly argued with the Bureau of Aeronautics that the plane should be smaller, and the number of systems reduced.

The Westinghouse J-34 engines caused endless problems after the airplane flew in March 1948. It was chronically underpowered because the engines never produced as much thrust as was required. In a later version more than 200 F3Ds were built.

The F3D served with distinction during the Korean War. A plane flown by Maj. William T. Stratton, Jr., with marine M. Sgt. Hans Hoglind destroyed a Yak-15 jet fighter on November 2, 1952. Thus the F3D became the first jet to destroy another at night in combat. The Yak was brought down by the F3D's 20-mm cannons.

The fighter was also equipped with Tiny Tim rockets, which were anything but tiny, each weighing over half a ton, with a 150-lb warhead in the nose of the 10.5-foot missile. It proved to be a stable and safe airplane, and a crew could exit in an emergency through a unique escape-slide system in the bottom of the fuselage.

Now that bombers were flying at speeds more than twice as fast as those in World War II, the safe dropping of bombs became a matter of grave concern to members of the Defense Department. Bomb shapes had not been changed since 1925, but speeds and altitudes had risen dramatically. The Douglas El Segundo Division was given a contract by the navy to design bomb shapes up to 2,000 lbs, with one exception. The United States Air Force was charged with responsibility for design of the 750-lb bomb. The new shapes were aerodynamically designed for release at any altitude or speed.

Arthur Raymond was in Montreal in April 1950 when he got a call from Douglas asking if he could go to Europe after attending the International Civil Air Organization meeting. He said Swissair was at the decision stage as to whether to purchase the Douglas DC-6 or the Lockheed Constellation. He said the sale probably would not amount to more than two aircraft initially, but that several other airlines might follow suit.

Raymond agreed and returned to Santa Monica where he and his wife Dottie and Jack McGowen, project engineer for the DC-6, prepared to fly to Europe.

They flew in a KLM Constellation by way of Gander, Newfoundland, and were met by Michel "Mike" Oliveau who was in charge of the European office at Zurich.

At a meeting with Walter Berchtold, president of Swissair, they presented the details of the DC-6 program. Berchtold said he would have to discuss the matter with his board, and he suggested they take off for a few days and see more of Switzerland.

They went to Wenger for a couple of nights, and on their last day took the cog-rail trip to the summit of the Jungfraujoch. There, during lunch, the concierge at Wengen called to say that they had a cable from Santa Monica via Zurich. Raymond, his long legs cramped by the telephone booth, made notes as the concierge read the cable in broken English.

Oliveau and Dottie thought Ray must have fainted in the booth because he was there so long. All they could see was the phone cord disappearing out of sight inside the booth. Raymond finally got the gist of the cable. It was a last-minute attempt to beat Lockheed in the competition by offering better contract terms.

With a smile Mike got a slate and wrote on it, "Douglas Aircraft Jungfrau Division," which he placed in the center of the table.

Raymond immediately called Berchtold at Swissair and offered the new terms. The following morning, back at Wenger, Berchtold called Raymond that his board had decided to buy the DC-6, but first they wanted the answers to seven questions. Raymond and his party boarded the train for Zurich, prepared to answer any questions Swissair might want to ask. En route Oliveau read them the headlines in the newspaper which said the Swissair board had agreed to purchase the Douglas airplane, and would buy six instead of two. They relaxed, knowing they had won the competition, and that remaining details were unimportant. Douglas was correct in assuming that a breakthrough with Swissair would bring in several more European airlines. KLM, Sabena, and SAS followed suit.

For some time American Airlines had been insisting upon a follow-on to the DC-6, an airplane that would make possible nonstop transcontinental service even against prevailing winds on west-bound flights. Douglas resisted C. R. Smith's pleas, but American's head believed one more propeller airplane should be built before the advent of the jets.

Douglas agreed reluctantly because the Wright R-3350 turbo-compound engine, which had proved so problem-plagued on the Boeing B-29 and the AD series, would have to be used. He had little confidence that Wright Aeronautical would ever completely resolve the engine's problems.

Douglas and Raymond had given much thought to a jet transport during the previous few years. They were aware that the military services were moving rapidly away from propeller aircraft, but they agreed that a few more years would be required to perfect jet commercial transports before they would be reliable and safe.

The 140,000-lb DC-7 went into service in the spring of 1956. Later, a longer-range DC-7B was built at the urging of Juan Trippe at Pan American that carried 100 passengers. Lastly, the DC-7C, which had an additional ten feet of wing span to increase range up to 5,000 miles, became the first true transatlantic transport.

In 1957, Harry Strangman, the company's vice-president of finance, talked to Ed Heinemann at El Segundo. He told him that Doug had asked him to tell Ed how much he appreciated what the El Segundo Division had accomplished. "You know we've got trouble with those Wright 3350 engines on the DC-7. Scandinavian Airlines are mad as hell. They said they will never buy a Douglas airplane again with Wright engines."

Strangman also revealed they were losing so much money on the DC-7 that Doug wanted him to know how much he appreciated the money his military aircraft were making for the company. Doug said, "If it weren't for the El Segundo Division, and the good work with the navy you are doing, we'd go under."

The DC-7C was the last of a distinguished line of Douglas propeller-driven commercial transports, and it followed the conservative pattern of evolution that Douglas had always insisted upon. In all 1,041 DC-6 and DC-7 aircraft were built.

Lockheed, meanwhile, had produced the 1049C, but the DC-7 was twenty-eight miles an hour faster than the Super Connie, and Douglas cornered the market for these types of aircraft. While Douglas continued to set the pace during these years, Lockheed kept rising to meet the challenge. The 1649A Starliner, designed to compete with the Douglas DC-7C, failed to do so because the "Seven Seas" had lower seat-mile costs and was cheaper.

It had been a long postwar battle, but Douglas finally won the competition with Lockheed hands down. Now, however, a new threat faced Douglas from an old adversary at Seattle.

The Douglas Company was not immune to the rising unrest among union workers for more pay and better working conditions after the Korean War broke out. When a strike loomed at the Long Beach plant in 1951 Arch Wallen, who had recently rejoined the company as manager of the plant's production and tooling department, called a meeting of his supervisors. He advised that the strike might last a long time, and that they had to be prepared. It was agreed that cameras should be placed on top of all buildings to record, through closed-circuit television, all activity violent or otherwise.

Wallen was disturbed by the tough talk among some of his superintendents. A few said they would do almost anything to break the union. Wallen tried to explain that Douglas did not particularly like unions, but wanted no part of goon squads.

One truculent superintendent told Wallen before the meeting, "You can count on me. No son-of-a-bitch is going to stop me from crossing that union line." Another superintendent proposed they arm themselves with short chains and hack their way through union picket lines at the gates. Wallen, knowing he had some rugged individualists on his staff, and, speaking for Douglas, warned there would be no rough stuff. Fortunately the strike was settled without violence.

After VE-Day the research papers of the eminent German aircraft designer Dr. Alexander Lippisch were read avidly by American designers. He had helped design the tailless rocket aircraft Komet 163. In his papers he had some provocative things to say about triangular-shaped wings.

Heinemann and Douglas studied Lippisch's reports after his papers became available. They were familiar with Jack Northrop's flying wing, and the work Heinemann and Northrop had done with a delta-wing aircraft called Model 25 in the late 1930s. A. M. O. Smith, one of the engineers who had gone to Europe to study the German designs, came up with some delta-wing shapes for Heinemann that were tested at Cal Tech's wind tunnel. Smith told Leo Devlin and Heinemann that the delta concept offered interesting possibilities.

One day in 1948 Heinemann was in Comdr. Turner Caldwell's Washington office in the Pentagon and learned that Caldwell and Comdr. Sidney Sherby were quite keen on delta designs for fighters, even though Rear Adm. A. B. Metzger, who headed BuAer's fighter branch, disagreed with them. Caldwell told Heinemann, "The navy needs a fighter that can climb to 40,000 feet within five minutes, or better, and intercept high-flying Soviet bombers before they can reach their bomb-release points."

Heinemann expressed interest and went home to get his engineers to develop an airplane that might even better Caldwell's performance figures. When he submitted a proposal for a delta-wing fighter, later called the F4D Skyray because of its resemblance to a manta ray, he said it would be able to climb to 38,000 feet in 2.5 minutes. Heinemann told Caldwell the Skyray would have four 20-mm cannons, and be able to mount two tons of bombs, rockets, or other stores under its wing. He said he had hoped to use the Westinghouse J-40 jet engine, but it would not be ready in time for the airplane so initially the Allison J-35 engine would be used even though it developed only 5,000 lbs of thrust, roughly half the anticipated thrust of the J-40. Not only Caldwell, but the Bureau of Aeronautics, expressed strong interest, and a contract was signed with Douglas.

Test pilot Larry Peyton flew the first Skyray January 25, 1951, and it was apparent they had a fine fighter in the making, despite numerous control problems and the fact that the one-thirty-second-inch-thick skin of the test aircraft really was too thin. The navy knew these were typical development problems that could be overcome, and they ordered the plane into production.

Heinemann would have preferred more extensive testing but, when the J-40 engine became available in February 1952, and Robert Rahn's flights proved so spectacular, he agreed to early production.

In retrospect a delay in production would have been advisable because tail buffet problems appeared by mid-1952, and Rahn almost lost an F4D when, close to the ground, the Skyray pitched up while decelerating through the transonic zone and he blacked out because of high G loads. Fortunately Rahn recovered quickly and he landed the Skyray safely. The F4D had to be scrapped, however, because the aircraft's thin skin was so wrinkled that the plane was too dangerous to fly again.

Heinemann's hopes that the J-40 engine would resolve many of their problems failed to materialize as problems multiplied with the new engine. An expensive retrofit, involving structural changes to accommodate the 10,000-lb-thrust Pratt & Whitney J-57, became necessary even while Skyrays were moving down the production lines.

With its new engine the F4Ds performance improved dramatically, and Lt. Comdr. James Verdin set a 3-km record of 754.4 MPH near the Salton Sea, and Robert Rahn flew 728.0 MPH over a 100-km course to set new world speed records. Later Maj.

Edward N. LeFaivre set five time-to-climb records. In one he reached 49,215 feet in two minutes, thirty-six seconds.

Heinemann and North American's Dutch Kindelberger received Collier trophies in late 1954 for their contribution to the advancement of aeronautical science. Heinemann won his for the F4D Skyray and Kindelberger for development of the F-100 fighter. President Dwight D. Eisenhower was so intrigued by the model of the Skyray that he was given at the White House ceremony that he asked Heinemann, "How does it fly without a tail?"

A total of 447 Skyrays were built, but they never saw combat. They were flown by two dozen marine and navy units from carriers around the world, and provided fleet protection from the late 1950s to the mid-1960s.

A later model, the F5D Skylancer, was canceled prior to production. The United States Navy found itself again in a money pinch, and ordered its Bureau of Aeronautics to cut back on experimental programs. At the time, there were three contenders for a new fighter. They included the Douglas F5D, the Chance Vought F8U, and the Grumman F-11. The bureau continued the Chance Vought program, saying it was a conventionally designed airplane, and the F5D was considered unconventional due to its delta-type planform wing. The Grumman airplane was eliminated because it did not have sufficient fuel capacity and, therefore, was deficient in range. The three experimental Douglas F5Ds were sent to Moffett Naval Air Station in California where navy pilots continued to fly them.

Weeks later a Moffett official called Heinemann. "Why in hell did the navy cancel this airplane?"

"The navy was short of funds," Heinemann replied.

"This airplane is two-tenths of a Mach number faster than the Chance Vought airplane," the navy official said.

This news pleased Heinemann because the Bureau of Aeronautics had cited as one of their reasons for cancellation of the F5D that it was slower than the Chance Vought airplane. In addition, later tests showed the F5D was not only faster, but had greater range.

The Skylancer was a good airplane and also was noteworthy because it was the first airplane to eliminate troublesome vacuum tubes in all its electronic gear. Heinemann had insisted that all systems should be solid state, and the equipment was designed and built by the division.

The F5D achieved speeds of 1,000 miles an hour, and the three test airplanes later served the National Aviation and Space Agency—the old NACA—with distinction in early space exploration programs.

Defense Secretary Louis Johnson had scrapped the navy's super carrier, the USS *United States*, in April 1949. Heinemann suspected this would happen, so when the Bureau of Aeronautics sought bids for a heavy bomber the navy believed should weigh 100,000 lbs, he was ready with a design that would not exceed 70,000 lbs and could be flown off existing carriers. Furthermore, he told BuAer that his concept, later known as the A3D Skywarrior, would be able to carry a five-ton nuclear weapon.

Capt. Joseph N. Murphy was in charge of BuAer's aircraft division. When Heinemann showed him his proposal, Murphy refused to believe an airplane with that performance could be built at such a weight. He accused Heinemann of lying to get new business.

Heinemann was furious. He picked up his drawings and started to walk out. "If you're not interested," he said stiffly, "I won't bother you."

Murphy had second thoughts. He admired Heinemann and, in the past, had usually found him correct. "Leave the drawings here. I'll have them checked," he said hastily.

Heinemann was still so mad he almost walked out without leaving his drawings, but calmed down enough to drop them on Murphy's desk.

BuAer's engineers evaluated Heinemann's proposal, and declared it feasible. The lighter design made sense because the airplane could be used on Midway-class aircraft carriers and still perform the mission the navy had envisioned for a heavy bomber.

The Douglas El Segundo Division was given a contract in July 1949, to build three A3D Skywarriors. It was decided to sweep the wing 36 degrees and intersect it with the fuselage at the top. This high-wing configuration was selected because the A3D was designed to carry nuclear and thermonuclear bombs that were five feet in diameter. Such large bombs had to fit under the center wing spar, and only a high wing would permit such an attachment. The A3D's Pratt & Whitney J-57 engines were slung on pylons in nacelles on each side of the fuselage.

The Skywarrior flew on October 28, 1952, and remained in production through 1960; 281 were built in seven versions. Ultimately the Skywarrior reached a weight of 84,000 lbs and served in a variety of roles other than its primary one of bomber. It was used extensively in Vietnam, particularly as a tanker to which fighters could insert probes and be nursed home when their fuel tanks were shot full of holes.

In the early days of flight testing, the A3D went through the usual number of problems. One involved a change in the center of gravity when a heavy nuclear weapon was released. Heinemann called Douglas over to review and resolve the problem.

Douglas carefully studied the reports. "I think you're all right," he said. As always Douglas backed him up, and he was a tower of strength at such difficult times.

During this period the El Segundo Division got into bomb design again when the Sandia Corporation found itself unable to get into production fast enough to build TX5 and TX7 nuclear bombs. The division actually built many of them until Sandia was ready to take over.

One January morning in 1952 Heinemann faced fifty navy officers in a conference room at the Bureau of Aeronautics. In one of his familiar talks he discussed the importance of weight reduction in aircraft design, and how it was directly related to aircraft production costs. He showed an illustration of a new lightweight interceptor his division had designed that did not exceed 8,000 lbs. "Every pound of extra weight costs $40.00," he said. "Any increase in weight inevitably reduces performance and increases costs. The result is an inefficient aircraft."

Rear Adm. Apollo Soucek had listened closely while Heinemann talked. He had no interest in the proposed Douglas interceptor, knowing that the navy had canceled such a requirement.

When Heinemann finished, Soucek said, "Would your growth factor apply to a light attack jet bomber as well as a fighter?"

"Yes, it would."

"How much would such a light bomber weigh?"

"About 12,000 lbs."

The room exploded with derisive laughter, but Soucek had too much respect for Heinemann to join in. "Will you come up with such a design for our consideration?"

"Yes, I will. I'll be back in a month."

The design for the new attack bomber called for a swept wing, but one so small that it would not need to be folded for carrier use. To save weight, Heinemann's engineers designed the wing so it could be constructed with single sheets of aluminum from tip to tip, with three spars for structural integrity.

Heinemann was as good as his word and appeared back in Washington in a month's time to present his design for consideration. There were still many skeptics at BuAer that such a 12,000-lb airplane could do the job expected of it. Heinemann assured them the airplane would have a 460-mile radius of action, and fly at 500 MPH with a 1,000-lb bomb. He explained that the British Sapphire engine, made by Allison in the United States as the 7,200-lb-thrust J-65, was the only suitable engine available although it did not have all the thrust he would like.

In response to a question, Heinemann said the new airplane, which he called the A4D Skyhawk attack bomber, would fly faster than the Russian MIG-15 fighter. Heinemann stoutly defended his design concept under a barrage of criticism. To one questioner, who said such a bomber would have to carry 2,000 lbs of bombs, Heinemann quickly did some calculating. "That's no problem, but it will raise the gross weight to 14,000 lbs."

Admiral Soucek was intrigued by the design, although his engineers had told him such an airplane would have to weigh about 30,000 lbs.

He took Heinemann to see Rear Adm. Thomas S. Combs, who explained, "Ed, we're up against it. We can't build an airplane like that because it will cost too much, and we can't afford it. We have to make sure that what we buy is the best for the money available. We believe a new bomber must not exceed $1 million per copy."

Ed assured the admiral his design could be built for that amount of money. "Airplanes are too complicated," he said. "They need to be simpler. If they are, costs will come down. I know we can build this airplane for the amount of money available in procurement funds."

Both admirals had their doubts, but they told him to prepare a definitive proposal for their appraisal. When Heinemann returned to El Segundo he called in his engineering staff and laid it on the line, explaining that everything in the new airplane must be designed with weight in mind as their number one priority.

In one of the most intensive programs in the industry, weight savings became so important that costs were slashed to the minimum. As a result, the A4D Skyhawk was a miracle of simplicity with clean, aerodynamic lines, and outstanding performance.

The first Skyhawk flew in June 1954, and a rudder buffet problem baffled engineers until it was solved by using an idea developed by North American Aviation. It was a simple fix, and called for placing the rudder's supporting ribs on the outside of the skin, instead of inside as in previous airplanes.

Lt. Gordon Gray set a world speed record by flying the attack bomber at 695.162 MPH—a speed that few fighters of that period could match. The A4D became known as "The Mighty Midget" or Heinemann's hot rod, and eventually almost 3,000 were built for the United States Navy and several foreign countries.

In service the design simplicity of the Skyhawk paid off because maintenance costs were only 40 percent of those for comparable aircraft. The A4D saw extensive service in Vietnam, where navy and marine pilots loved its ruggedness and the ease with which it flew. Like many Douglas airplanes it was a forgiving machine for even inexpert pilots.

Although Douglas kept his eyes on the jet age, he listened intently when Juan Trippe, head of Pan American World Airways, proposed that the DC-7 be converted to a turbo-prop transport. At first Douglas found the idea attractive, particularly when Trippe said he would give him a letter of intent for twenty-five such airplanes. Raymond's department was instructed to study the matter, finally telling Douglas that it was too late for a turbo-prop airplane, and that the next step should be pure jet. Douglas and Trippe both agreed that Raymond's arguments were sound when he pointed out that the cost of operating a DC-7D would be about the same as a jet, but that a pure jet would be 150 miles an hour faster.

Douglas knew a jet transport could have been built as early as 1952, but he told Raymond that it would not be a very good airplane. At the time, he had said, "Anyway, American Airlines and the other big ones don't want it now. They want to amortize the planes they already have."

Airline presidents who urged Douglas to consider getting into the design of a jet transport were told, "I don't want to go ahead with the jets until we've gained experience similar to what we obtained with the DC piston models."

Company jet-power experience dated back to World War II, and valuable knowledge was gained from the design of the D-558 program that was useful in developing new jet aircraft for the navy. Jet bombers and fighters went into production in the early 1950s as the company explored the possibilities of commercial jets.

Douglas Aircraft now had a formidable rival in the Boeing Airplane Company, which had produced hundreds of jet bombers for the United States Air Force since World War II. When this vast knowledge and experience were used to build a passenger prototype of the 707, Boeing gained a significant advantage.

Douglas delayed entering the jet commercial market for several reasons. As he told his associates, "The airlines have a billion-and-a-half dollars worth of propeller airplanes. Many of them are almost new. If we bring out a jet transport too soon the airlines will face financing difficulties."

He and his top associates also were aware of what could happen unless the way was paved carefully with solid engineering data. They had watched the DeHavilland Comets come along and, at first, it seemed the British would capture the world market for jet transports. When two of them blew up, killing 110 passengers and their crews, the people at Douglas suspected metal fatigue, because their early experience had given them ample warnings that a jet passenger cabin needed new design techniques to withstand pressures that were twice those of the DC-7.

After the Comets crashed Douglas sent a cable to DeHavilland offering sympathy and any technical or theoretical aid possible. His action was typical of the industry. No matter how hard they competed with one another, they joined forces when one of them got into trouble.

Despite constant pressure from some of the company's oldest customers Douglas remained stubbornly adamant that he would not give the go-ahead until tests had simulated 100 years of flying, and 300,000 simulated climbs and descents were made to approximate the life of a commercial jet transport in actual service.

The company had started its research in 1950, although the performance and reliability of jet engines had been under study long before that. In secrecy, a special project office was established in

June 1952 to start definitive design for a new series of commercial transports to be called the DC-8. Douglas now was personally satisfied the company could build an economical and safe commercial jet transport. His time-honored theory that all new aircraft should be evolutionary, and in series, paid off again. Over half the world's passengers now rode in Douglas-designed transports, and the DC-3, in less than its first quarter-century, had flown 600 million passengers a total of seven billion miles.

It was a great heritage, but the financial risks of getting a toehold in the age of jet transportation were staggering. Some called it a billion dollar expression of faith in the future of air travel.

American's C. R. Smith said of Douglas at this stage, "I have never known him to be content with a product that did not substantially exceed requirements. The country is a better country and a safer country by reason of his genius. We salute him!"

Shortly before he relinquished the presidency to Dwight D. Eisenhower, Harry S. Truman told Republican Douglas that Democratic presidents had always favored Douglas airplanes. With a chuckle, Truman said, "Now we'll see whether a president of your own party will still buy Douglas."

Douglas ruefully admitted later that Truman was right after Eisenhower authorized the purchase of a Lockheed Constellation as his personal airplane, supposedly because his wife Mamie liked the airplane's nickname, "Connie."

When Eisenhower was reelected president in 1956, Douglas wrote him a letter of congratulations. President Eisenhower replied, "I am more than grateful for your note of felicitations on my reelection. Of course I find reassurance in the vote that the principles and policies of the present administration are supported by the majority of the American people—and that reassurance naturally makes easier the difficult decisions of these critical days."

He signed the letter, "With warm regard."

His "warm regard" did not extend to any favoritism towards the Douglas Company and the company actually fared worse under Eisenhower than under any previous president.

13

"Well, She's Up"

Douglas and his wife Charlotte were divorced in 1953 after a long estrangement. During the divorce trial Charlotte named her husband's long-time companion and executive assistant, Mrs. Marguerite "Peggy" Tucker as corespondent. While newspapers sensationalized Charlotte's revelations, Doug's intimates learned a new facet about their boss's private life about which most of them had had no knowledge. For many, the revelations placed their taciturn boss in a new and more human light because to their surprise, he, too, had normal human failings. While sympathetic, his friends kept their thoughts to themselves, knowing from long experience that any invasion of his privacy would not be tolerated. For Douglas, exposure of his private life was a shock, and the divorce cost him half his fortune.

Superior Court Judge Thomas J. Cunningham granted the divorce after thirty-seven years of marriage on March 3, 1953. Under the property settlement, Charlotte Douglas received $897,059.71 in investments. Also included was the couple's $70,000 home at 1433 San Vicente Boulevard in Santa Monica.

Charlotte told the court that her husband's attitude had changed since 1949, and charged that he and his fifty-one-year-old assistant, Mrs. Tucker, took frequent trips on his yacht on weekends. "If the weather was sunny, he would leave on Friday nights and spend the weekends on his yacht," Charlotte said bitterly. "If the weather was foggy, he'd come back home. His assistant did not care for fog," she said, with a biting sarcasm that brought a ripple of laughter in the courtroom.

Charlotte formally dropped her earlier charges of misconduct during the final days of the trial, but she got one final dig at her husband despite her attorney's efforts to silence her. "What I want to know is why he didn't leave with this woman twenty-one years ago! I would have been much better able to take care of myself twenty-one years ago!" Her remarks were ordered stricken from the record by Judge Cunningham.

Just before the judge approved the divorce, he asked Charlotte whether she was satisfied with the property settlement.

"I have to be!"

In exasperation, her attorney Jerome J. Mayo replied, "You don't have to be, if you're not! Are you?"

"I am, but only if the other letters are brought in."

Her husband had agreed to two other provisions, which were included in two letters. One was an agreement that Douglas would pay $125 a month to each of their twin sons while they were attending a university. They were twenty-one years old at the time. The second letter involved a contract stating that Douglas's father had agreed to bequeath one-half of his estate to the five grandchildren.

While Douglas's lawyers agreed to permit Judge Cunningham to read these letters, Charlotte demanded to know, "Can that will be canceled tomorrow?"

Judge Cunningham refused to advise her, but her counsel assured her that the letters were binding and were her best protection. In addition to the other terms of settlement, Douglas agreed to give Charlotte 15 percent of his salary, and he also agreed to leave the bulk of his estate to his five children. Only $90,000 was permitted for other bequests.

Under terms of the property settlement, Douglas retained his yacht *Endymion,* a home at 421 Homewood Avenue, Los Angeles, two cars, and $833,011 in securities. The following year Donald Douglas married Peggy Tucker, and she remained his executive assistant. Her retention as an employee of the company undoubtedly was a means of protecting her financial interests in the event of Doug's prior demise.

Douglas's relationship with Peggy Tucker evidently began in 1932 when he met her in a rather casual manner at the Yacht Club in Santa Barbara. At the time, neither gave a thought that their relationship would develop in the way it did and cause such heartbreak to so many. Their abiding love for one another made their relationship something special, however, and, despite the agony it cost them at times, overrode all other considerations.

Throughout the trial his two oldest sons, Don and Will, remained steadfast in support of their father. Don had known the trauma of divorce when he and his wife Molly were divorced after World War II and the two children remained with their father. In 1950 Don married Jean Cooper, and this marriage proved far more durable and happy than the first one. Undoubtedly Don's loyalty at a particularly difficult time in his father's life was influential in helping his father reach an important decision on his son's career at a later date. Loyalty was a basic facet of the elder Douglas's nature. That loyalty was to be reciprocated when Don also faced the most crucial period in his own life.

The divorce had a traumatic effect on all the children. Barbara, who had married General Arnold's son William in 1944, felt obligated to stand by her mother, although she adored her father. The young twins remained with Charlotte. Each of the children wished it had not been necessary to take sides.

Before Charlotte died in 1976 she told Barbara that she wanted her to renew her association with her father. After her death, Barbara reestablished a close relationship with her dad and, after seeing how devoted Peggy had been to her father, she was grateful to her.

Boeing's president, William M. Allen, invested $16 million of his company's money to develop a prototype jet transport, based on plans for a jet tanker they hoped to build for the air force. This prototype for Boeing's 707 flew in July 1954. During competition for an air force jet tanker Boeing had the edge because of the prototype, but Douglas spent $650,000 to make a presentation of his own.

In February 1954, Douglas expected that the air force jet tanker contract would be split between Boeing and Douglas. When air force secretary Harold Talbott awarded a preliminary order for twenty-five tankers to Boeing, insuring they would win the competition, Douglas realized Boeing would have the advantage over his company in price and delivery schedules. Now, in the competition for a commercial jetliner, Douglas knew it would be all but impossible to compete against Boeing. He cried foul, but to no avail. Douglas never sold a DC-8 jet tanker to the air force despite repeated attempts to do so.

Talbott justified his decision because of the urgent need for tankers for the strategic forces in the shortest possible time. And Boeing had a prototype in flight status while Douglas did not. Douglas had to make a decision as to whether his company should go it alone on a new jet transport, or abandon the field to Boeing. After much soul-searching Douglas decided to proceed with the DC-8. He was fully aware of the financial risks, but he knew his company had to remain in the commercial transport field to retain its world leadership in commercial aviation.

The company actually was in sound financial health, paying regular dividends to its stockholders, who considered the company a blue chip stock. An investor who put $1,000 in Douglas stock in 1928 found his investment worth $33,000 in 1954.

Sales staffs went out for orders in July 1955, headed by Nat Paschall, vice-president of sales, and Project Engineer Ivar Shogran. The DC-8 was still a "paper" airplane so Paschall and Shogran listened to what the airlines had to say. They found a great difference of opinion. Some airlines wanted just a transcontinental airplane, while others insisted upon intercontinental range. It was a difficult position for the salesmen because Douglas had given strict orders that changes were to be held to a minimum to keep costs down. When major changes were suggested by airline officials, Shogran tried to explain how difficult some of them would be. "It's like moving your heart from the left to the right side. It displaces a lot of other organs in your body."

Despite Boeing's lead, and some of the airlines' reluctance to believe Douglas actually could go ahead with the DC-8, Paschall told them over and over, "We're going ahead with the airplane."

After one of these sessions Shogran kidded him, "What do you mean by going ahead?"

"I don't know," Paschall said ruefully. "We can't go into production unless we get orders, and we can't get orders until we go into production." It was the familiar treadmill both knew so well.

Boeing's lead was not one-sided. Douglas had a vast background of research on high-flying, high-speed jet aircraft in many different types of configurations, so the eccentricities of jet flight were well known since many company military aircraft had already probed the unknown. And big airplanes had been produced by the company for many years. C-124 Globemasters had logged nearly a million flying hours covering a distance equal to a trip to the sun and back, or 8,000 times around the world. It was an ungainly looking airplane, but a necessary one.

Ted Conant, senior vice-president and vice-chairman of the board, met constantly with Douglas during the decision-making process to determine what kind of an airplane the DC-8 should be. Conant was against a large DC-8 because he felt Boeing had too great a lead and that traffic growth would not support another big jet.

In the final analysis, the airlines "sized" the airplane and both continental and intercontinental models were agreed upon. Once the decision was made, Douglas believed the program had a reasonable chance of success.

The race was on for orders. Much was at stake to make the DC-8 a success, but it was tough going from the start because the 707 undoubtedly would be in service a full year ahead of the DC-8.

The net jetliner was a challenge the company met head-on. It would weigh about 100,000 lbs more than the DC-7, and could fly about 200 MPH faster than piston-engine airplanes and at altitudes up to 40,000 feet.

The biggest single factor was to reduce the sound of the jet engines. At this stage little was known about silencing powerful jet engines and, certainly, they had to be quieter than their military counterparts because most of the world's air terminals were close to heavily populated areas.

Although Douglas could not positively tell airline officials DC-8 engines would be silenced effectively, he did say that progress was being made in altering and reducing jet noise. "I have every reason to believe that the sound created by the DC-8 will be acceptable to the public."

Ground testing of an airplane's parts and systems had always been a phobia with Douglas. Particular emphasis was given to cabin windows because that was where the Comet's troubles had started. Triple panes were used for absolute safety, and the airplane was designed so it could dive rapidly from high altitude to a safer altitude in less than a minute in the event a window should give way. Even with a hole that let 350 cubic feet of air per second escape, the cabin system would retain normal atmospheric temperatures.

With the thought of the British Comet's trouble always in mind, window and door frames were reinforced with forged titanium. Such reinforcement would stop the spread of a crack, such as those that developed in Comet window frames, which had progressed until explosive decompression destroyed two airplanes. Although titanium was costly, no expense was spared in the airframe, which was guaranteed for a minimum of 30,000 flight hours.

The first step was to make clay and steel wind tunnel models of various parts of the aircraft. Then, a full-sized wooden cabin and cockpit were built at a cost of $7.5 million. The DC-8 eventually took 6.6 million man hours to design, in comparison to the 740,000 hours for the DC-6. The company spent more money developing the DC-8's landing gear than it spent developing the entire DC-3.

The basic design was established by September 1955, although some items were kept flexible to meet airline requirements. More than 28,000 drawings (themselves equalling the weight of one DC-8) were needed to build the airplane. National Air Lines was first to order DC-8s from Douglas in 1955, and Pan American split its order down the middle—half from Douglas and the other half from Boeing.

United's Pat Patterson, after hearing Air Commodore Frank Whittle speak in 1947 about the future of jet-engined aircraft, had called in Jack Herlihy, who headed his engineering staff. He told him how impressed he had been with the claims made by Whittle, who had designed Great Britain's first military jet engine in World War II.

"If what he says is so," Patterson said, "the jet era is almost here." Herlihy agreed.

Patterson reminded him of the need to maintain United's leadership in the airline business, saying that a jet committee should be set up to learn all there was to know about future jet aircraft.

Herlihy promptly established such a committee under engineer Ray Kelly. It was responsible for studying turbine engines and the impact jet transports would have on United's system, which was geared to propeller airplanes.

Three years later Kelly and Herlihy went to England and were given a demonstration ride in a British Comet. Back home they told Patterson the Comet flew smoothly, but that it was too small to be economically viable on United's routes, and that its range was too short.

It was now clear to Patterson that availability of commercial jet transports might be eight or nine years away so, in 1952, he authorized the purchase of the seventy-passenger DC-7 for $1.8 million each, specifically for United's routes to Hawaii.

After ordering these long-range propeller aircraft, he asked Herlihy to give him a prediction of when jet transports would become available. Much had happened to the industry since Herlihy's formation of a jet committee so he could speak now with more confidence. "Seven years," he said.

The original prototype for the 707 had seats for 100 passengers, which Patterson and his staff considered inadequate. They liked their flight in the 707, but insisted that the fuselage would have to be widened to permit six-abreast coach seating.

Pan American ordered 707s for their overseas routes, and Patterson was eager to be the first domestic carrier to order jet transports. The $6 million cost per airplane was a consideration of the greatest magnitude, Patterson realized, because if the jet transport failed to live up to specifications, it could bankrupt them.

After reviewing all aspects of such a purchase Patterson told his staff he was willing to invest $175 million, but he insisted on some hard bargaining with Boeing officials. He had already seen some of the preliminary sketches for the proposed DC-8 jetliner, noting that it and the 707 were practically identical in size, speed, range, and number of passengers. The DC-8 cabin was wider, and would permit six-abreast coach seating.

When he and his experts sat down with Boeing's Bill Allen and his chief engineer Wellwood Beall in Seattle, Patterson came right to the point. "Can you change the cabin's dimensions and make it two feet wider?"

Allen turned inquiringly to Beall.

"We can make the cabin longer, but not wider."

Patterson stood up, saying he wanted to see what Douglas could offer. In Santa Monica the next day, Patterson told Douglas what he wanted in the way of a jet transport, specifically mentioning his insistence on a wider fuselage. After consultation with his top engineers Douglas assured United's boss that the DC-8 fuselage could be widened even more to accommodate more coach passengers.

Patterson was disturbed to learn that the DC-8's delivery date would be a year later than the one contemplated for the Boeing 707. He was willing to take the delay if he could get precisely what he wanted.

United announced its decision to buy the DC-8 on October 25, 1955, expressing its confidence in Douglas by ordering thirty jetliners. Patterson was frank when he made the announcement. "This is the most important decision in our history. If we make a mistake, we're busted." Although not expressed in such blunt language, all airline officials felt much the same.

Patterson said of the $175 million order, "We don't want to lose twenty-two years of Douglas experience with us, and our experience with Douglas." He said his engineers had worked with Douglas since 1936, ever since United bought its first DC-3. He also said these DC-8 transports would shrink the world by at least 40 percent. "They will provide the fastest, most comfortable, most dependable air service ever conceived."

Patterson knew his airline would need more long-range DC-7s in the interim so United's board of directors authorized $60 million to purchase thirty-three more, bringing the total to fifty-eight.

After losing the United order, Boeing decided to widen the 707 after all.

Herlihy's seven-year prediction about the start of jet service was to prove amazingly accurate. He missed the target date by only four months.

The DC-8 was an entirely new airplane in every respect, but it adhered to Douglas's personal philosophy that its conservative design be based on tried engineering principles. There were no radical departures in design techniques, and one of the world's leading aeronautical engineers, Arthur Raymond, made certain his engineers kept their feet on the ground.

Although the DC-8 cost more than twice as much as the DC-7, it was expected to produce two to three times as much revenue for an airline. In relation to the DC-6, the most economical airplane ever built for its size and capabilities, the DC-8 was designed to have a 22 percent lower operating cost over comparable distances. When plans for production were announced in the fall of 1955, ten major lines had ordered 105 DC-8s.

A new $20 million assembly plant was built at Long Beach where the C-133 Cargomaster was being built for the air force. The latter was a huge airplane capable of carrying twenty-six tons of military equipment up to 4,000 miles at an average speed of 320 MPH.

An even larger cargo transport was in the design stage at Tulsa, Oklahoma, but the C-132 was arbitrarily killed by the air force before it could go into production. Douglas denounced the decision as one the air force and the people of the United States would regret in later years. He never made a truer statement.

American Airlines' President C. R. Smith, long a stout admirer of Douglas and his company, chose the Boeing 707. His decision was hard to take because Smith had always been a Douglas partisan. He had been the first to switch his entire fleet to the DC-3.

At the time of the American DC-3 purchase Douglas had said of Smith, "His tremendous faith in us and in the future of air travel, his boundless energy and clear vision, and his uncanny knack of making and inspiring the right decision at the right time, were the catalytic agents that greatly influenced us in taking the steps to build the DC-3."

Now Smith had turned away from his old friend, and it was a tragic loss to the company.

Of the decision, Smith said publicly, "Selection of the right airplane to buy was the hardest we've had to make since 1932. Both the Boeing and Douglas airplanes are excellent in design and use the same engines. But Boeing has a jet transport flying and the price is less."

The loss of American reflected the tremendous stakes both Boeing and Douglas had in their respective airplanes. The Boeing 707 was cheaper—$250,000 a plane less, due in large part to their tanker contract with the air force. Some company officials urged Douglas to lower the price of the DC-8 but he refused to "buy" in. Douglas told Raymond that if he had been in Boeing's position, with a prototype flying, and the DC-8 still a paper airplane, Douglas would not have gotten a single contract.

Many airline officials, appreciating Douglas's personal integrity and his reputation for fair dealing, trusted him. Through the years his personal association with them and the fact that his company had established a strong commercial design experience and an intimate knowledge of airline problems were decisive factors at this stage in their selection.

Many are convinced that the Douglas company's eventual collapse started during these years. Donald Douglas's failure to invest corporate funds to build a prototype jetliner at the time Boeing was doing so started an inevitable chain of events.

The DC-8 went through many design stages, starting out as a much smaller airplane than what eventually materialized because of the insistence by airlines on greater passenger capacity. It finally ended up with a 142-foot wing, a length of 150 feet, and a passenger capacity of 122 in a mixed first-class-tourist configuration.

Boeing's original advantage of having a flying prototype was somewhat alleviated because the increased size of the DC-8 forced Boeing to increase the cross section of the 707's cabin, and also increase range and payload.

Sales efforts were the most intense anyone at Douglas could remember. Douglas personally worked with the sales teams. Normally, he did not say much because airline officials knew that anything Douglas's staff said had the Old Man's approval. The efforts to win Eastern Air Lines reached their climax after Rickenbacker told Paschall, "I don't want to talk to sales teams any more. I want to talk to Don."

When they met in New York Rickenbacker insisted that Douglas guarantee noise levels. "I want a noise level no higher or even less than the DC-7. Can you guarantee that?"

"I'll have to confer with my engineers," Douglas said, and they walked out to talk privately in another room.

Douglas and his engineers had gone over and over their efforts to reduce jet noise, and they were confident of success but not to the point of making a guarantee.

Raymond said, "We've made fine progress and chances are we'll be able to do it by the time the DC-8 is certified for service."

"What about right now?" Douglas said.

"We can't guarantee it."

Douglas was resigned to loss of the vital Eastern contract. "Let's go back in."

He was deeply troubled, and he walked into Rickenbacker's office with a solemn face. "Eddie, we can't promise it."

"Hell, I know you can't. I just wanted to see if you're still honest. You've just sold $165 million worth of airplanes. What I'm buying isn't the DC-8. It's integrity!"

On their way out Rickenbacker said, "I hope you're going to keep working to get that noise level down."

Douglas assured him they would do everything humanly possible. His integrity had always come first, even at the risk of losing a large order. Rickenbacker's decision reaffirmed one of Douglas's basic beliefs that honesty pays off in the end.

Douglas was honored in 1956 when he was presented the Elmer A. Sperry Award. It was given "in recognition of his distinguished contributions which had advanced the art of transportation through the development and production of the DC series of airplanes." That same year he also received the National Defense Transportation Award.

Douglas participated in a unique venture that same year called "Operation Heartbeat" with the world-famous heart specialist Dr. Paul Dudley White and the National Geographic Society. Scammon's Lagoon, off Mexico's Baja California coast, each winter is the breeding ground for California gray whales. Dr. White was interested in checking the heartbeats of the huge mammals in hopes that some of the secrets of the human heart might be revealed. He hoped to find whether there was a correlation between the number of heartbeats per minute and the size of a living creature.

Douglas made his company's yacht, *Dorado,* available, and with the knowledge developed through years of experience with guided missiles it was hoped that by using crossbows and hand-thrown harpoons with trailing wires connecting to a telemetering boat that the beat of the whales' hearts could be recorded. The first attempt was not successful, and they realized they needed better equipment and more scientific techniques.

They tried again in 1957 using a helicopter to hover over the forty-foot whales as they frolicked lazily in the calm waters of the lagoon under a bright blue sky. This time the government of Mexico, the U.S. Army's Aviation Branch, and the U.S. Fish and Wildlife Service, with its boat with naturalist Dr. Raymond Gilmore on board, participated to assist Dr. White's cardiographers.

At first they tried to plant electrodes in an old cow and her calf from the chase boat *Ballena* with Donald, Jr., at the helm, and his father and Ted Conant handling the harpoons. As they chased the whales out to sea the mother whale turned unexpectedly and headed directly for the *Ballena*. She slammed the boat, tearing off its rudder and propeller. Now, with the rescue skiff manned by industrialist Charles Langlais, and the Douglas Company's D. W. "Bud" Gardiner racing towards the *Ballena* as it rolled helplessly in the water, the whale charged again. This time she hit below the waterline. The *Ballena* shuddered, and a torrent of water poured through her shattered planks. The younger Douglas grabbed a couple of life jackets and jammed them into the sides of the sinking boat as the rescue craft neared. He spared only a quick glance at the whale, noting with relief that she and her baby were heading out to sea. In danger of sinking, Douglas's son beached the *Ballena,* and ran canvas underneath it so it could be towed to the Douglas yacht *Dorado* where it was hoisted aboard.

Later Douglas and Don, Jr., went up in an army helicopter armed with high-powered rifles to fire harpoons. Two harpoons had to enter a whale as far apart as possible to detect the beat of a whale's heart. They made five connections out of eleven attempts and one in particular was highly successful. When the giant gray whale surfaced, the helicopter moved into position. The Douglases fired simultaneously.

"A hit!" Douglas shouted.

Now it was up to the telemetry boat, being towed by lines attached to the harpoons embedded in the whale as it rushed away. The small, orange-colored boat with its bobbing antenna rode the calm waters well, and contact with the whale lasted four hours as the delicate vibrations of the whale's heartbeats were transmitted back to receiving stations.

After several days they headed home. Douglas stood at the rail of the *Dorado* as they left the bay, watching whales do belly flops, at times almost fully rising out of the water as if they were standing on their tails, before slamming down with loud slaps on the Pacific's surface.

He turned to his son, "I suppose that's their way of saying thank Neptune those sons-of-bitches are leaving."

Although the tracings from the electrocardiographs were studied for months by Dr. White and his associates, results were inconclusive. The expedition did prove that highly technical equipment could be used to further man's knowledge of the human heart.

After Heinemann's younger daughter, Jean, tragically was killed in an automobile accident in 1957, and his wife was confined permanently to a hospital, Charlotte Douglas called Ed and invited him and his other daughter, and her husband, to dinner. The graciousness and kindness of his hostess during this difficult period in Heinemann's life was appreciated.

The following week Ed received a call from Doug inviting him to go out on his boat. "I'll be glad to go," he said, welcoming the chance to get away from the pressure of constant work for a few days. The boat was anchored off La Paz in Baja California, so they flew down to spend a few days at sea. When he returned, Heinemann wrote Charlotte a thank-you note for the lovely dinner he had had at her house before the trip. Evidently Charlotte had learned he had been aboard Doug's yacht because he never heard from her again. Heinemann felt bad because he sincerely liked Charlotte. It was one of the tragic aftermaths of the Douglas divorce and remarriage wherein long-time associates had to take Charlotte's side or be ostracized. It was a most difficult position for everyone.

Douglas tried to get to sea during this period as often as possible so he could relax with a few selected friends aboard the *Dorado*. With his time limited, Douglas had his boat crew anchor the *Dorado* in the bay off La Paz near the tip of Baja California each fall and keep it in that area until April or May.

One weekend, with his weimaraner Wunderbar with him, he flew to La Paz to spend a few days on board. Douglas's affection for dogs began early in life and he was hardly ever without one. Although he loved each dog, perhaps his favorite was Wunderbar, or Bar for short. When Douglas returned from a trip, associates had learned to stand clear because Bar would charge up to him and anyone who got in his way would be bowled over.

Bar loved the boat trips to La Paz, but for some unaccountable reason he refused to relieve himself on board. Therefore, several times a day he had to be rowed ashore in the skiff so he could answer nature's call. One day Douglas rowed Bar ashore because he had been told the dog had a favorite rock he always used. Sure enough, Bar headed straight for a large rock. Douglas looked at the rock with a speculative gleam in his eyes. He wondered if they brought the rock on board whether Bar would use it there so they wouldn't have to row him ashore.

Back on board he told his associates what he had in mind. They, too, were fed up with rowing the big dog to shore, and agreed it was a good idea. Several rowed to shore and struggled mightily with that heavy rock until they had it safely in the skiff.

Once it was placed discreetly by itself on the *Dorado,* they waited expectantly to see what would happen. Bar hurried to see what they were doing. He sniffed around the rock while they waited breathlessly to see if he would use it. Bar, however, turned up his nose and pranced disdainfully away.

Douglas told them it was too soon for Bar to need to go again, and that they should be patient. Several hours later Bar began to pace back and forth on the deck, indicating he had to go again. They pointed to the rock, but Bar would have none of it, and hurried to the fantail where the skiff was located.

Douglas exploded. "Come back here!"

Bar ignored his master, barking incessantly that he had to go ashore. Douglas was furious, telling the others that he'd either use the rock or else. As time went on, and Bar still refused to go near the rock, his agony was obvious and his eyes seemed to almost bulge out of their sockets as his need to relieve himself became more acute. Glenn Snyder told Douglas that this situation could not continue, and that he would row Bar ashore.

When the skiff was lowered, Bar excitedly jumped into it, and Snyder laboriously rowed the large dog across the bay. As the skiff bumped into the shore, Bar sprang out and set a beeline to where the rock had been. When he found it missing, he began to howl piteously, but still refused to relieve himself. Snyder coaxed the dog to perform but finally had to admit defeat and rowed Bar back to the *Dorado*.

Douglas was at the rail when the skiff came up to the boat. "What was all that howling about?"

"That was Bar."

"I didn't think it was you," Douglas said with sarcasm. "What was he howling about?"

"He won't go until he gets his rock back on shore."

"What!" Douglas's face was flushed as his anger mounted. Then he began to laugh uproariously.

They all struggled with that large rock until finally they had it back on shore in its identical place. They were exhausted, and flopped on the beach as Bar raced happily toward his rock and, to their vast relief, lifted a hind leg.

When Bar died of throat cancer in 1958 the tears that came so readily to Douglas's eyes were not easily staunched. They had been together for eight years, and their mutual affection touched all who saw them together. Bar's death left him heartbroken and inconsolable for days.

Donald Douglas, Jr., had been with the company since 1939, moving up through the ranks in various steps until he became director of contract administration in 1948, and of the company's research laboratories at Santa Monica in 1949. Two years later he was elected a vice-president of the company, and in 1953 became a member of its board of directors.

Active in many California and national organizations and societies, he had always been concerned with the welfare and problems of youth and, for eleven years, was president of the Crescent Bay Council and member-at-large of the National Council of Boy Scouts of America. A hard-driven young man, he was named president in 1957 by action of the company's board of directors and took over responsibilities for the day-to-day running of the company while his father remained as board chairman.

"Let him make the decisions now," his father said. "One of these days I'll just disappear from the plant like steam off hot water."

Douglas and some members of his family stood outside on a balcony overlooking Long Beach Municipal Airport the morning of May 30, 1958, as the first DC-8 taxied to the end of the runway. Quiet and casual as always, his brown eyes intent as the DC-8 slowly gained speed, Douglas watched the DC-8 as it thundered down the runway and lifted off in a cloud of black smoke caused by water injection into its engines to increase their thrust.

He turned to Raymond. "Well, she's up."

Raymond said with a chuckle, "That's the same thing you said when the DC-1 first took off."

"More Guts and Less Gobbledegook"

light tests of the DC-8 proved it to be a rugged, comfortable airplane but there were basic design deficiencies. Despite problems, airlines continued to place orders, and United's Patterson reaffirmed his faith in the company by increasing his original order to forty DC-8s. Sales efforts were intensified and Boeing and Douglas made broad concessions to gain new orders. Foreign airlines, in particular, remained largely loyal to Douglas and their orders increased the total backlog.

Fifty million dollars were allocated to Raymond's engineering department to correct deficiencies, but few of them were corrected. Douglas's face showed the strain but he remained calm and unruffled before his executives, telling them, "We promised the airlines a good airplane, and we'll make it right no matter what it costs."

When some of Patterson's engineering people protested that the DC-8 was not living up to some of its expectations, he told them bluntly, "I know Don. He'll make it right."

The stakes for the company were high. Failure of the DC-8 to live up to its warranties and guarantees could easily break the company.

In analyzing what happened, Raymond told Douglas, "We were optimistic on the low side in our wind tunnel analysis. Too many things worked out on the high side."

Douglas brushed a hand through his hair, now perceptibly graying, and said, "I know. But we've got to stand behind the airplane."

His attitude was typical. No matter how bad the news, all one had to do was tell him the truth, and he would back a person all the way.

The great engineering team Arthur Raymond had established through the years had developed serious personnel deficiencies. Normally a strong administrator, Raymond became seriously ill due to the strain and was unable to wield the strong hand that in the past had kept tight reins on his department. His illness further compounded the problems with the DC-8, and later became so severe that he was forced to resign.

For United in particular, the waiting period to get their DC-8s was agonizing because its rivals with their 707s were already nine months ahead of them when UAL placed its first DC-8 into service in September 1959.

Patterson said at the time, "We're glad we waited for the DC-8."

Douglas replied that in ten years the few months' delay in getting the DC-8 into service would make little difference.

At the time, Patterson and Arthur Raymond had a long discussion about Douglas.

"You know, Ray," Patterson said, "before we made our decision to buy the DC-8 we took all the Douglas commercial planes, and some of the military, and put them together as representative of what the DC-8 would be." He paused deep in thought. "I don't think Doug knows how important he is to his own organization. He's not only an outstanding engineer but he's never permitted himself to be distracted from current problems, and he's always been a man who could mediate between manufacturer and customer, and he's never failed to reconcile the two. Added to this, he could always see the hint of a major problem and set about solving it." He chuckled. "If anyone came into his office firing a cannon, he'd approach the man coolly. God gave Scotsmen what he didn't give the rest of us—a shrewd analytical capacity."

Raymond agreed. "I'd also add consistency and an almost uncanny ability to give the right answer intuitively."

In the midst of his troubles Douglas found time to sympathize with Lockheed in 1960 when its Electra tore itself apart in the air. During the worst of the crisis he called Robert E. Gross, board chairman of the Lockheed Aircraft Corporation, to tell him to keep his flag flying and to keep up his courage. "In the end things will work out well."

For some time Douglas had been working on the design for the interior of a motor sailer called *Lady Fair,* and he helped in the building of it more than any previous yacht. When she was launched in 1960 he was as proud of her as of any boat he had ever owned.

Douglas still managed to get away with intimates once in a while and occasionally went to the Douglas-owned White Oaks Ranch in the Simi Valley to hunt. One day he joined Charles Lick, chairman of the Pabst Brewing Company, and Charles Jones, president of Richfield Oil, for a hunting trip. Both were members of the company's board of directors, and longtime friends.

As they prepared to leave Douglas called Lick over and whispered something in his ear. Lick agreed with a chuckle, and wandered down the road as Jones's chauffeur arrived in a limousine to take his boss home. Jones was a likeable, but rather formal, person with a dignified manner. He bade Douglas good-bye as he entered his limousine and Douglas watched the car drive away. As Lick, hidden in the trees alongside the road, tossed a handful of gravel at Jones's car as it passed him, Douglas simultaneously fired his shotgun. The limousine screeched to a halt, and Jones charged out and strode angrily back up the road to the grinning Douglas, cursing him for firing at his Cadillac.

Douglas's body shook with laughter. He tried to soothe the irate Jones by saying, "Charlie, you don't think I'd actually fire my shotgun at your car, do you?"

Jones glared at him, saying nothing, his face flushed and his eyes flashing.

"You didn't answer my question," Douglas said.

"Hell, yes!" Jones roared. "I wouldn't put anything past you when you get an idea in your head to devil somebody."

Then he noticed Lick grinning beside him, tossing a handful of gravel up and down. He started to walk towards his car, but turned back. "You owe me a drink." Douglas put an arm around Jones's shoulders and led him back to the clubhouse.

Ed Heinemann, who had been brought to Santa Monica earlier as vice-president of combat aircraft systems by Douglas, was called to the president's office in May 1960. He was told his position was being abolished in a major reorganization of the company, and he was offered the position of vice-president of the European Division to head the company's sales office in Geneva. Ed was shocked. He and his new wife Zell had just purchased a home, and he believed he was making a contribution to the company's combat aircraft programs.

Company president Donald Douglas, Jr., asked him first to explore whether the company's European offices should be moved from Switzerland to Paris. Despite serious doubts that such a move was in his own best interests, or those of the company's, Heinemann agreed to go to Europe for thirty days.

In Switzerland he became more and more convinced that acceptance of the European post would be a mistake. Mike Oliveau, who had long headed the office, had done a superb job and was well liked by airline officials. One of them told Heinemann, "Don't take the job. You're respected in design circles, and it would be a mistake to get on the cocktail circuit."

Heinemann dutifully checked all aspects of the desirability of moving the company's offices to Paris. After a talk with a leading lawyer in Paris, who advised him that Douglas would be forced to pay prohibitive taxes, he returned to Santa Monica and advised Douglas to keep the Geneva office.

Heinemann faced a dilemma. The younger Douglas had specified that Ed either had to return to Switzerland and take over the job, or return to his old post at El Segundo as chief engineer. He rejected the latter. Leo Devlin now had the position and was doing his usual capable job. He had no intention of getting his old friend demoted. He went in to discuss the problem with Doug.

"You were a damn fool to agree to go over there in the first place," Douglas said. "Let me talk to Don."

The father failed to convince his son to change his mind, and Heinemann realized he had no recourse but to resign. He knew the younger Douglas considered him an impediment and wanted to surround himself with his own men, who did not owe allegiance to his father. Heinemann submitted his letter of resignation July 19, 1960, and offered to continue as a technical consultant. His resignation was accepted.

So one of the nation's true aeronautical geniuses, a stubborn, unassuming man who had earned the respect of military and commercial customers alike for the fundamental simplicity and durability of his innovative designs, was forced out. His departure helped to seal the company's fate seven years later.

The DC-8 had been improved greatly, but the production line was down to a one-a-month rate. Nineteen sixty was a bad year for commercial aviation as air travel declined due to a sluggish national economy, and the Douglas Company bore the brunt of it. One hundred and sixty DC-8s worth $675 million had been sold, far below the number required to break even on the program, and well below Boeing's orders for the 707.

Boeing obviously was far in the lead, prompting Douglas to tell Paschall, "If we'd been flying a prototype and been as early as our competition and hadn't shut them out, I'd have fired you."

Although most of the uncommitted airlines now were going to Boeing with their orders, there were many who stood stalwartly behind Douglas and his company. When Scandinavian Airlines System accepted its first DC-8, an executive told him, "In ten years we'll be very glad we're flying a Douglas airplane."

Tomás Delgado, chairman of the board for Iberia Air Lines of Spain, spoke more colorfully. "At this time, when air traffic is changing from propeller to jet for the greater worldwide enjoyment of our civilization, it is deeply moving to consider the figure of Douglas whose name covers the whole of our air-traffic history."

Of the DC-8, he said, "The feats of the DC series assure us that the DC-8 will continue the story of its predecessors—that quality which we call in Spanish breeding—and will contribute to the well-being of the present generation which will see materialize its greatest dream—that of being carried any place on earth to any other place in one day."

It was the most frustrating period in Douglas's life and the lines on his face were more deeply etched than ever as the company went into the red and dividends were suspended for the first time in years.

It was during this difficult period that the company's advertising director misjudged the temper of his boss, and emerged from the experience a shaken and wiser man. O. B. "Ben" Marble was persuaded by his staff that his department needed a trilinguist because of the company's associations with European countries. In particular, the company's agreement to market the Sud Aviation's Caravelle twin-jet airliner supposedly had created a situation where many Douglas employees at all levels were working with Sud personnel who did not speak a word of English. So, it was theorized, someone should be hired to teach supervisors to speak French. The fact that the company had been doing business with France for at least three decades without the need for a linguist evidently did not cross Marble's mind.

Marble believed the hiring of a linguist was mandatory, despite a freeze on hiring salaried employees. A French woman with impeccable credentials was hired at $3.62 an hour, or $585.00 a month as a salaried employee, which at the time corresponded to the pay of a good artist in the advertising department. She was well qualified for the job, being a French citizen who also was fluent in Spanish and understood some Italian. When she was hired she volunteered to brush up on her Italian, and pay for the lessons herself. In taking the Douglas job, which was approved by the younger Douglas, she turned down another position as manager of the Berlitz School in San Francisco.

Douglas, Sr., heard about her indirectly and, in a handwritten memo on board chairman stationery dated October 6, he wrote Marble: "I can't believe what I hear, that you have a French girl employed at a handsome salary to teach French here! This is ridiculous and not in line with my policy to cut unnecessary expenses. Also I am told we are now paying for this gal to learn Italian. Is everyone going nuts around here? Get rid of her pronto."

Five days later Marble wrote Douglas saying, "I can easily see why you would be disturbed about the new employee in the Advertising Department with the limited information available to you on the job description." In his three-page memorandum, Marble sought to justify her hiring, explaining the need for her talents.

Douglas responded with another memorandum the same day. "I have read your surprising memo of 10-11-60 in respect to the work you have for a French translator. It still does not ring true to me. You have a number of people here including Cardenas and MacArthur who are thoroughly capable of doing translations.

> This employee's hiring smacks of a boondoggle. She should be terminated. I would think any employee who wants to learn a foreign language should pay for instructions himself and take them on his own time. The woods are full of language teachers. If we are to teach languages, why do we not also teach wives cooking,

men social usages, and even go to the extent of teaching our salesmen golf, drinking procedures, sailing and hunting?

From the reports to me, this employee is doing no work to speak of as you have listed. You state that in the last 2 years we produced 15 DC-8 sales films in several languages. How did we accomplish this at that time without this "tri-lingual" woman who now must go to school to learn Italian?

Your cost reductions are commendable. Is this why you were saddled with the expense of this employee? You had better rid yourself of her and maintain your good record.

Marble caved in under such an onslaught by the company's board chairman, and the unfortunate woman was laid off.

This was a typical reaction by Douglas once he got wind of unnecessary hiring during a critical period in the company's finances. When he was president, as well as board chairman, he personally authorized the hiring of any salaried person at the corporate level. The fact that department heads had to get his personal approval, even in good times, injected a good deal of caution in their requests for additional salaried employees. Now, with Douglas's son as president, there were far too many people on the payroll about whom he knew nothing.

Eventually Douglas's faith in the DC-8 was justified and hundreds were built in later versions, and it proved a worthy successor to the famed propeller airplanes.

During these critical years Douglas's contributions to the advancement of aviation were recognized as never before. He had been named "Man of the Month" by the National Aviation Club and was made a life member in 1957. That same year he was elevated to Officer of the French Legion of Honor and, much to his embarrassment, was kissed on both cheeks by Maurice Chevalier. He was also named the nation's top businessman for the 1950s. The Franklin Institute presented him with their medal in May 1958 for creative engineering in the field of the aeronautical sciences.

The following year he shared with Lockheed's Robert E. Gross the honor of being named California Industrialist of the Year. He was cited for the development and production of the DC-8, and for the part he played in the first operational deployment of the Thor missile in the United Kingdom.

During the summer of 1960 Douglas and his wife, Peggy, led a sales team to Mexico City to help sell DC-8s to Aeronaves de Mexico. His reputation there was so great that President López Mateos and his entire cabinet flew with him on a demonstration flight. Douglas, his eyes wide with wonder and astonishment, told a company official, "It's incredible the confidence they have in a Douglas airplane. If it had crashed the entire government of Mexico would have been wiped out!" For once Boeing salesmen were left out in the cold as the big jet took off with its passenger load of Mexican VIPs.

At a news conference in Mexico City Douglas was asked why his company, world leader in commercial aviation, had abandoned the next step into supersonic commercial transports. He paused. A short time before, he had personally directed that all research into an SST be abandoned by the company. His reply was calm. "It's a bad interim step. We're talking about putting man on the moon. If we can do that, why not wait until a huge rocket can be designed to fly passengers from coast-to-coast or continent-to-continent? If we can make a soft landing on the moon, it certainly can be done in New York, Paris, Mexico City, or anywhere else."

More importantly, he said he did not believe a supersonic transport could pay for itself because initial costs would be astronomical, and operating costs would be considerably higher than for subsonic jet transports. The later fate of the British-French *Concorde,* and the Soviet *Tupolev* supersonic transport sustained his judgment. Although each proved that passengers could be carried safely and in comfort, neither airplane was sufficiently economical to show a profit, even when passengers paid premium fares.

There is no question that a huge passenger-carrying rocket could fly from the United States to the most distant parts of the world. A flight from the west coast of the United States to Australia, for example, could be made in less than an hour. Again, it is a matter of cost. Would passengers pay an additional premium of $500 over the normal price of a ticket to make such a hypersonic flight? It is rather doubtful in the foreseeable future, but that time will come. One of the greatest advantages of rocket flight is the higher utilization possible due to greater frequency of flights because each would average less than an hour's time.

Douglas's remarks in Mexico were widely publicized because there were many, even then, who believed that a supersonic transport would only cause a massive boom miles each side of its flight path as it rode above the earth and would create more problems than it was worth.

Aeronaves bought the DC-8 and, in many ways, their confidence in Douglas dated back to the time many years before when General Obregón bought his first Douglas airplane and paid for it in gold.

The Youngest Vision

D ouglas's office was simply furnished with a desk like those used by managers throughout the company. One wall was full of books and airplane models. There was a picture of his yacht, the *Endymion,* and a picture of his daughter Barbara Jean. Always beside him was a dog who received a reassuring pat on the head from time to time.

Douglas's love for the sea endured since he first sailed on Long Island Sound as a youngster. He loved his travels on the Pacific Ocean with a few intimates, particularly when he needed to get away and relax from the daily tensions of the plant. His wife Peggy, who also acted as his executive assistant within the company, encouraged him to take these trips, knowing better than anyone how much he needed to get away occasionally from the company's problems. She did not share his love for the sea so she remained at home most of the time. As the company's crisis worsened, she worked long and hard to ease the heavy burden he was carrying, but his appearance became more haggard each day.

On these cruises one ritual never varied. Dr. Charles "Doc" Rooney, an early company medical director who before he died in 1945 had often been with Douglas on his yachts, was remembered. As they passed Rooney's "rock," on the west end of Catalina Island, Douglas would cut the engines while those on board sang a song Douglas had composed about "Old Doc" Rooney and they drank a toast. At times, when the tide was strong, they were in danger of foundering on the rock, but Douglas insisted that the song be completed before he would turn the engines back on.

Informality was the rule on the boat, with Douglas often replacing Luther Gift as cook, and he prepared many of his own specialties. The latter were enjoyed despite his heavy hand with butter.

While production of the DC-8 continued, the company expanded its activities in the missile field. Before World War II ended, it was evident to strategists that antiaircraft systems were woefully obsolete, and that future aircraft would need wholly new missile systems to counteract them.

The army's Frankfort Arsenal's Fire Control Department Office had had the problem under study for some time. When a young lieutenant proposed a rocket or jet-propelled "controlled projectile" in 1944, his ideas were submitted to manufacturers. The army discussed the proposal with officials of the Bell Telephone Laboratories and they, in turn, talked it over with Douglas. He approved the company's role as the principal subcontractor to design and develop missiles and their launching equipment. Bell was made responsible by the army for the design of the radar, communications, and guidance systems.

Nine years later, the first results of this association were evident when the tactical Nike Ajax went operational in December 1953 in Maryland. Simultaneously, a more advanced Nike was under development to carry a nuclear warhead at longer ranges to seek out high-altitude bombers. It became known as the Hercules.

The engineering organization that started missile work in 1940 now had extensive experience in guided missile systems and supersonic aerodynamics. Through the years this team produced more than 50,000 individual units. Among them were the "Bumper-Wac," which established new speed and altitude records in 1949. A second stage of the Wac Corporal reached an altitude of 250 miles at speeds of 5,000 MPH. Douglas also built the airframe for the navy's Sparrow I, an air-to-air missile.

This research and development team designed a part of the Nike-X antimissile system, later called Zeus, for use in destroying ICBM/nuclear warheads far away from and above a projected target. In response to the army's request for a surface-to-surface missile

Douglas developed Honest John, which is used like an artillery gun.

Out of all this vast experience came the sixty-five-foot Thor, an intermediate-range ballistic missile that was also used as a booster for space vehicles. For the Thor, Douglas was named by the air force as prime contractor. The Soviet Union's advances in missiles gave an added impetus to the project, so the program was assigned top priority. Thor was the only interim system available to counter a Soviet missile attack against the United States, but it was limited to a 1,500-mile range. In the late 1950s and 1960s Thor was superceded by intercontinental ballistic missiles, but its usefulness was not at an end. Perhaps its greatest achievements were in its reliable launching of space systems.

There were other important developments, including the high-velocity air-to-air rocket MB-1 Genie, which was built for the Air Force Defense Command and went into service as a nuclear rocket for fighters in 1957. Genie was so potent that it could destroy an entire formation of attacking bombers at high altitudes.

In 1958, Douglas appeared before the Senate Armed Services Subcommittee on Preparedness to give the benefit of his knowledge and experience as to how the United States could overcome the Soviet Union's apparent lead in missile and space programs.

At the start, he said, "I do not share the opinion of so many that the race for weapon supremacy has been lost forever, and that we are permanently doomed to the role of a secondary power. I am one of those who have boundless faith in the basic strength, rugged integrity, courage, and determination of the American people. Given a proper understanding of the nation's defense needs, they will do their part magnificently, as they have in every crisis we ever faced."

He told how the Douglas Thor intermediate-range ballistic missile had been developed and tested in less than two years, and how the production line was ready to turn them out in any quantity desired.

He also discussed the Zeus antimissile missile and said all that was needed was the "go-ahead" signal to bring it to the same status. He cited Zeus as a conspicuous example of government failure to make early and firm decisions.

"Nearly two years ago we felt this weapon was sufficiently

feasible to warrant a go-ahead. But so far only a small fraction of the necessary funds have been made available."

In reference to the successful firing of the Thor, he said his company waited from August to December for an order to increase production. He said one of the military services estimated that an average of 333 days was required to process a facilities request, and that needless paper work for the government forced an addition of 30 percent more technical manpower, pointing out that his company spent upwards of 400,000 man-hours a year to prepare unnecessary reports.

He put the entire matter succinctly when he said, "Delay and indecision on the part of many in the defense establishment can be as damaging in the long run as any action by a potential aggressor. In other words we need more guts and less gobbledegook."

He was roundly applauded for his forthright stand.

One of Douglas's most frustrating moments during this period was the cancellation of Skybolt. This program was initiated in the spring of 1959 by the air force for an air-launched ballistic missile with a nuclear warhead to be carried by B-52s and British Vulcan bombers.

Although it was successfully tested, and would have permitted American and British bombers to remain safely a thousand miles away from enemy defenses, it was canceled in 1962. There had been the usual problems with Skybolt, but none were insurmountable. Actually, the B-52 would have needed costly structural beef ups if the program had continued.

Douglas's personal involvement in space systems paralleled company advances in the missile and rocket fields. Scientists had prepared a study for him in 1946, which was called "Preliminary Design of an Experimental World-Circling Spaceship," at a time when such a possibility was considered science fiction.

After the USSR launched its first Sputnik as a space satellite on October 4, 1957, space programs took on a new urgency in the United States. Fortunately for U.S. supremacy in the field, the Douglas-built Thor was a proven, reliable booster, permitting Pioneer I to reach an altitude of 70,700 miles, the farthest space penetration made by any man-made object up to that time. Although Pioneer I failed to reach escape velocity, it was the forerunner of many others that did.

The basic Thor was modified several times to accommodate second-stage vehicles to carry a host of scientific and military payloads. So successful was Thor for the Discoverer Program, a research program to carry out preliminary and general space explorations, that it performed perfectly in thirty-five out of thirty-eight launches. Its reliability in all its different types of launches was exceptional. For a period of eight years it proved reliable 92 percent of the time during more than 200 space firings.

When the company was selected to build S-IV, an upper stage of Saturn I, and the more powerful S-IVB, it placed the full resources of a new Missiles and Space Group behind the project to help man land on the moon in the Apollo program. So successful was the S-IV that the company later won the contract to develop a Manned Orbiting Laboratory in which a crew could live and operate in space on orbital flights for as long as thirty days.

Douglas approved another step in 1965 when the company bid on and was successful in establishing a new firm called Douglas-United Nuclear, Inc. This was a subsidiary combining the company and United Nuclear to command a half-billion dollar reactor and fuel fabrication operation near Hanford, Washington. As part of the operation, the Donald W. Douglas Laboratories were engaged in research in the use of nuclear energy and energy-conservation systems for future space explorations.

The company submitted a formal report to Congress on the performance of its launch vehicles in early 1966. The report said that through December 1965, there had been 268 successful and 70 unsuccessful launches by all United States space vehicles. Of this number, Thor launched 189, and all but 9 were successful. All Saturn launches were successful and, of the 195 launches of all missiles using Douglas equipment, 186 were successful.

The company took part in 58 percent of all United States launches and 69 percent of all successful launches of space hardware. It was an achievement of which any company could be proud, and at the top was a man of seventy-four with the youngest vision of anyone in the company.

"Fix It!"

Boeing proposed a smaller jet transport to the world's airlines in 1957 with a shorter fuselage and a smaller wing, but having much in common with the 707 series. The decision by Boeing to build the 720 was a crucial one for Douglas because the company could not afford to embark on another new commercial transport. To further complicate Douglas's position with the airlines, Boeing came up with the 727 trijet in 1961. It appeared to many that the Douglas company's inability to go ahead with a new airplane would turn most of the commercial market for airplanes over to Boeing.

During the years between 1959 and 1962 a rather serious recession hit the United States and commercial airlines felt it strongly. Although some DC-8s were sold, the assembly line in Long Beach remained almost constantly on a one-a-month level because of a lack of orders, although the performance of the airplane had been improved and deliveries were on schedule.

The Douglas problem was compounded by the fact that, for several years, airlines had been clamoring for a short-range transport—one that could be economical at ranges from 100 to 800 miles. A twin-engine DC-9 had been on the drawing boards for some time, waiting for the moment when airlines could financially handle such a new jet transport, and also for the time when Douglas's financial position would improve to the point where a go-ahead was possible.

In 1961, the company was reorganized and split into separate divisions, one for missiles and space and the other for all types of aircraft. At that time, Douglas, his son, and Jack McGowen, vice-president and general manager of the Aircraft Division, frequently discussed the proposed DC-9. McGowen pointed out that his analysts had found a bulge on their market projection charts, indicating a sizable market for a small twin-jet aircraft. Airline officials told him that such an airplane must be economical at short ranges, with a minimum of mechanical complications and maximum reliability, and with speed and comfort comparable to the DC-8.

It was a bold and challenging task for the Aircraft Division to come up with an airplane with a swept wing that would be shorter in span than the DC-3, have a fuselage low enough for quick loading and servicing on the ground, and would be about the length of the DC-4. A departure from the previous Douglas practice of mounting engines on the wing to facilitate loading and servicing was agreed upon and the two turbo-fan engines were mounted on the aft fuselage. McGowen told the Douglases the simplicity of the design would pay off because the DC-9 could take off on a 500-mile flight with seventy passengers and baggage from a 5,000-foot runway, and land in less than half that distance at maximum landing weight.

The Aircraft Division's general manager had been pushing strongly for such an airplane after studies indicated the need for a short- to medium-range jet to replace propeller transports. Twenty-eight of the forty-eight cities analyzed were without jet service despite the fact that almost seven million passengers made flights with an average trip distance of 200 miles. He knew the DC-8 was not economical at such ranges, so the market potential for a smaller jet was great. Studies went forward, with both Douglases concurring on the need for the DC-9. By 1962 the corporation's cash position had improved, and it appeared to Board Chairman Douglas that the company could handle design and production of a new airplane.

The final design was an airplane powered by two Pratt & Whitney JT8D-5 turbo-fan engines, each capable of generating 12,000 lbs of thrust. Although the wing area was slightly less than the DC-3, the cabin had the capacity of the DC-4.

McDonnell Aircraft in St. Louis, meanwhile, was also studying the market for a twin-engine commercial transport. Until now McDonnell had concentrated on military aircraft. After Robert E. Hage joined the McDonnell Company in 1958, following twelve years with the Boeing Airplane Company, he became vice-president and general manager of McDonnell's transport division. His first proposal was for an executive aircraft called Model 119/220.

When no buyers materialized, Hage recommended to company founder James McDonnell that they build a forty-passenger, four-engine transport. It was quickly apparent that a commercial jet of such size would not be large enough to interest airlines.

Hage next explored a twin-engine transport, with engines mounted on the tail, much like the one under study by Douglas. The early success of the French Caravelle intrigued the entire industry. The twin-engine jets proposed by Douglas and McDonnell would seat eighty passengers, and would have the same range for the short- to medium-range market.

The two companies had worked together on supersonic research for several years for the Federal Aviation Agency. During this period McDonnell discussed several cooperative projects, but Douglas had no interest. McDonnell constantly reminded the elder Douglas that they had both gone through a period when economic necessity forced the merger of several automotive companies, and that only a few remained. He told Douglas he believed the aerospace industry was headed down the same road.

Douglas conceded that Jim McDonnell was probably correct in saying the aerospace industry eventually would follow the same path as the automotive industry. In the spring of 1963, however, when McDonnell openly discussed a merger of their two companies, Douglas was adamantly opposed to such a union, and his board of directors backed him up. Commercially, Douglas knew McDonnell's expertise would add nothing to his company's relations with airline officials, and frankly, he thought such an association would worsen them. The McDonnell Company had no experience in building commercial aircraft, and Douglas believed any joint venture would hurt future sales prospects. McDonnell, who personally and through his company had bought up a large number of Douglas shares at their depressed levels, now sold them at a handsome profit.

Douglas told intimates, "He'll be back."

A variety of interior arrangements was agreed upon for the DC-9, along with plans for conversion of the airplane to all cargo, or a combination of passengers and cargo for either commercial or military use. In the first of the series it was decided the seating would be arranged so fifty-six passengers could be accommodated in a four-abreast arrangement or eighty-three passengers could be accommodated five-abreast. The cruising speed was raised so it would be twice the speed of the propeller aircraft it would replace—an important economic factor for airlines. Because the DC-9 was designed to operate from shorter runways, 26 percent more airports would be opened to jet service.

There was no question about the need for such a transport, and Douglas considered McGowen's reports long and carefully before he recommended that the board of directors approve a go-ahead. He knew that to stay competitive the decision had to be made. When it was given April 8, 1963, McDonnell canceled his own company's proposal, knowing airlines would never purchase a McDonnell commercial jet when they could deal with companies such as Douglas and Boeing.

McGowen's sales representatives, meanwhile, continued their intensive drive to get American Airlines to buy the airplane. C. R. Smith actually implied before the go-ahead he would buy the DC-9, but when American's bid to merge with Eastern was turned down by the Civil Aeronautics Board, he inexplicably changed his mind and made the decision to buy the British BAC-111.

Douglas officials were stunned. They had known Smith was close to officials of the British Aircraft Corporation, and was favorably disposed to Rolls-Royce engines, but his action caught everyone by surprise. Smith later ruefully told McGowen, "I really didn't think you could go ahead with the DC-9."

His decision was based on the premise that the BAC-111 would be delivered earlier than the DC-9, and the fact that it was cheaper. Actually the 111 had a fatal crash of its first test airplane thereby delaying deliveries, so the DC-9 was delivered first.

The next major sales effort was to get United signed up, and there was confidence this could be done. At this point Boeing announced a new twin-jet airplane called the 737, so Patterson told Douglas he had to wait until his engineers could consider the Boeing offer. United eventually bought the 737, a decision that really shook the Douglas Company. Patterson gave his reasons as the commonality of the 737 with his large Boeing fleet, and the fact that he, too, did not believe Douglas could go ahead.

During this critical period Donald Douglas was presented the Wright Brothers Memorial Award in 1963 by the Aero Club of Washington, D.C., on the 60th anniversary of the Wright brothers' flight at Kitty Hawk.

Meanwhile DC-9 production continued without orders until Delta Airlines made the first purchase.

The drag problem of the original DC-8 design, which proved to be 13 percent higher than estimates based upon wind tunnel evaluations, was 10 percent above airline guarantees. Douglas's response to the problem was typical. "Fix it!" The Boeing 707 also had a drag problem, but it was not so severe.

For the DC-8 the greatest effect of the problem was on the range guarantees for the intercontinental airlines. Although engineering changes solved some of the problems, Douglas offered a cash settlement of $230,000 an airplane after it became evident that meeting the original guarantees was impossible. The airlines agreed to accept the airplanes at this reduced price.

In 1963 Scandinavian Airlines System began to think seriously of switching to the Boeing long-range 707s because, as its president Karl Nilson said, "Our extremely long flights from Scandinavia to Los Angeles, and to other parts of the world, need an airplane that can make these runs nonstop."

McGowen's engineers had been investigating various ways to improve performance of the DC-8 but it was apparent that just fixing the original DC-8s was not the answer because the result would be only a 2 percent improvement. A whole new series was needed using longer, slimmer engine pods, cut-back pylons underneath the wing, and other improvements. The cost was high but failure to proceed with a new series might bring the entire DC-8 program to an untimely end.

After discussion with Douglas and his son, McGowen was told to take a look at what would be gained by a new engine pod. "You can go ahead," they said, "if these changes provide a 7 percent performance improvement."

First results were disappointing, indicating only a 2 percent improvement. Later, after more extensive wind tunnel tests, aerodynamicists told McGowen, "We can do better than we thought. About 4 to 5 percent." This was encouraging, but still below the 7 percent McGowen needed to go ahead. Long discussions took place between McGowen and the two Douglases, and it was evident that a cut-back pylon also was needed to reach performance goals.

Meanwhile, United's Bill Mentzer, vice-president of engineering maintenance, protested to McGowen that Douglas was designing a new airplane for SAS but "you're doing nothing for us."

Mentzer and McGowen then went over improvements that United wanted, particularly an airplane with a longer fuselage to increase passenger capacity. They agreed on an airplane 36.5 feet longer than the original DC-8. Engineering analysts said that by using the all-cargo DC-8, the structure was strong enough so no other changes need be made. This became the Super 61, which United and Eastern bought in quantity.

SAS specifications called for new engine pods, cut-back pylons, and wing-tip extensions to provide a 10 percent improvement in long-range characteristics, but with a fuselage length increase of only 6.5 feet. The airplane so pleased SAS that it remained with Douglas and they signed a contract for Super 62s. After the airplane was flight-tested it proved to even exceed its performance forecasts.

The final version of the new series, the Super 63, retained the long fuselage of the 61 series, and also all the changes to improve performance that were in the Super 62. It proved to be the most aerodynamically perfect of any of the DC-8s.

Although development of this new series proved a financial burden to the company, particularly after the DC-9 went into production, the decision to proceed proved sound because years later, when the DC-8s went out of production in 1972, 556 airplanes worth $2.5 billion had been sold. This was almost twice the original estimate.

At Long Beach the DC-9 program moved ahead concurrently with the DC-8, and assembly of the first twin-jet started on schedule March 6, 1964. The wealth of experience accumulated in the production of Douglas transports, particularly the DC-8, was used to achieve a relatively simple, reliable, and easily maintained airplane that would assure lower airline operating costs. About one-third the size of the DC-8, the original DC-9 was distinctive because of the high-level horizontal stabilizer atop the vertical stabilizer, commonly known as a T-tail, and its two engines mounted on the aft fuselage.

After the first of the series was produced and successfully flown on February 25, 1965, its performance proved so remarkable that orders poured in by the hundreds—particularly after it went into service in December of that year.

With the first of the series under way, the airplane was "stretched" as so many others had been in years past. While Donald Douglas operated the company, five DC-9 versions were produced, proving to be one of the company's most reliable commercial transports.

In addition, the Air Force Airlift Command ordered a version for transporting sick and injured servicemen between hospitals in the United States. Designed as the C-9A Nightingale, this aircraft accommodated up to thirty litter patients, forty ambulatory patients, or a combination of the two.

Everyone was exuberant over the success of the airplane after its agonizing start. It met all guarantees and some called it the jet-age successor to the venerable DC-3. For the first time in commercial aviation history the DC-9's direct operating costs came close to one cent per passenger mile.

So successful was the Aircraft Division in producing the airplane, and the DC-8 along with it, that the division had not missed a schedule in five years. Stockholders were so impressed by the huge orders pouring in that the price of each share soared in value. It peaked at over $100.00 a share, and there was elation throughout the company. Douglas now fully believed that the company's historic preeminence in the commercial field would be reestablished. The younger Douglas, as president, and Jack McGowen, head of the Aircraft Division, believed they had been vindicated by their actions despite the dire predictions of many old timers.

Douglas's son, in particular, had borne the brunt of intense criticism for his handling of the company since he became president. The criticism had been harsh both within the company and among its stockholders. He was jubilant over the sharp turnaround of the company's standing. He had never been popular among the company's old guard and, within three years of his accession to the top, all but one corporate vice-president had resigned. Some did so knowing their status had changed drastically for the worse under Junior and they were bitter, expressing themselves in no uncertain terms. As a result, morale throughout the company had dropped measurably since he became president. At one point before the resurgence of orders, Nat Paschall, the vice-president of commercial sales, told the company's chairman that his son's management of the company was leading it to disaster. Thoroughly aroused by the accusation, Douglas told him, "That's none of your business."

Paschall replied, "I'm making it my business. I quit."

These blunt words shook Douglas as nothing had before because he well knew the enormous respect Paschall had acquired among airline officials. His departure from the company could have damaging effects. He tried to reason with him, saying he knew Paschall was overwrought and should take time off to reconsider.

Paschall said he would take three months leave of absence, but he still intended to resign at the end of it. He kept his word. Now Douglas was in a quandary because all former men at the top who had served under him as president, with one exception, had departed the company. These were men who had helped to make the company great. Their loss did much to accelerate the situation that soon developed.

Douglas's son, whose manners at times were unnecessarily abrasive in his dealings with his top executives, refused to concede that he was at fault. It was a trying time for his father, who had to weigh his love for his son against the strong emotional ties he felt for his former top staff men.

For one of the few times in his life Douglas failed to act decisively to reconcile the growing conflict of personalities. At the root of the problem was the fact that the president was his namesake.

After the tremendous surge of orders materialized for the DC-8 and DC-9 Douglas felt a reaffirmation of his earlier faith in his son. When the last of the original top vice-presidents was forced out by Douglas, Jr., he did nothing to intercede in the man's behalf, despite his long tenure with the company. Privately, he said later, when you give a man the responsibility for running a company, you cannot dictate whom he should have reporting to him. This was a basic philosophy that he had always adhered to and, despite the hurt it caused to many individuals, no one could fault the basic premise.

Bankruptcy

Thee Vietnam War had a severe impact on the company's commercial operations. At first the seriousness of the situation was not apparent to the elder Douglas. During analytical studies prior to the start of the production of the DC-9 and the new series of DC-8s it was known there were 10,000 trained aircraft workers available for jobs, more than enough to complete both programs successfully.

Now, with other defense industries tapping this potential work force, it rapidly diminished, creating the problem of hiring untrained people and trying to make precision craftsmen out of them. Costs mounted as the Aircraft Division spent dollars to train unskilled workers, and paid premium prices for scarce materials.

During the decline in orders for the DC-8, the division's workforce dwindled to as low as 7,500 people from a high of 27,000. Much of the supervision needed during this great expansion of the DC-9 program was not available, having been laid off during massive cutbacks the previous five years. Available management was spread so thin it compounded all other problems. Worst of all, there were shortages of material because contractors with Vietnam orders had first priority over commercial production.

In the spring of 1966, President Donald W. Douglas, Jr., announced the company was in one of the most satisfactory phases in its history. His father told stockholders that the company's first-quarter earnings should exceed the $14.6 million it earned in 1965. If true, such profits would be the highest since 1958. It appeared that the corporation had gotten over its financial problems resulting from its losses on the DC-8 program. The company's indebtedness was only $24 million, and there was a $3 billion backlog. And, early in the year common stock rose to $112.00 a share.

DC-8 and DC-9 sales were almost unbelievable, and the military programs were all doing well and earning profits. Board Chairman Douglas was so confident of the future that he authorized approval of the design for a DC-10 wide-bodied jetliner.

The company's financial position appeared so strong that Douglas told his bankers the $200 million line of credit would no longer be needed, and it was reduced to zero. He personally reached a gentleman's agreement with bankers, however, that, if needed, money would be made available.

In the middle of a $75 million debenture offering, company profits disappeared in the second quarter, and a loss in excess of $3.4 million was announced. Rumors quickly spread that the Douglas Company was in serious trouble, particularly after the value of its stock plummeted to $30.00 a share in October. Stockholders were shocked. They had suffered a paper loss of $359 million, and were even more disturbed when Douglas announced suspension of dividends.

The impending catastrophe stunned financial analysts who had been overly enamored of the company's huge backlog, including 500 orders for the DC-9, and who had assumed Douglas's problems were in the past. Executives freely admitted they had not foreseen the downturn in the company's fortunes, which only added to the distress of the financial community. Douglas officials now admitted there had been a serious breakdown in corporate communications and management controls. The sales department at Long Beach had signed up all comers for new contracts, agreeing to production schedules that were impossible to meet. With rising production costs, delays in delivery of material from suppliers, and the need to train thousands of new workers who had never been in the business before, the situation at the Aircraft Division got completely out of hand.

When the division was formed, Harold Hynd, perhaps the company's most skilled production and cost-control expert, refused to accept the deputy position under McGowen. Jack McGowen had proved himself in engineering as a project engineer, and was well known and liked by airline officials in his later capacity of vice-president of the company's commercial sales. As vice-president and general manager of the Aircraft Division, however, he acquired total responsibility for the division's operations, which he might have been able to handle in a less troublesome period. Through the years Harold Hynd had established tight controls over the El Segundo and Long Beach divisions when they got in trouble. These divisions now had been merged to form the Aircraft Division. McGowen was shocked when Hynd chose to leave the company rather than work for him. Both Douglases joined McGowen in pleading with Hynd to change his mind, but he stubbornly refused. Earlier, Hynd had expected to replace Ted Conant as senior vice-president of manufacturing, and when the job went to another man he became so incensed that his bitterness against the company's top officials turned into an obsession. Many of the company's problems that now developed were directly related to Hynd's departure. This strong, feisty individual was one of the last of a tough breed that used to be so common in top management circles. A self-made man who worked his way up, he had achieved a top job in the company through merit even though he had never graduated from high school. Many managers who had worked for Hynd and who respected his abilities now were faced with ostracism by the new division manager. Such was the alienation that many longtime managers chose to leave as more and more outsiders were brought in until the division management became top-heavy with unnecessary people.

The Douglases should have realized the growing problems at the Aircraft Division when its entry into the C-5 contest came out in third place in September 1965, behind Lockheed and Boeing. The poor showing occurred despite the fact that McGowen had enlisted the support of former Air Force Air Transport Command officers who were given high-paying jobs. The C-5 contract loss proved critical because the Douglas Company was now shut out completely from the important military transport market, a field in which they had formerly been preeminent. This lesson cost the company $20 million, which they could not spare.

Several years earlier the company had wooed Bobby Kennedy in hopes of getting a contract for a military transport based on the DC-8. At the time his brother was president of the United States. Bobby promised much, in return for large donations to the Democratic party. When McGowen and Douglas, Jr., were brought before the president by Bobby to state their case, an astonished John F. Kennedy told them, "But Mr. Douglas, I can't just give you a contract!" The coffers of the Democratic party were the only gainers in this odd exercise in high-level marketing.

Without the Harold Hynd manufacturing expertise, some of the forty-three DC-9s delivered in the first nine months of 1966 were up to three months late. Earlier in the year, the company had to amortize $100 million of the DC-9's development costs. Now the loss on each $3.3 million DC-9 was approximately $600,000. And, it was quickly apparent that such losses would continue. Obviously no company, regardless of its initial soundness, could withstand such losses for long.

In the fall the company sought a loan of $100 million from a consortium of eight banks. Earlier in the year these banks loaned the company $125 million. Some bank officials now talked openly of the necessity for top management changes before they would loan the company more money. Even some members of the Douglas board were convinced changes had to be made, and quickly, if the company was to survive. They focused their accusations against Douglas, Jr., but the elder Douglas continued to back his son. It was a difficult period for the son, and he lashed back at his internal critics. Both Douglases were strong willed, but otherwise quite unlike one another. Whereas the father was a retiring, somewhat aloof individual except with cronies, the son was aggressive and outgoing. Douglas, Jr., had always had a variety of interests. At the time, he was part owner of a 470,000-acre cattle ranch, and an aluminum yacht business that failed. A prominent Boy Scout organizer, the son was also an enthusiastic member of several gourmet clubs and an avid horseman, hunter, and fisherman.

Despite his critics, and they were numerous inside and outside the company particularly among some airline officials and members of the banking community, it must be kept in mind that Douglas's son inherited a sick company. Due to serious design deficiencies, the DC-8 program almost brought the company down. In the four-year period after 1957, only 47 DC-8s were sold in comparison to Boeing's jetliner sales of 172 aircraft. The Douglas Company reported losses of over $108 million before tax credits for the years 1959 and 1960 while Boeing's earnings exceeded $37 million. Without its military problems in 1959, which accounted for 88 percent of total sales,

Douglas would have collapsed. Douglas Aircraft's plight worsened when it was unable to compete with Boeing's new medium-range 727, and long-time customers such as United and Eastern went to Boeing for their future aircraft procurement.

During the late 1950s the Douglas board of directors had viewed the continuing problems with the DC-8 with dismay. Some voiced their opinions that the program should be canceled. Board chairman, Douglas, Sr., resisted such a step, knowing that once it was taken the company would forever be out of the commercial business. Still, with $300 million invested in development costs and only 154 DC-8s sold after six years, something had to be done. There were many executives who were convinced that the DC-8 program would never recover its costs. To do so, at least 250 aircraft had to be sold, and that seemed impossible. Despite the success of the DC-9, by 1966 Boeing was still ahead in total sales of all jet transports, delivering 216 jets compared to 100 for Douglas.

The younger Douglas refused to concede that the DC-8 program was washed up. To assure its success, and to permit production of new jet transports, he reorganized the company into two divisions; one for all aircraft at Long Beach under Jackson R. McGowen, and the other for missiles and space with Charles R. Able at Santa Monica until a new space center could be built at Huntington Beach. Both division heads were old friends in their late forties, about the same age as the company's new president.

This drastic reorganization cut overhead costs by eliminating the huge El Segundo Division with its excess of 2.5 million square feet of unneeded floor space, and tightened up the overall command organization. His father, while president, had twenty-seven top managers reporting directly to him. Douglas, Jr., sharply reduced this number with only two division heads and a few at corporate headquarters reporting to him. Such action quickly eliminated the old guard and a further exodus took place, eventually leading to the retirement, forced and by choice, of all eleven top vice-presidents who had served his father for so many years.

Despite dire predictions of many of the remaining lower echelon old-timers, the action of Douglas, Jr., seemed to improve the company's prospects. In 1961 the company showed a profit of almost $6 million, because DC-8 development costs had been written off. To the relief of stockholders, earnings improved and in March 1965 the company paid cash dividends for the first time in six years. Meanwhile the company's commercial backlog rose from three-quarters of a billion dollars in 1961 to over two billion dollars.

Prospects for the company were not all upward during this period. The United States Air Force suddenly canceled the Skybolt program, which was valued at a billion dollars.

Douglas's son had to face the reality that the company was losing out in missile programs, and he decided to emphasize space programs instead. His father and the board of directors authorized a new Space Systems Center at Huntington Beach. The center seriously depleted Douglas's available funds, but the gamble paid off when the company was awarded the main contract for the Air Force's Manned Orbiting Laboratory in August 1965.

James McDonnell had been quietly acquiring Douglas stock, and now owned 200,000 shares, with another equal number of stockholders pledged to him if he chose to make a takeover move. Apparently the elder Douglas forestalled such a step by requesting that McDonnell not make the attempt.

Although sales of the DC-8 were improving, Boeing was still far ahead in total sales at a time of dwindling orders for the whole industry.

The company concentrated now on its commercial production to maintain the rising demand for Douglas jet transports. For a time its stretched DC-8 proved popular, but the company was in no financial position to compete with Boeing's huge new 747, which could carry 490 passengers. Long-haul carriers in particular again abandoned Douglas to invest in the new Boeing behemoth. Actually the 747 proved much too large for the time, and only became economically successful as an airline transport years later.

DC-9 production costs continued to escalate in 1966 so there was no hope of reaching the break-even point for manufacturing costs on the twenty-first airplane, which had been forecast. Instead, each of those first thirty airplanes cost an average of $1.25 million over estimates. Even after fifty airplanes were produced, manufacturing losses on each averaged $200,000. In addition, an equal amount had to be added for overhead, increasing the loss per plane to $400,000.

Management explained these losses by saying they were writing off estimated costs in excess of sales value for the first ninety DC-9s, which, it was hoped, would help the company by bringing it closer to the day when the DC-9 program would show a profit.

These manufacturing losses now had to be added to the $100 million that was spent to develop the DC-9. Under the older Douglas's policy of writing off development costs as they were incurred, in conformance with his conservative financial beliefs, the impact on earnings was only temporary. Under that policy, after a new plane had written off its development costs, profits per airplane went as high as 20 percent to the great satisfaction of stockholders.

Douglas, Jr., ordered that development costs of new aircraft be postponed until deliveries started, and thus ease the impact on earnings. He argued that the $100 million development costs should be considered as "deferred charges." His financial advisers agreed to spread the $100 million over 500 DC-9s. If manufacturing costs had been held to a reasonable level his plan would have worked. Matters were made worse, however, when manufacturing costs spiraled beyond projections, and the delivery schedule for both DC-9s and stretched DC-8s fell behind. With late deliveries in 1965 and 1966, final payments for many aircraft were not made on time, increasing cash-flow problems.

Delivery of airplanes was hampered by failure of Pratt & Whitney and manufacturers of systems and assemblies to maintain their contractual schedules. One of the greatest problems was with DeHavilland of Canada, which had contracted to produce the DC-9 wing and tail assemblies. When the Canadian firm ran into trouble, Douglas had to buy a portion of DeHavilland for 86 million scarce dollars. Another Canadian company, which had signed to build DC-9 flaps and ailerons, also got into financial trouble and faced bankruptcy. Again Douglas had to bail this company out, increasing the cost of these assemblies by $11,000 each.

To critics, who complained that the Aircraft Division accepted airline delivery schedules that even in normal times might have been almost impossible to meet, President Douglas said, "When you're fighting your way uphill, trying to achieve parity with an outfit like Boeing, you have got to be gung-ho or die by attrition."

Boeing, meanwhile, was making so much money that its profits in 1965 were 12 percent above the previous year.

The Douglas problem boiled down to one basic fault. It had lost control of its costs and even worse, it did not know it. Young Douglas tried to stem the tide by appointing Jesse L. Jones, the number two man at the Missiles and Space Division, to head manufacturing operations at the Aircraft Division. McGowen was not demoted, but remained as group vice-president. To assist the hard-driving Jones, the president sent Tom Gabbert to take over financial management of the division. At the corporate level, Douglas, Jr., brought in a new controller. Each of these steps was taken on an emergency basis, and the individuals involved were charged with the responsibility of improving cost controls.

Along with tightening management controls at the Aircraft Division in Long Beach, Jones also put forth a maximum effort to get airplanes out on time. He told President Douglas, "I'm a firm believer in the principle that if you miss a schedule, that's your last day of employment. I intend to apply it here."

When the 1966 second quarterly report was released, $3 million in losses were reported, and rumors spread like wildfire that the Douglas Company was in serious trouble. Many were even more convinced when the third-quarter loss exceeded $16 million.

After the extent of the poor financial condition became apparent to the chairman and his board of directors, Douglas personally took charge of the company's operations. There were reports that losses might exceed $75 million, and the banks absolutely refused to lend any more money despite their gentleman's agreement. Under the circumstances, their refusal is understandable. They were convinced that the company would go broke unless there were changes in top management. With financial troubles mounting daily, there were days when corporate officials were not sure on Wednesday whether the large weekly payroll could be met on Friday.

Ballooning costs reached astronomical proportions and the value of Douglas stock plummeted. It was now apparent to the senior Douglas that at least $250 million was needed to continue to produce the large number of commercial transports already sold.

With bankruptcy staring him in the face, Donald Douglas showed the deep anxiety he felt, but never once did he condemn McGowen during this traumatic period. Instead he constantly sent messages of encouragement and of his personal confidence in him, saying, "Keep up your spirits, Jack."

At board meetings, when some members condemned McGowen

and Douglas Jr., Douglas defended them strongly, reminding the board that theirs was a speculative business and that projected costs could only be estimates. This was a lesson he had learned well in past crises.

The disastrous change in the world environment, due to the Vietnam War and the tight money market, were to prove fatal but Douglas and his executives fought back trying to stave off disaster as, almost daily, the company's stock plummeted in value.

To the end Douglas remained loyal to his son, refusing to consider insistent demands by financial institutions that he be fired, even though a spokesman for the banks said that money would be forthcoming to bail the company out if he did so. He reminded them all that, as board chairman, he was as responsible for what had happened to the company as his son.

Douglas deeply resented the criticisms of his son, feeling they were overly vicious attacks by people who refused to believe that his son had any redeeming qualities. He was equally bitter about attacks upon his wife, Peggy. Some airline officials and bankers charged that, as his executive assistant, she was overly protective, refusing to let them discuss important matters with him on a private, personal basis.

For many years the Douglas Company had a line of credit, averaging $150 million, with seven banks. Chase Manhattan, First National City, and Morgan Guaranty were the informal leaders for the other four.

Douglas's son hired A. V. Leslie in 1962 as the company's financial vice-president. Previously, Leslie had been treasurer and senior vice-president for Trans World Airlines. At Douglas he negotiated a new line of credit, and formed the Douglas Finance Corporation so this subsidiary could help airlines purchase the company's products.

Leslie's financial arrangements included Bank of America, which became the second West Coast bank to be involved in loans to the company. Security First National of Los Angeles had been involved with the company for some time, with a representative on the Douglas board. Leslie's arrangements, however, changed the familiar pattern of having lead banks represent the others. Inevitably, with little cross-sharing of information about Douglas among them, a division of opinion among the bankers created serious doubts about what was happening within the company. They blamed Leslie for his failure to keep them advised, but Leslie evidently was not kept as knowledgeable about the Aircraft Division's true financial status as he should have been. Actually, the financial problems that began to appear in the spring of 1966 came as an almost total surprise to everyone at the top of the company.

Formation of the Finance Corporation was a good idea because banks normally will put up three dollars for each one a company puts up to sell its products through a financial subsidiary. Perhaps the primary reason this subsidiary got into so much trouble so quickly was that the Aircraft Division's salespeople were giving airlines such favorable time-and-interest terms that airlines flocked to the subsidiary for financing. Many airlines were such good credit risks that they easily could have gone elsewhere to borrow money.

With the elder Douglas now in charge of daily operations, he called a board meeting for October 7 because the banks insisted that he take steps to end the crisis. It was believed that, after tax credits, the 1966 loss would exceed $27 million. With long-term debt now exceeding stockholder equity, the banks insisted that $121 million in development costs, which had been deferred, be written off immediately. It was now believed that about $330 million would be needed over the next eighteen months to keep the company solvent. Both Douglases continued to insist their troubles would be over if the banks would only lend them $200 million. Bankers insisted on management changes, or that the company be merged with some well-run company, which could provide new management in depth to correct the Douglas Company's serious deficiencies.

Father and son stonewalled their position and Morgan Guaranty and some of the other banks threatened to abandon the company to its fate. They considered the Douglas proposal to raise $50 million in equity capital unrealistic because stock was selling for $30 a share and the money would be difficult to raise. They pointed out that Douglas Aircraft Company's total equity had fallen to $64 million and, if the $75 million that had been raised in convertible bonds in July was added that the capital base would be raised to $139 million. Against this sum, they added, Douglas already had $91 million in long-term debt, and company officials were asking for an additional loan of $200 million. To clinch their argument, they said the Douglas capital base was considered as subordinate to any new loan. In reality the bankers had lost faith in the company, and would only act to preserve it if its founder and board chairman agreed to remove his son as president.

Douglas was desperate by November and discussed his problems with private investors and companies. One of those who helped him in New York was his eastern representative, Ted Stern. Douglas asked him to arrange a meeting with Laurance Rockefeller. Douglas had known the wealthy philanthropist for years, and he hoped that he could talk him into a special loan to bail out his company.

Stern talked to Rockefeller, who readily agreed to see Douglas. He implied that he might be able to help his old friend out. On the day of the interview Douglas and his son went to Stern's office in the Graybar building. Stern called Rockefeller, saying, "I have them here. Can we come over?"

"Who's 'them'?" Rockefeller asked.

Stern explained that Douglas and his son wanted to see him.

Rockefeller said he would be happy to see the father, but he flatly refused to meet with the son.

Stern explained the situation to Douglas, who refused to go alone to Rockefeller's office. The circumstances were explained by Stern to Rockefeller and the interview was canceled.

There was some concern that Howard Hughes might use part of his enormous personal fortune to take over the Douglas Company in a shotgun marriage. Hughes told intimates privately, when questioned whether he would consider such a takeover, "Are you out of your mind?"

While in New York the Douglases called on Nate Cummings, chairman of Consolidated Foods. After they told their story Cummings called Henry Crown, suggesting to the man who had bailed out General Dynamics, and later made money on the deal, that he might be interested in offering similar salvation to the Douglas Company. "It's another General Dynamics situation all over again," Cummings said.

"If you're right," Crown replied, "that's the best reason for me not to be interested." Later, when General Dynamics became interested in a merger with Douglas, Crown initially was involved.

During their stay in New York bankers suggested to the Douglases that they seek a Wall Street firm, or even an influential individual, to try to raise money for the company. Merrill Lynch Pierce Fenner and Smith had underwritten a convertible offering by the Douglas Company, and had long been the company's permanent underwriter. They were being sued, along with Douglas, by some of those who had bought debentures, charging that the prospectus had been misleading. Douglas told the firm that he considered such an association inadvisable under the circumstances, and they agreed with him.

Instead, the Douglases talked to Andre Meyer, one of the legendary financial figures on Wall Street, who headed up the New York firm of Lazard Freres, international investment bankers. Meyer agreed to have his firm review the Douglas position.

A team of analysts, led by Meyer's partner Stanley de Jong Osborne, came to Santa Monica on November 28 to go over the Douglas books. Most banks were convinced a merger was the only way out for Douglas, but Osborne believed his first obligation was to the company that had hired his firm.

In reviewing the company's financial status Osborne quickly learned that forecasts were not reliable because they kept changing. After talking with many officials of the company, and reviewing their records, Osborne concluded that any attempt to raise money by a public offering was not feasible. The convertible debentures, sold in July, were selling in the low 80s. When he realized that nothing whatsoever had been done about management problems, he was convinced no company or individuals would risk the millions necessary to bail out the company.

Osborne and his associates also determined that, even with a merger, up to $400 million would be needed to produce the commercial aircraft on order. Few companies had that kind of credit. The banks and Douglas had already tried to get airlines to advance more money than they had contracted for; they hoped for $100 million. It was also hoped the company might borrow up to $75 million on the basis of its successful military projects. V-loans were another consideration. The Defense Production Act of 1950 permitted the Defense Department to guarantee private loans to finance inventories on military contracts. It was hoped that the company's suppliers might also lend a hand. Finally, a possible loan from the Export-Import Bank was considered to finance the building of jetliners for foreign airlines. Douglas pointed out that the commercial backlog for the next two years amounted to over $500 million just for overseas airlines, with a potential of $1 billion a year in the future. The company's bankruptcy, Douglas said, would have a serious impact on the nation's balance of payments. Leslie explored these possibilities with government officials, including the heads of the Federal Reserve Bank offices in San Francisco, which handled V-loans, but he met with a complete lack of understanding about the gravity of the Douglas situation.

Two weeks after his arrival in Santa Monica, Osborne told Douglas that he should call an emergency meeting of the board of directors and he would report his findings. At the meeting, Osborne was blunt. Despite its huge backlog, the Douglas Company was bankrupt. The news stunned most directors. They had known the situation was bad, but only now after this independent audit was the truth laid bare. Osborne advised them that Douglas's only solution was to seek a merger partner.

Honor Above All Else

The Douglas board met several times in emergency sessions during December, and agreed to seek bids from possible merger partners. Four companies expressed interest initially, including General Dynamics, North American Aviation, Martin-Marietta, and McDonnell Aircraft. Douglas was not surprised by the latter's interest.

A special committee was established by the board because it was known that $400 million might be needed to keep Douglas solvent, with much of it needed immediately in cash. The merger partner, therefore, had to be a corporation with an impeccable credit rating.

On December 12, 1966, Harry Wetzel, head of Garrett Corporation, a subsidiary of Signal Oil, urged his parent company to seek a merger with Douglas. His father had been Douglas's executive vice-president for years prior to his death, so his son had a special interest. Signal had prepared a detailed proposal, offering to buy five million shares of a proposed new 6 percent preferred stock to be offered at $20.00 a share. This would give Douglas $100 million, and would be convertible into Douglas common stock on the basis of two shares of preferred for one of common. In effect, Signal's offer amounted to $40.00 a share, for shares which were then selling for about $45.00. Signal, therefore, would end up with 29 percent of Douglas's common stock. Signal also asked for voting rights that would permit it to elect a majority of directors on the Douglas board. Signal made the offer with an expiration date of December 29. On that date Douglas asked Signal to extend their offer to January 13, and it agreed to do so.

All candidates for merger sent their officials to question Douglas's management about the true state of the company's problems. Meanwhile, the Douglas board established a special negotiating committee with the elder Douglas and three of the company's outside directors, plus Lazard Freres's Osborne, to serve as their adviser. One of the early guidelines was to assure that each company's bid would be kept confidential, and not used to improve someone else's bid. Douglas insisted that his company's shareholders should be protected insofar as possible. Key criteria for selection of the successful bidder included $100 million available in equity capital or subordinated debt and possibly more if it should be needed, management availability for all levels of Douglas supervision, and a company with a proven record of tight controls over operations.

Potential merger partners at last had a clear picture of the tangled finances of the Douglas Company. It was now realized that the 1966 loss, before taxes, would exceed $50 million, and there was little doubt of a substantial loss the following year.

Those within the lower ranks of the company feared that tight new controls would eliminate many of their jobs. There was no question that the payrolls at each of the divisions were excessive due to an overabundance of employees compared to actual work needs.

In late December Sherman Fairchild, the top man in Fairchild-Hiller and Fairchild Camera, and probably the largest single stockholder in IBM, decided to submit a proposal. He and Robert Lehman, who headed Lehman Brothers, went to the Lazard Freres's office in New York and told Andre Meyer they were prepared to invest $75 million in Douglas. Meyer encouraged them to make a bid, and Fairchild was brought up to date on the Douglas situation.

George Bunker, president of Martin-Marietta, who had made a rather vague offer of a $50 million loan and merger, withdrew January 11. He realized that Douglas's salvation would cost Martin-Marietta more than he was willing to risk.

When the negotiating committee met January 9 to hear each company's presentation, James S. McDonnell spoke first on behalf of his firm. He now owned 300,000 shares of Douglas common stock, which made him the largest single stockholder in the company. In contrast, Douglas and his son owned only about 9,000 shares.

With his president, David Lewis, and investment banker Ferdinand Eberstadt, he proposed the immediate purchase of 1.5

million shares of Douglas common at about $43.00 a share, to be followed as soon as possible by a merger of the two companies. He kept repeating that "Old Mac," evidently referring to his company as much as himself, and Douglas supplemented one another. He promised to provide whatever resources were needed to give the combined company total systems capability.

Prior to Douglas's problems, McDonnell Aircraft had split itself into three separate, autonomous divisions, much like Douglas had done. He said now it would be simple to add another Douglas division to his corporate structure.

Charles Jones, the rugged board chairman of Richfield Oil, and long an associate of Donald Douglas and a member of his board, grew increasingly irritated as McDonnell kept calling himself "Old Mac." "Just call me 'Old Charlie,' " Jones said, getting a laugh from everyone, but the remark did not faze McDonnell.

The negotiating committee agreed that McDonnell's offer of $43.00 a share for Douglas common was inadequate, and McDonnell said he might go higher. One committee member chided McDonnell about his company's relationship with subcontractors, which, he said, was not impressive, although he admitted improvement had been shown of late. McDonnell's expanding capital base and years of profitable operations were in the St. Louis firm's favor, and it was conceded by the committee that its middle management was young and aggressive.

Signal Oil appeared the following day with its president Forrest Shumway, senior executive vice-president William Walkup, and Garrett president Harry Wetzel. Earlier the committee had received a copy of a letter from the Bank of America that it would give Signal a $100 million loan between January 3 and May 31 if their offer to merge was accepted. Shumway said that the Douglas Company was more a victim of unfortunate circumstances than anything else, citing the excuses Douglas officials had long used. He said that Douglas Aircraft basically had sound management, but needed stronger direction, which Signal could provide with a new board dominated by them. Wetzel, he said, would become chief executive officer. It was an attractive offer, and would pose no antitrust problems because Signal's only aerospace operations were with Garrett Corporation.

General Dynamics president, Roger Lewis, appeared before the committee on January 11. He said he understood the Douglas situation, perhaps better than others because his firm had already gone through a similar situation. He proposed that his firm put money into Douglas by buying an issue of Douglas preferred stock and then merging the two companies. Perhaps his most persuasive argument was that the two companies would complement one another. General Dynamics, now out of the commercial business, was involved only in military programs. He said General Dynamics wanted to get back into commercial production, and this was the best way to do it. Years earlier the disastrous Convair 880-990 jet transport program had almost brought about the company's collapse. Only Crown's intervention had saved the company.

Committee members pointed out that General Dynamics appeared unable to raise most of the capital required, but Lewis successfully countered that argument. He reminded them that his company was under a court antitrust order to sell its Liquid Carbonic division, and the money from this sale could be used to provide the necessary capital.

Next morning it was North American Aviation's turn. Board chairman and president J. L. Atwood, who started with Douglas back in the early days of the company, said he was speaking more as a friend trying to help a neighbor in distress. He was listened to with respect because he headed a conservatively run corporation, with over $2 billion in sales and over a half billion in assets, and his plants in the Los Angeles area were neighbors of the Douglas company.

Atwood's offer involved an issue of senior securities by Douglas that North American would purchase, control of the Douglas board, and, if the Justice Department approved a merger, 1.2 shares of Douglas common to be traded for 1 share of North American common.

That afternoon Sherman Fairchild, representing Fairchild-Hiller, offered to invest $75 million in Douglas and provide managerial talent for the beleaguered company. Actually, Fairchild-Hiller, a producer of commercial turboprops for short-range operations, had little to offer such a merger.

Signal now sent a revised proposal and offered to buy $100 million of preferred stock at $43.00 a share convertible to Douglas common on a share-for-share basis. Further, Signal said it would vote the preferred share for share with the common instead of its previous offer to vote it separately, which would give Signal a 27 percent voting interest.

The Douglas committee dropped Fairchild-Hiller from further consideration on January 13. General Dynamics lost out next because the committee did not believe it had sufficient long-term capital. If General Dynamics had not retired approximately $100 million of preferred stock held by Henry Crown the previous April, it might well have been the successful bidder. The committee considered that the sale of liquid carbonic might not result in the necessary capital soon enough.

Signal Oil failed in its proposal primarily because the committee did not believe it had the in-depth management to take over the huge Douglas organization.

With the contest narrowed between North American and McDonnell, James McDonnell sweetened his proposal by offering to buy one-and-a-half million more shares of Douglas stock, in addition to the 300,000 shares he already owned, and pay $45.80 for them. This offer was more than the stock's market value, and would give the Douglas company $68.7 million. His offer would stand even if the Department of Justice disapproved the merger. In a merger, Douglas common would be valued at 1.75 shares of McDonnell common.

Privately, McDonnell agreed to give Douglas's son a contract for seven years at $100,000 a year, and make the father honorary chairman of the new board at a salary of $50,000 a year. McGowen and Able, group vice-presidents for the two major Douglas divisions, were also offered seven-year contracts. North American Aviation's Atwood refused to increase his company's bid so on January 13, 1967, the Douglas negotiating committee unanimously recommended a McDonnell-Douglas merger. James McDonnell's offer to purchase additional Douglas stock, without regard to Justice Department action, won the day. The other contestants tried to buy in at minimum risk, and so lost out. The Department of Justice approved the merger April 26, and it formally went into effect two days later. Douglas was named honorary chairman, but he no longer had any control over the company he had founded forty-seven years before.

McDonnell had no difficulty in getting ten banks to come up with $300 million in a revolving-credit fund. McDonnell teams, headed by David Lewis, went over the Douglas Company department by department, and there were many changes in operations as tight fiscal management policies were adopted. They were so successful that, by the end of 1968, the new corporation had net earnings of $94 million.

At the time of the Douglas collapse, the younger Douglas as president bore the brunt of criticism within and without the company. Much of the criticism was emotional and unfair, and did not correspond to the facts. In retrospect, it is apparent that the three men who dominated the company throughout most of its corporate existence—the elder Douglas, Ted Conant, and Arthur Raymond—had difficulty keeping up with changing events as they grew older. They seemed unable in the final decade of the company's independent existence to adapt to priorities in a rapidly expanding aviation world. When the DC-8's engineering problems became apparent, the pressures upon Arthur Raymond were almost intolerable. He became seriously ill and later was forced to retire. When his usually strong leadership was most needed, engineering management was largely left in the hands of lower-echelon managers.

Donald Douglas had run his company with a firm hand. Some accused him of cronyism, which, in part, was true, but he surrounded himself with strong managers at the top and right down through the ranks.

The younger Douglas also was guilty of cronyism, but there was a difference in the way he and his father handled people. The younger Douglas incurred the inevitable hostility of many of his father's most intimate associates and, despite his father's appeal to them to give his son all possible assistance in running the company, they could not or would not do so because of strong feelings that the younger Douglas could not possibly fill his old man's shoes. They looked upon him as the kid they had once known, ignoring the fact that he had risen successfully in the company under his father's watchful eyes. Although their attitudes are understandable, they proved catastrophic in the effective running of the company.

The son retaliated against those whom he considered enemies, and made personnel management appointments at the mid-management levels, replacing experienced administrators with those who had joined his team. Many appointees had to be trained on the job, at a time when experience was vital to the company. Douglas's son completely ignored the teachings of old-timers who used to say, "Experience teaches us the difference between reasons that sound good, and good sound reasoning." Or, as Arch Wallen used to say when talking of particularly inept managers, "men of action with no time lost in thinking."

A new group of management leaders was developed during World War II, but many of them became discouraged and left the company when it needed them most after the younger Douglas placed key friends in high positions. Normally a large corporation can suffer disastrous setbacks, but it will rebound if its managers are experienced. Many of Junior's friends lacked that experience.

While his son was in operational control, Douglas and Conant acted as elder statesmen, providing the final authority for key decisions. The tight controls they had established during their years of operational oversight no longer worked because lower management levels had been decimated by firings and resignations, and the newer managers had not yet learned their jobs.

Toward the end, airline customers and top military officers wanted to talk to the old man when problems developed. They had always done so, and they resented any attempt by the son or his top associates to intervene. This was a ticklish and aggravating situation. All too frequently the response of Douglas, Jr. was explosive anger, a normal reaction but one that did nothing to resolve the growing conflict.

One of the basic faults of the younger Douglas's regime was its failure to establish effective controls over costs, schedules, and quality assurance. Conant and Douglas had always stressed that no matter how well a part was designed, the manufacturing engineer must plan to produce it economically. If a part was over-tooled or under-tooled, costly hours were lost in assembly and production costs snowballed.

Managers such as Arch Wallen had always stressed strong planning and manufacturing controls to see that parts were made and delivered as close to schedule as possible. When Wallen and hundreds of other managers left the company, newcomers did not have time to learn their jobs.

Father and son were so different in makeup that they almost did not seem to belong to the same family. The father always selected the best men in the company to place in top management positions, whereas the son frequently made misjudgments in character.

Therefore, the lack of experience led the son's management team to fail to consider where the costly functions were in the DC-8 and DC-9 programs, and chaos resulted.

There are many former Douglas employees who firmly believe some collective force conspired to bring the company down. Either that, or the younger Douglas and McGowen were primarily responsible for its collapse. Neither is true. The causes of the bankruptcy were varied, and many date back to the failure of the corporation to take the risk and build a prototype commercial jet transport as Boeing did. Failure of Santa Monica's Engineering Department to design the company's first jetliner with a minimum of design deficiencies, and later its inability to correct serious defects, both contributed to the company's decline.

After the merger, Douglas's son became the favorite whipping boy because of the loss of his father's company. Such charges are nonsense. Actually, his father so dominated the company that it is doubtful if anyone from within the organization could have saved it. Like all great adventures, this one, too, had to come to an end.

Erik Nelson, the army pilot who flew one of the World Cruisers around the world in 1924, died in Hawaii in May, 1970. At his request his body was cremated, and, because he was born in Sweden, he specified that his ashes should be scattered over the North Sea. Donald Douglas came out of retirement and asked that a memorial ceremony be held at Douglas Park on Santa Monica Boulevard, the exact spot where Nelson had signed the contract with him to build the World Cruisers, to honor this great airman.

In a moving tribute, Douglas personally gave the eulogy, saying that Erik Nelson was basically responsible for the Douglas Aircraft Company's early leadership in the commercial transport field. He said Nelson's insistence on the design of the World Cruisers, and his determination that the around-the-world flight should succeed, made the Douglas name and its products known throughout the world.

On Douglas's eightieth birthday in the spring of 1972, his former associates arranged for a huge party at Century Plaza in Los Angeles.

James B. McDonnell, in an oddly phrased memo, sent his regrets. "I want to felicitate you on having completed 80 meaningful orbits around the Sun, and wish you many more vigorous years to come." He said he would be with Douglas in spirit and that his nephew Sandy would be there in person to pay the respects of the McDonnell branch of "our joint clan and present you with our check for ten thousand dollars for the 'Donald Douglas Prize Fellowship Fund.'"

In his memo dated May 5, McDonnell wrote,

> Last Friday on the fifth anniversary of the merger of our two companies, our Board again unanimously elected you 'Honorary Chairman of the Board' for the coming year.
> In appreciation of your existence,
>   Sincerely,
>   OLD MAC

Douglas's private thoughts about this communication are not available. Those who knew him well agree they would have been earthy.

For those who knew Donald Douglas, he will always remain one of the true geniuses of the twentieth century. With each passing year the Douglas legend grows, and it becomes more evident that he was not just another businessman, or one who designed and built airplanes, but through the force of his extraordinary personality he has left an imprint on this century that will endure for generations to come. Other outstanding men have been responsible for the advancement of aviation in this century but none of them, including the man who took over a bankrupt company and made it solvent, will ever be remembered with the same respect and admiration as Donald Douglas. The reason is simple. He was first of all a brilliant creator, and not just a builder of airplanes.

In describing men like Douglas, his old friend Dutch Kindelberger once said, "Pioneers are men with arrows in the seat of their pants." Douglas had a quiverful in his.

Douglas summed up his feelings about loss of his company during his last day in office, and there's more truth in his words than anyone else has ever written. "One should never grow old where one was once great." Through the years banks and stockholders made fortunes as the result of Douglas's genius as a brilliant design engineer and industrialist. At the end, most deserted him in his final hour of need. If he felt any bitterness he kept such thoughts to himself, bowing out with the same pride and dignity that characterized his long and productive life.

Douglas died on February 1, 1981, at the age of eighty-eight, only a few months after James McDonnell passed away. At his request, his ashes were scattered over the Pacific Ocean, where he had spent some of the happiest days of his life.

He had always been a superb engineer, but he also had that rare gift of vision, leaving his indelible mark on an industry he helped to pioneer, and one that created the modern miracle of global air transportation. To those who knew him well, and they number in the thousands, his integrity as a human being will always be remembered. They knew him as a man whose word was his contract, whose friendship was a strong bond—a man who believed in honor above all else.

During his retirement years, Douglas continued to find solace in writing poetry, an avocation he had enjoyed since childhood. As always, his favorite theme involved sailors and days at sea. One of his most revealing poems was written in 1969. It could well be his epitaph.

> As we grow old and the shadows lengthen
> Old friends close ranks and old bonds strengthen.
> Old times together now bathe in the gold
> Of our youth and our strength and bold
> Deeds of old.
>
> So here's to all sailors, old or young,
> Here's to all seamen of every tongue.
> May your deeds and your memories ever be
> Softened and strengthened
> And washed by the sea.

INDEX